READER'S DIGEST

all-season guide to gardening

late spring

READER'S DIGEST

all-season guide to gardening

late spring

PUBLISHED BY

THE READER'S DIGEST ASSOCIATION LIMITED

LONDON · NEW YORK · SYDNEY · MONTREAL

contents

foreword

The *All-Season Guide to Gardening* provides a complete practical and inspirational guide to making the most of your garden season–by–season, with year-round detailed information to help you plan, plant and enjoy the garden of your dreams. Each of the volumes is presented in four key sections:

inspirations offers a source of design and planting ideas taken from contemporary and traditional gardens photographed during the season. The plants featured have been identified to enable you to re-create or adapt the ideas to your own garden scheme.

practical diary is a guide to the most important tasks to be done in the garden at this time of year. The information is divided into subject areas – such as Perennials, Climbers,

or Patios & Containers – that reflect particular gardening interests. The headings appear in the same order in every volume in the series, so you can easily find the information you need. Under each heading is a list of the season's main tasks. The most important jobs are then explained in more detail, with step-by-step photographs and expert tips. The Healthy Garden, at the end of the section, is a full checklist of priority seasonal tasks for the whole garden. Since many jobs require follow-up attention in a later season, a 'Looking

useful terms

alpine Although this strictly refers to a mountain plant that grows naturally in free-draining soil at high altitude, the term is used by gardeners to mean any plant suitable for growing in a rock garden.

annual A plant that grows, flowers, sets seed and dies in one growing season.

anther The part of the flower that produces pollen.

aquatic plant In its widest sense, this can mean any water plant, but usually refers to plants such as water lilies that grow in deeper water, rooted in the bottom of the pond or in special baskets.

bareroot This refers to plants, usually trees and shrubs, that have been dug up and supplied to the customer without any soil on their roots. Roses are often supplied in this way.

bedding (plant) A plant used outdoors for temporary or seasonal display, often as part of a planned 'bedding scheme'.

biennial A plant that completes its life cycle in two growing seasons.

biological control The treatment or prevention of pests, diseases or weeds by natural, rather than chemical, methods, usually involving a naturally occurring parasite or predator.

cloche A glass or plastic cover used to shelter plants from cold or windy weather. Cloches are available as separate units or in tunnel form, often called 'continuous cloches'.

coldframe A low, unheated structure with a transparent top, in which plants can be grown in protected conditions.

cordon A plant restricted by pruning and training to a single, unbranching stem. Examples include apples, tomatoes and sweet peas grown on canes.

corm The swollen stem base of plants like crocuses and gladioli, where food is stored during winter. A new corm forms each year on top of the shrivelled remains of last year's.

cultivar A distinct, named plant variety that has originated in cultivation, rather than in the wild. Cultivars are often simply (but incorrectly) called 'varieties'.

deadhead To cut off the spent flowers.

die-back The result of attack by a fungal disease, which causes shoots or branches to die back from their tips.

direct sow To sow seeds in the ground where the plants are to grow, rather than starting them indoors or in a temporary seedbed for later transplanting.

drill A furrow or channel made in the soil at the correct depth for sowing seeds.

ericaceous Any plant belonging to the erica or heather family, for example pieris and rhododendrons. Also refers to the acid conditions these plants like and the special lime-free compost in which they are potted.

espalier A tree such as an apple or cotoneaster that is pruned and trained as a single upright trunk, with side branches

extending horizontally to form symmetrical layers or 'tiers'.

foliar feed Liquid fertiliser sprayed or watered on the leaves of plants, usually applied for rapid results or when plants are not actively absorbing nutrients through their roots (after injury or in cold weather, for example).

glyphosate A chemical weedkiller that is absorbed through leaves and moves through the plant so that all parts, including roots, are killed (see systemic).

habitat The natural home of a plant growing in the wild. Not to be confused with habit, which is the typical form or shape of a plant.

harden off To gradually acclimatise a plant previously grown indoors to unprotected conditions outside in the garden.

hardwood cutting A piece of this year's shoot taken for propagation from a shrub, tree or climber during the autumn, when their stems are hard and ripe.

heel A small strip of bark torn from the main stem when a sideshoot is pulled off to make a (heel) cutting.

heel in To bury the roots of a plant in a temporary hole or trench when it is not to be planted immediately.

humus The dark, water-retentive component of soil that results from the decay of organic material.

in situ Literally, in position, or where plants are to grow permanently.

internodal cutting A cutting that is trimmed midway between two leaf-joints, rather than immediately below the leaves.

layering A method of propagation in which a shoot is rooted while still attached to the

ahead' feature indicates when you will find details of follow-up action in another volume.

plant selector is a directory of the plants which are at their best at this time of year, as selected by our gardening experts. Within each subject grouping the plants are arranged by colour, and within each colour sequence they are generally listed alphabetically by botanical name. Each plant is shown in a photograph, with information supplied including the plant's common name, size, site and soil preferences, best uses, general care and suggestions for good companions. Each plant is also given a 'hardiness' rating:
● 'Hardy' plants can be grown outdoors in all parts of the British Isles.
● Plants rated 'not fully hardy' can be grown outdoors in milder parts of the British Isles but elsewhere will need some protection in winter.

● 'Half-hardy' plants can withstand temperatures down to 0°C (32°F). They are often grown outdoors in summer displays, but propagated and kept under glass between autumn and late spring.
● 'Tender' plants require protection under glass for all or part of the year.
At the end of the section, there are lists of the plants best suited to different garden conditions and soil types.

garden projects offers ideas and instructions for garden improvements, ranging from building a patio, pergola or raised bed to designing and planting up a new border or pond. Major DIY projects are illustrated with step-by-step photographs and all the projects are within the capabilities of a fit, practical person. Although some projects are specific to a season, many of them can also be undertaken at other times of the year.

parent plant. Rooting a branch where it touches the ground is called simple layering, while serpentine layering involves rooting a long flexible stem in several places; long stems can be tip layered by burying their growing tips.

loam A type of soil that contains a balanced mixture of sand, clay and organic material.

marginal plant A waterside plant that is grown at the edge of the pond, either in shallow water or on the bank.

mulch Any material used to cover and protect the soil surface. Organic mulches include straw, manure and lawn mowings, while polythene sheet and stones are examples of inorganic mulches.

naturalise To deliberately plant, or allow plants to grow and spread, as in the wild.

node The place on a plant's stem where a leaf forms.

nursery bed A piece of ground specially reserved for raising young plants.

organic This literally refers to any material derived from decomposed animal or plant remains. It is also used to describe a gardening approach that uses little or no obviously chemical substances such as fertilisers and pesticides.

perlite A granular, absorbent soil or compost additive made from expanded volcanic rock.

perennial (correctly herbaceous perennial) A durable non-woody plant whose soft, leafy growth dies down in winter, but grows again the following year.

pinch out To remove a growing tip, using finger and thumb.

pot on To move a potted plant into a larger container.

pot (up) To transfer a plant from a seedtray or open ground into a pot.

prick out To transplant seedlings from where they have been sown to a container or piece of ground where they will have more space to grow.

rhizome An underground root (strictly, a stem) that behaves like a bulb by storing food from one season to the next. Also used to describe the buried creeping shoots by which some plants, especially grasses, spread underground.

rootballed This describes plants packaged for delivery by wrapping their mass of roots and soil or compost in a net bag.

rootstock (or stock) The rooted portion of a grafted tree. This usually influences the habit and ultimate size of the selected variety joined onto it (the scion).

seedbed A piece of ground for raising seeds, specially prepared by removing all weeds, stones and large lumps of soil.

semi-ripe cutting A section of this year's stem cut off for propagation, usually during summer while the tip is still soft but the base has become firm and woody.

softwood cutting A cutting prepared from a portion of a young new shoot that has not started to harden.

spit A measurement of depth equal to the length of a spade-blade (about 25cm/10in).

standard A trained form of woody plant with a single upright stem that is clear of all leaves and shoots. Full standard trees have trunks about 1.8m (6ft) high, half-standards 1.2m (4ft). Standard roses are about 1m (3ft) high, while half-standards have 75cm (2ft 6in) stems.

subsoil The lower layer of ground below the topsoil (see below). Often paler and relatively infertile, this is usually coarser in texture and hard to cultivate.

sucker A shoot growing from below ground and away from the main stem of a plant, sometimes from its rootstock.

systemic A type of pesticide, fungicide or weedkiller sprayed onto leaves and absorbed into all plant parts in its sap.

tender perennial A plant that can live for several years but cannot tolerate frost or very cold conditions.

thin out To reduce the number of plants, buds or fruit so that those remaining have enough room to develop fully.

tip cuttings Softwood cuttings (see above) formed from the outer ends of young shoots.

top-dressing An application of fertiliser, organic material or potting compost spread on the surface. Also refers to replacing the top layer of compost in a large container with a fresh supply.

topgrowth The upper, visible part of a plant above ground level.

topsoil The upper layer of soil, usually darker and more fertile than the layers below (see subsoil), and where plants develop most of their feeding roots.

tuber A fat, underground root (in dahlias, for example) or stem (begonias), constructed differently from a bulb or corm but used in the same way for storing food from one season to the next.

variety Botanically, a distinctly different variation of a plant that has developed in the wild, but commonly used to mean the same as cultivar (see left).

Everyone's garden looks
beautiful in late spring –
the grass is never greener,
the trees never fresher and
flowers never prettier. From
the delicate beauty of
spring blossom to the
carpets of fresh ferns and
late flowering bulbs, the
whole landscape is full of
sweet promise. Among all
your endeavours in this
loveliest of gardening
seasons, be sure to take a
little time off to enjoy the
floral abundance.

inspirations

beautiful bulbs

Bulbs are the mainstay of spring in all their glorious colours and extraordinary flower forms. When they have finished flowering, they gradually disappear below ground, to build up their resources for the following year.

Crown imperials (*Fritillaria imperialis*) are the largest of the fritillaries. They require a rich, well-drained soil in sun or semi-shade.

An American dog's-tooth violet (*Erythronium oregonum*) thrives with the European native *Cyclamen repandum* in dappled shade (right).

Lily-flowered *Tulipa* 'West Point' is a mid to late flowering hybrid that is an excellent choice for containers.

A meadow-land plant, snakeshead fritillary (*Fritillaria meleagris*) in its white and purple forms naturalises well in moist grassland (below).

Summer snowflake
(*Leucojum aestivum*) is a
superb bulb for dry shade
and best left alone once
planted (left).

A naturalistic planting
(below left) combines
Anemone blanda and wild
daffodils (*Narcissus
pseudonarcissus*) with
wild violets and primroses.

Tulips look best massed
in groups according to
colour (below right).
These are Darwin
hybrids 'Apeldoorn'
(red) and 'Apeldoorn's
Elite' (yellow).

*Hyacinthus
orientalis* 'Carnegie'

carpeting the ground

The garden floor is never fresher or more colourful than in late spring. Naturalised bulbs look charming in grass or mixed with biennials as ground cover in shaded borders.

Geranium macrorrhizum

This chequerboard design of gravel and turf could also be achieved using thyme or chamomile instead of grass. Though fiddly to maintain, the effect is striking.

In this bulb meadow the big Dutch hyacinths are in perfect scale with the *Tulipa kaufmanniana* hybrids, giving the planting a surprisingly natural look.

A delightful cottage garden effect is achieved with forget-me-nots, wallflowers and tulips. The tulip in the foreground is *Tulipa* 'Queen of Night', with the lily-flowered yellow 'West Point' behind.

Bleeding heart (*Dicentra spectabilis*) and forget-me-nots surround the sinister flowers of *Trillium sessile*.

Vinca minor 'La Grave'

In the dappled shade beneath an acer (below), self-seeded forget-me-nots nestle in the long grass.

Unfurling fronds of the ostrich fern (*Matteuccia struthiopteris*) pierce clumps of *Erythronium* 'Pagoda' (below). Both plants enjoy the same moist woodland conditions.

inspiring beds & borders

There's something new every day in late spring beds and borders. Now spring flowers merge with those of summer, punctuated by the fresh foliage of plants to come.

Candelabra primulas and globe flowers (*Trollius*) bring colour to this border on moist soil, set off by the dark leaves of *Lysimachia ciliata* 'Firecracker' in the background (left).

Forget-me-nots and scented wallflowers are the mainstay of many a fine spring border. Remove them when flowering is finished and replace with a summer scheme.

Paeonia mlokosewitschii, with its showy creamy yellow blooms (above), is an eye-catching plant for the late spring border. It is teamed here with the lime-green-flowered *Euphorbia palustris*. The peony flowers are followed by handsome seed heads.

Bowles' golden grass (*Milium effusum* 'Aureum') (right) associates well with the ferny leaves and creamy white blooms of sweet cicely (*Myrrhis odorata*).

Tulips, threaded through mixed borders (top left), pull a spring garden together to create a harmonious display.

Blue comfrey (*Symphytum officinale*) and *Iris germanica* (above) make a strong highlight in cool colours in this lush planting.

Doronicum x *excelsum* 'Harpur Crewe'

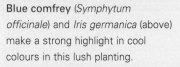

Columbines, happiest in partial shade, cheerfully co-exist alongside sun-lovers *Stachys byzantina*, *Iris orientalis* and white valerian (*Centranthus ruber* 'Albus') at the edge of this woodland planting.

features & focal points

A focal point is easy to create, with strategically placed plants or a feature. Even something as functional as a gateway, if it is dressed up with style, will draw the eye and transform the scene.

With its concave outline and echoing arch, this gateway not only frames a view but is a delightful focal point in its own right.

In this white garden a stone seat makes a functional focal point, enhanced by 'White Triumphator' tulips and snow-white azalea.

Clipped evergreens, such as these box spheres (right), can be replicated in a formal garden to make a year-round feature that works equally well on a large or small scale.

A tall, shapely pot placed among vegetation can create a strong focus, blending the planting together.

Tulips, though spectacular, come and go quickly, whereas this sundial makes a permanent point of interest that can preside over seasonal planting.

A small statue adds a sense of mystery to the dense, dark growth of rhododendrons. Such a feature needs to be 'discovered', so place it in a woodland setting or a secluded corner out of the main view.

Raised on a plinth, these softly rounded stone doves create a sculptural focus in an informal planting scheme (below).

container blooms

Containers are excellent for speedy transformations in any season, but in spring, pots, baskets, troughs or even buckets can be planted up with beautiful bulbs or speedy herbaceous plants for a colourful effect.

Viola

Grape hyacinths (*Muscari armeniacum*), seen here with violas (right), will grow happily in the smallest of pots. Later, they can be planted out to naturalise in the garden.

Show auriculas, fashionable in Victorian times, have been bred especially for display in individual terracotta pots. Grow them under cover as rain spoils their 'painted' flowers.

A repeating line of miniature standard salix shows their fresh spring foliage. They form a shapely outline grown in shiny galvanised buckets, pierced in the base for drainage.

The lily-flowered tulip hybrid 'Maytime' makes a fine display in this stone trough. After flowering, the bulbs can be discarded or planted in the garden to die down naturally, making room in the container for a summer display.

White-stemmed *Betula utilis* are grown in galvanised planters large enough to accommodate their extensive roots. Spring-flowering thrift clothes their base.

Individually potted pansies make a pretty grouping (below). If regularly deadheaded, they will continue blooming for months.

A deliciously fragrant mix of grape hyacinths, *Scilla siberica* 'Alba', pansies and *Narcissus* 'Cheerfulness' makes a wonderful window-box planting (bottom).

walls, doors & structures

Never overlook the immense value of vertical surfaces. In a small garden, they can provide a larger growing area than the ground, and will more than double the impact of your displays.

A stone retaining wall is made bright with a cascade of yellow *Aurinia saxatilis and* purple aubrieta. Both plants thrive in the well-drained conditions of a raised bed.

A rustic screen (below left), swathed in the climbers *Vitis coignetiae* 'Claret Cloak' and *Clematis* 'Madame Julia Correvon', casts pretty shadows in the late spring sun.

Ornamental quince (*Chaenomeles*), tightly clipped and trained against a wall, makes a handsome springtime feature (below). At its foot are lemon euphorbias.

Vigorous, rambling climbers such as *Clematis montana* (left) look best when allowed to hang in generous swags over the tops of walls. After flowering, they create a pleasant green background for border plants.

Laburnum, trained to form a tunnel on a series of arches (left), provides a spectacular, though brief, display when in flower.

Chinese wisteria (*Wisteria sinensis*, above) is the best late spring climber of all for a warm, sunny wall. For reliable flowering, buy a named variety, and prune each year in late summer, and again in winter.

Clematis macropetala 'Markham's Pink'

ornamental trees

Late spring is blossom time, when most ornamental trees are at their best. Even those that bloom at other times of the year look fresh in their bright young foliage.

A clipped cypress (top), with bare stems and green dome, makes a sculptural topiary form. Be prepared to clip at least twice a year to keep it so immaculate.

Flowering crab apples (above) are great year-round trees. They have a shapely outline, good autumn colour, fruits for jelly – and superb blossom in late spring. This is *Malus floribunda*.

Magnolia stellata (right) is one of the most robust magnolias in cultivation. Its starry spring flowers are produced before the leaves appear. Unlike several magnolia species, this one is fully lime-tolerant.

A formal planting of pleached limes makes an elegant division in a large garden. Here the trees are underplanted with pale-flowered bearded iris.

Ornamental maples make perfect trees for the small garden. *Acer pseudoplatanus* 'Brilliantissimum' (below) is a pale-leaved cultivar whose early buds are shrimp-pink. Grow it in semi-shade to avoid leaf scorch. A golden form, *Acer platanoides*, frames a vista (bottom right). The pair of trees is underplanted with a soft, pastel scheme that includes *Veronica gentianoides* and golden lemon balm.

Sweet harmony is achieved in Claude Monet's garden at Giverny. The flowering *Malus*, with aubrieta and tulips planted beneath, shows that startling colour combinations can work well.

The Judas tree (*Cercis siliquastrum*, below), flowers on bare branches and looks more natural if grown, like this, with multiple trunks.

The Japanese cherry *Prunus* 'Shirotae' (below) is a superb ornamental specimen.

With late spring comes the busiest planting time. New shrubs and hardy perennials planted during these months will have a whole growing season to become established before winter. Seeds of hardy annuals sown now will provide gorgeous colours in high summer and, once the danger of frost has passed, it is safe to plant out such tender species as pelargonium and heliotrope. As the soil warms up, you can enjoy setting out your kitchen garden, too, and watch with pleasure as the vegetable seedlings emerge. Late spring may be a busy time, but as you plant, prune and sow, you are laying the groundwork for a colourful and rewarding year.

practical diary

perennials

Herbaceous perennials keep you busy in late spring with a range of tasks that allow plant growth to be as swift and as healthy as possible. On top of routine maintenance, give some thought to the future, as this is the best time to propagate the next generation of plants, either as fillers for gaps in the border or for next year's display.

now is the season to . . .

■ **put supports or stakes in place,** well before tall perennials begin to flop over.

■ **water thirsty young plants** that are still developing a root system, if more than a few days go by without rain. Soft leafy perennials that have just been planted need plenty of water to maintain their rapid pace of growth – in dry weather this means up to 5 litres (1 gallon) per week per plant.

■ **mulch to reduce water loss and suppress weeds:** cover the soil around plants with an organic mulch, such as composted bark, well-rotted manure or garden compost. Before you mulch, make sure the soil is thoroughly moist and clear of perennial weeds. Then lay the mulch at least 7–8cm (3in) deep to prevent light from reaching the soil and stimulating weed seeds to germinate.

■ **take steps to control slugs and snails** by a range of means (see opposite).

■ **remove weeds regularly,** otherwise they will compete for food, space and moisture.

■ **deal with aphids** as they settle on the soft growth of perennials: vigilance is important. Apply a precautionary spray with a systemic insecticide or, if you prefer not to use chemicals, choose an organic oil-based spray that kills the pests as they feed.

■ **take basal cuttings from plants** that produce an abundance of new shoots at ground level and insert them in cuttings compost to root (see page 29).

■ **acclimatise and plant out young perennials,** to give them time to establish before winter (see right).

■ **lift and divide mature perennials** to rejuvenate them as well as to increase stock (see page 28).

■ **lift and discard some of the more invasive plants** such as creeping Jenny (*Lysimachia nummularia*) with its low spreading habit; this will check its rapid rate of growth in early summer.

■ **encourage sideshoots to grow** from the base of new plants. Whether they have been raised from seed or from cuttings, make them bushier and stronger by removing the growing tip of each shoot, pinching between thumb and forefinger, once they reach a height of 10cm (4in).

supporting perennials

Herbaceous perennials have soft, non-woody stems, so when they reach a certain height they tend to flop. This can result in considerable damage to both stems and flowers, especially after rain when the blooms, heavy with water, cause the

Put a support of twiggy birch stems in place before tall perennials grow too high.

stems to keel over and collapse. Once a plant flops or is beaten down by rain it never recovers; however carefully you arrange its stems it will always look awkward.

Give extra support to tall-growing plants long before it is needed, and certainly before they have reached half their mature height. Ideally, the supports should be no more than two-thirds of the plants' ultimate height, so that their shoots and leaves grow through the supports and obscure them. Use any of the following:

● **twiggy stems of birch or hazel,** known as brushwood, with the tips bent over.

● **bamboo canes** (though these are more difficult to obscure).

● **specially designed stakes or supports** that link together to form a frame around the plants as they develop; push these deep into the soil initially and ease them up as plants grow.

acclimatising overwintered plants

It can take perennials raised from seed two full years from germination until they flower. If you sow in late summer or early autumn and grow the plants under the protection of a coldframe, greenhouse or conservatory for the first winter, this period can sometimes be shortened.

Perennials raised in this way, or propagated from root cuttings taken in late autumn or winter, will need to be acclimatised gradually to garden conditions, or 'hardened off'

Dicentra spectabilis 'Alba'

easy cuttings

Some plants, such as aster, doronicum, erigeron and phlox, form roots at the base of the new shoots as they develop. Known colloquially as Irishman's cuttings, these roots and shoots can be detached from the parent plant and potted up immediately.

dealing with slugs and snails

The new shoots of herbaceous perennials are soft and succulent and, being at soil level, make easy meals for slugs and snails. Try one of these methods to trap them:

● **hand-pick offenders,** particularly after rain and in the evening.

● **set beer traps,** or a 50:50 beer:water mix; slugs and snails are attracted by the yeasty aroma and then drown.

● **lay a grapefruit half** (flesh scooped out) near vulnerable plants. It will attract large numbers of slugs and snails, so check underneath each morning

● **grow leafy perennials in pots,** raised off the ground.

● **lay slug pellets** sparingly to act as bait. They are frequently used in far too great a quantity: 10 pellets per m² (1 per sq ft) should provide adequate control for one week.

(see page 65), by standing the pots outdoors on warm, sunny days. Bring them under cover at night to protect them from cold and frost. This ensures that the plants will not suffer a serious check in their growth when they are eventually planted out.

Once the plants are fully acclimatised and the risk of heavy frost has diminished, plant them out in the garden (see page 28). With a full growing season ahead of them, they will be strong enough to survive outdoors throughout the following winter season.

PLANTING TIP New perennials raised over winter and divisions from established plants will be smaller in size than those bought at a garden centre, so plant them in groups of three or five of the same species. They will soon appear to merge into a single clump, making much more of a visual impact than if they were planted singly.

Leafy hostas are particularly vulnerable to attack by slugs and snails. Take precautions as soon as their shoots emerge through the soil, otherwise their foliage will be shredded.

perennials/2

planting and propagation

Late spring is a time of rapid growth and lush fresh foliage, so catch the opportunity to lift and divide mature perennials. This is also the time to plant out young plants grown from seed or cuttings, particularly those with hollow stems.

planting perennials

While many perennials can be planted in autumn or early spring, those with hollow stems are vulnerable to weather and must be planted now. They include anchusa, delphiniums, euphorbias, hellebores, helianthus, kniphofias, liatris, phlox, ligularia, poppies (*Papaver orientale*), *Sedum spectabile* and symphytum. If these perennials are planted out in autumn and made to spend their first few months sitting in cold, wet soil, rainwater can collect within their stems and cause them to rot. Disease may then easily be spread to the rest of the plant.

Before planting, dig the site thoroughly, removing all perennial weeds, and incorporate some organic matter, such as well-rotted manure or garden compost. Allow the soil to settle for a week or two, then clear any remaining weeds and roughly rake the soil level before planting begins.

Dig a planting hole large enough to accommodate the whole root system. When you take a bought-in plant from its container, remove the top 1cm (½in) of compost from the surface of the rootball, as it may contain weed seeds and moss that would otherwise be introduced to the garden.

The planting depth of perennials is critical. Most perennials have a shallow root system, with the body or crown of the plant either at or just below soil level.

- **for perennials with fibrous root systems,** such as asters, carex and stachys, the top of the roots should be 1cm (½in) below the soil surface.
- **perennials with fleshier roots,** such as acanthus, bergenias and *Dicentra spectabilis*, need setting slightly deeper, at about 2–3cm (1in) below soil level.
- **it is better to plant slightly too high** and add more soil or mulch later, than too deeply and risk the plant rotting.

PLANTING TIP Buy an established perennial in a large pot rather than several smaller ones. When you get the plant home, remove it from the pot and divide it into smaller pieces, each with several growing shoots and roots, and plant them out as normal.

dividing perennials

Lifting and dividing perennials will rejuvenate mature plants that have formed large congested clumps. This can be done in either autumn or spring. Wait for any that flower early, like bergenias, to finish blooming before you disturb them.

- Lift the clump with a border fork when the soil is moist.
- Divide the clump into pieces by pulling it apart, cutting it

some perennials to divide **in spring**
- achillea • bergenia (after flowering) • *Geranium sanguineum* • hostas • *Helleborus orientalis* (after flowering) • *Iris sibirica* • *Lysimachia punctata* • *Scabiosa caucasica* • *Sedum spectabile* • thalictrum • *Tradescantia* Andersoniana Group

planting perennials

1 **Water the plant** thoroughly and leave to drain. Remove the plant from its pot by gently supporting the stem and foliage, and tapping the container with the other hand.

2 **Holding the plant** by its rootball, position it in the hole at the correct depth. Pull the soil back around the plant and firm it gently into place with your foot.

3 **Leave a slight depression** round the base of the stem, and water into this straight after planting.

taking a basal cutting

1 Remove young shoots from the base of the parent plant at soil level, using a sharp knife. Trim off any leaves from the bottom third of the cutting.

2 Dip the base of each cutting into an appropriate rooting hormone preparation. Cover only the cut surface at the base of the cutting as the rooting hormone may injure the stem.

3 Fill a pot to the rim with cuttings compost. Strike off the excess so the surface is level with the rim, but do not firm. Holding the cuttings vertically, gently insert them into the compost so their bottom third is covered. Water gently.

looking ahead . . .
☑ LATE SUMMER Sow seeds of perennials and raise under cover.
☑ WINTER Take root cuttings of perennials.

perennials **to raise from basal cuttings**
- achillea • campanula
- chrysanthemum
- delphinium • erigeron
- gaillardia • helenium
- lupin • phlox
- scabious • veronica

with a knife, or using two forks back to back.
- Replant the young outer sections of the clump in the border. They will become established quickly.
- Discard the old central portion and any sections carrying old flower stalks, as they rarely produce any further flowers.

taking basal cuttings

Basal cuttings are a variation of softwood cuttings. They are particularly well suited to perennials that produce an abundance of new shoots at ground level in mid to late spring, such as delphiniums or lupins (see above). Select very young, healthy shoots 8–10cm (3–4in) long and insert them into pots of cuttings compost. An 8cm (3in) pot will take a single cutting, a 13cm (5in) pot about six cuttings.

Hostas form large clumps, which can easily be divided. If necessary, cut the clump into pieces using a knife or spade blade.

A clear plastic drinks bottle, with the base cut off, makes an ideal cover for a single cutting. Unscrew the cap regularly for ventilation.

annuals & biennials

Spring biennials are now drawing to an end and autumn-sown annuals will soon come into bloom: late spring is the time to ensure an abundance of summer-long flowers. It is also the best time to sow next year's spring bedding in a vacant patch outdoors, but if you do not have time or space to raise your own annuals from seed, you can still buy young bedding plants.

now is the season to . . .

■ **harden off young plants** sown indoors earlier in spring that are nearly ready for planting out (see page 65). Remove cloches and fleece from protected seedlings outdoors, and open cold frames on mild days to acclimatise young plants.

■ **prick out and pot up greenhouse seedlings** to make large specimen plants.

■ **clear away exhausted spring bedding plants** and prepare the ground for summer annuals.

■ **plant out hardy annuals** sown in spare ground last autumn.

■ **buy summer bedding** at the garden centre and plant out (see opposite).

■ **sow annuals where they are to grow,** especially those that dislike being transplanted. Do this from mid-April to mid-May in milder areas, two to three weeks later in colder parts of the country or where soils are slow to warm up.

■ **sow biennials in drills outdoors** (see opposite) or start under glass for potting up or transplanting later.

■ **grow a few annuals for filling seasonal gaps** later or for planting up pockets left in permanent displays; sow in rows in a vacant patch elsewhere in the garden, as for biennials, or sow under glass. Transplant the seedlings when large and robust enough.

■ **weed regularly between established annuals,** and protect younger plants from slugs and snails (see page 71).

■ **collect seed** from any outstanding spring annuals and biennials, and sow now or dry and store for later use.

and if you have time . . .

■ **sow a few pinches of quick-growing annuals,** like candytuft, where bulbs and early perennials are past their best, and also round spring-flowering shrubs for successional colour.

■ **sow fast-growing half-hardy annuals** such as marigolds (*Tagetes*), mexican sunflower (*Tithonia*) and mallow (*Lavatera*) in the greenhouse.

■ **take soft-tip cuttings** from vigorous plants of petunias, *Begonia semperflorens* and other tender annuals; choose non-flowering shoots or remove flower buds, and root the cuttings in a propagator or on a windowsill indoors (see page 63).

■ **sow leftover seed of taller annuals** in rows at the side of vegetable beds, where they will provide a decorative edging and armfuls of flowers for cutting.

■ **sow late flowering annuals** like asters, chrysanthemums and zinnias, either under glass or outdoors with frost protection.

direct sowing hardy annuals

Many hardy annuals will have been sown in autumn or early spring ready for planting out now, but fast-growing annuals like candytuft, as well as those that dislike being transplanted, such as california poppies and love-in-a-mist, can be sown directly into the soil now. Do not add fertiliser as most annuals will flower best in poor soil.

Biennial forget-me-nots (*Myosotis sylvatica*) self-seed freely.

● **prepare the ground thoroughly** as for a seedbed: rake and level the surface to a fine, stone-free texture.

● **scatter the seeds thinly over the area** and rake them in lightly, or cover with a sifting of fine soil, to about twice their depth. Then water the sowings with a fine spray.

buying bedding plants

If you do not have the time or space to raise your own annuals from seed, you can buy young plants in containers during spring. Do not buy them too early unless you can keep them frost free until it is safe to plant them out.

Avoid leggy plants and yellowing foliage, often symptoms that the plants have been growing for too long and have exhausted their compost nutrients. Also steer clear of trays with dry compost or masses of roots growing through the base. Choose compact bushy plants, well spaced out and all the same size, with healthy-looking foliage and plenty of buds, even the first open flower. Water and feed them when you get home, and plant out as soon as possible, or keep them in a warm (but not hot) sheltered place until you are ready.

planting out bedding

Clear the ground of spring bedding and weeds, and rake level. Mark out with sand, or lines scratched in the surface with a cane, the areas where different varieties are to go.

● **most bedding needs** 15–30cm (6–12in) spacings to produce shapely, bushy plants, but ideal planting density varies according to the size and vigour of the variety, so check labels or catalogue descriptions.

Digitalis purpurea

biennials **for sowing in late April and May**

These plants will flower the following spring and summer:

● brompton stocks (*Matthiola incana*)
● canterbury bells (*Campanula medium* and *C. pyramidalis*) ● clary (*Salvia sclarea*) ● double daisies (*Bellis*) ● forget-me-nots (*Myosotis*)
● foxgloves (*Digitalis*) ● giant thistles (*Onopordum, Silybum*) ● honesty (*Lunaria annua*) ● iceland poppies (*Papaver nudicaule*)
● siberian wallflowers (*Cheiranthus* x *allionii*)
● sweet williams (*Dianthus barbatus*)
● wallflowers (*Cheiranthus cheiri*)
● winter-flowering pansies (*Viola*)

sowing biennials

1 **Prepare a seedbed** outdoors in a spare piece of ground in good light. Mark out straight, parallel drills 15–20cm (6–8in) apart in moistened soil, just deep enough to cover the seeds to double their depth in soil.

2 **Sprinkle the seeds** thinly using finger and thumb (from your palm, not straight from the packet). Carefully cover the seeds and firm gently with the back of the rake.

● **choose a mild, still day** after the threat of frost has passed. Water the plants in their trays and pots, and leave to drain while you dig out planting holes with a trowel. Plant at the same depth as in their containers, firm lightly and water well.

sowing biennials for next spring

Forget-me-nots, wallflowers, sweet williams and foxgloves all need to make plenty of growth this season so that they overwinter outdoors successfully and flower prolifically next year. Sow them outdoors in drills in a nursery bed or vacant piece of ground during May and early June (see above). Cover the bed with netting if you think that birds, squirrels or cats are likely to be a problem.

When the seedlings are large enough to handle, thin to about 5cm (2in) apart; discard the thinnings or transplant them elsewhere. About two weeks later, thin again to leave small varieties 10cm (4in) apart, larger ones 15–20cm (6–8in).

Water as needed and feed once or twice in summer. In autumn, lift plants with a trowel and transfer them to the beds or containers where they are to flower.

looking ahead . . .

☑ SUMMER Deadhead to prolong the life of plants.
☑ AUTUMN Sow hardy annuals. Transfer biennials to their flowering positions.
☑ WINTER Order seed, and protect hardy annuals.
☑ EARLY SPRING Sow annuals under glass.

bulbs & tubers

You can mow bulbs planted in grass six weeks after flowering, or leave them until midsummer if they are intended to seed themselves (see inset picture).

This is the time to tackle spring bulbs that have finished flowering. But remember that bulbs are not exclusively for spring: tender or more exotic species can be planted now, ready to take starring roles in the summer border.

now is the season to ...

■ **plant dahlias and begonias** as dormant or sprouted tubers. Fork the ground deeply and work in plenty of rotted manure or garden compost; just before planting apply a top-dressing of balanced fertiliser at 125g per m² (4oz per sq yd).

■ **cut large begonia tubers** into sections; ensure each piece has at least one bud, and plant as normal.

■ **plant** *Anemone coronaria* in April for flowers in August.

■ **plant a batch of gladioli** every two weeks until late May for a succession of blooms.

■ **plant lily bulblets** and gladiolus cormlets, saved in autumn, in pots or nursery rows, to flower in a year or two.

■ **note dense clumps of spring bulbs** that did not flower well; they are probably overcrowded. Mark their position now for digging up and dividing later in the year.

■ **inspect lilies** for bright red lily beetles and their orange-black grubs; remove by hand or spray with permethrin.

■ **tie tall flower stems** of lilies, galtonias and gladioli to supporting canes, if your garden is windy.

■ **deadhead bulbs** as flowers fade so they conserve energy.

and if you have time ...

■ **feed spring bulbs** with high-potash fertiliser after flowering.

■ **sow seeds of summer bulbs** in seed trays in a cold frame.

■ **rake soil over holes** left by dead bulb leaves, to deter narcissus flies.

planting dahlias

1 **Dig a hole** about 15cm (6in) deep and wide enough for the tubers. Check the size by placing the rootball in the hole. For tall-growing varieties drive in a 1m (3ft) cane off-centre.

2 **Spread out** the roots carefully before planting, then place in the hole and work soil between them. Cover so the base of the old stem is 5cm (2in) below soil level. Leave a slight depression in the soil surface to act as a watering 'saucer'; water well after planting.

lilies **in pots**
Lilies planted now may bloom two to three weeks later than those planted in autumn, but will readjust to the normal flowering time next year. Choose late flowering cultivars such as 'Sterling Star' or 'Pink Perfection' (left), oriental hybrids like 'Star Gazer', or variants of *Lilium speciosum* and *L. lancifolium*.

looking after your spring bulbs

Bulb foliage continues to build up food reserves for next year's display for several weeks after flowering, so it is important not to remove, trim or knot the yellowing leaves for the sake of tidiness until their work is done.

● In the border hide the dying foliage of permanent bulbs by teaming them with leafy planting partners, such as hardy geraniums, or sow a fast-growing annual such as candytuft (*Iberis umbellata*) to camouflage dying foliage after the bulbs have finished flowering.

● Move bulbs used as spring bedding out of the way if you want to plant out summer flowers. If the leaves are already yellow, fork up the bulbs, clean off most of the soil and spread in a single layer to dry under cover, preferably in a greenhouse or a shed. If the bulbs have just flowered or the leaves are starting to discolour, lift them with as much soil on their roots as possible and replant in groups in a vacant patch (such as the vegetable garden if room), to finish ripening. Give them a liquid feed and let the foliage die down naturally. Then lift, dry and store the bulbs under cover until autumn.

planting bulbs for summer flowers

Whereas spring bulbs make the greatest impact massed in large colonies or naturalised drifts, summer bulbs and tubers look more effective in small, strategic groups. Plant them now to provide local colourful highlights in flower borders as well as to rectify any midsummer gaps in beds and borders left by earlier flowering perennials.

There are many summer-flowering bulbs and tubers to fit the bill. Tigridias and butterfly gladioli are useful 'dot' plants, or high points, or are good for cutting; begonias, cannas and dahlias create hot spots of lively colour; some lilies have a wonderful scent; and galtonias and crinums make stately plants that contrast strikingly with the softer, rounded shapes of many herbaceous perennials.

● **for containers**, use a trowel or bulb planter, and plant most of these bulbs at twice their depth in a pot of rich soil-based compost. Then stand the pots outdoors, feed regularly from six weeks after potting and avoid over-watering.

● **with large bulbs** like lilies, plant three or five (odd numbers tend to look better) halfway down a 25–30cm (10–12in) container. Use them to brighten the summer patio or to plunge into borders where gaps occur.

● **plant begonias, cannas and dahlias** as dormant tubers about six weeks before the last frosts are expected for your locality. Space them 60cm–1.2m (2–4ft) apart, according to expected size.

● **alternatively**, if you took dahlia cuttings in early spring or set the tubers to sprout (see Winter), plant them out once the threat of frost has passed (see opposite).

looking ahead . . .
☑ SUMMER Mulch dahlias and pinch out growing tips.
☑ LATE SUMMER Dig up overcrowded clumps of spring bulbs while dormant.
☑ WINTER Sprout dahlia tubers for taking cuttings or planting out.
☑ EARLY SPRING Take softwood cuttings of dahlias.

---

summer bulbs **for planting in late April and early May**
● alstroemeria ● *Anemone coronaria* ● begonia ● bletilla ● canna ● crinum
● crocosmia ● eucomis ● galtonia ● gladiolus ● *Nerine bowdenii* ● schizostylis
● tigridia ● *Tropaeolum tuberosum* ● zantedeschia ● zephyranthes
Explore bulb catalogues for more unusual species.

Crocosmia x *crocosmiiflora* 'Emily McKenzie'

roses

Roses have begun their transformation, now sprouting fresh foliage and strong new shoots, even a few early buds. By the end of May, the flowers of the earliest-blooming roses could be fully open.

now is the season to . . .

■ **finish pruning,** especially if spring is frosty and late, but try to complete this by mid-April (see Early Spring).

■ **continue planting container-grown roses.** They will benefit from being well established before midsummer.

■ **hoe round established plants** regularly to deter weeds and keep bare soil loose and crumbly; hoe only the top 2–5cm (1–2in) of soil to avoid damage to rose roots. Deeper weeds should be hand-pulled or carefully dug out with a trowel, or spot-treated with weedkiller.

■ **remedy moss** and green slime on the ground – indicators of soil compaction, especially after a wet winter and spring – by shallow forking and hoeing.

■ **feed roses** with a powdered or granular feed once spring pruning is finished, and again in midsummer (see below).

■ **give a foliar feed** where soil is poor or plants are ailing, at monthly intervals up to the end of July (see below).

■ **mulch roses** as soon as the ground warms up in May and again after feeding (see opposite).

■ **plant ground cover** and edging perennials in rose beds.

■ **check stakes, supports and ties** on climbing, rambler and standard roses, and loosen or renew them where they are worn or too tight.

■ **shorten some of the oldest** and thickest stems of climbing roses by half their length, to stimulate new main branches to appear lower down.

■ **start disbudding hybrid tea roses** grown for top-quality blooms by rubbing or pinching out all but the main bud at the end of each shoot.

■ **inspect the new growth** on bushes and standards for overcrowded or inward-growing shoots, and pinch them out at their base or at a low bud.

■ **check daily for the watering needs** of roses under glass as they come into flower, and give them a liquid feed every 10–14 days. Watch out for health problems, including red spider mites. Ventilate freely and shade the glass to keep temperatures down. When flowering has finished, stand the pots outside.

■ **water roses planted in early spring,** especially during prolonged dry weather.

Shrub rose *Rosa xanthina* 'Canary Bird', with its attractive single yellow flowers and fern-like foliage, is one of the first roses to flower.

and if you have time . . .

■ **sow miniature roses,** in warmth under glass in April. As seeds germinate erratically, sow them thinly in a large seed tray and prick out the individual seedlings when they are large enough.

feeding roses

Roses are greedy plants, and feeding is an important part of their annual care routine. Always use a fertiliser that is specially formulated for promoting flower production. A rose or tomato fertiliser contains all the necessary major nutrients and trace elements. Follow the manufacturer's instructions, and apply the fertiliser to moist soil around all established roses when you have finished spring pruning, ideally before the leaves open fully. Hoe or rake in lightly (see opposite). Repeat this at midsummer to sustain later growth and flowering, but do not feed after mid-July.

Where the soil is poor, plants are ailing or top-quality blooms are wanted, you can supplement this feed with a foliar feed of dilute liquid fertiliser at monthly intervals from now until the end of July.

mulching

Mulch roses after feeding them. Cover the soil around the stem with a 5–8cm (2–3in) layer of garden compost, rotted manure or composted bark, to suppress weeds and keep the soil moist. Leave a small clear space around the plant's stems.

pests and diseases

The first signs of problems can occur as soon as growth revives in spring, and you should decide whether you are going to spray regularly as a precaution, only treat specific ailments as they occur, or leave the plants to cope without your interference (see page 70). Plants can often tolerate many diseases if they are kept well watered and regularly fed, so control weeds, mulch plants generously, pick off badly affected leaves, and foliar feed infected plants.

MOSAIC VIRUS TIP Look for yellow lines, veins or bands, which show up on new leaves; feed infected plants well and do not use for taking cuttings.

planting roses

Unless there were good reasons for delay (climate or soil conditions, for example), bare-rooted roses will have been planted in early spring and will now be showing signs of life. In more northerly gardens, or where the ground was frozen or waterlogged, plant bare-rooted roses as soon as possible. Container-grown roses can be planted all through the season.

planting container-grown roses

The planting technique for container plants differs only slightly from bare-rooted plants (see Early Spring).

● Prepare the ground by digging deeply on a site where roses have not grown before, and make sure the drainage is adequate. Remove all weeds and pieces of root, and work in plenty of compost or rotted manure.

tying in **new stems of climbers**

Space out and secure vigorous new stems on climbing and rambler roses, using soft garden string to attach them to their supports. If possible, arch the stems sideways on walls and trellis, and spiral them around vertical posts to promote flowering. You could, at the same time, remove one or two of the oldest branches and replace them with new stems.

● Both the rose and the ground should be moist at planting time. Dig a planting hole 15–20cm (6–8in) wider than the container and a little deeper. Mix garden compost or a tree planting compost with the excavated soil, and line the bottom of the hole with a 5cm (2in) layer of this mixture.

● Stand the container in the hole, with the compost surface at ground level, and cut or slide the container off the rootball. Back-fill around the rootball with the loose, prepared soil mix (see above). Firm it as you go, using your fingers or a trowel handle. Level the surface and rake in a dressing of bone meal or rose fertiliser.

● Prune the main stems of all roses except climbers back to about 15cm (6in) immediately after planting.

● Water well in dry weather, and apply a mulch once the ground warms up in May.

PRUNING TIP Prune the rose while it is still in its container. This saves bending down to ground level later.

feeding and mulching

1 **Hoe the soil** lightly round the plant, removing any debris and weeds, before scattering on the fertiliser over the root area.

2 **Cover the fertiliser** with fresh compost to act as a mulch and soil enricher, as well as to help to suppress weeds.

looking ahead . . .

☑ SUMMER Spray, mulch, feed and deadhead roses.

☑ AUTUMN/WINTER Prune roses and tie in climbers.

☑ EARLY SPRING Plant out bare-rooted roses.

climbers

Many early flowering climbers have finished their display and are ready to prune, while others are just coming into growth. Correct pruning keeps the plants to the desired size and shape, but also encourages strong growth and plenty of flowers for next year.

now is the season to ...

■ **prune early flowering climbers** such as *Clematis alpina, C. armandii* and *C. macropetala.*
■ **take cuttings** of late flowering clematis.
■ **train the growing stems** of climbers into their supports.
■ **plant** new climbers (see page 38).

Flowering wisteria and *Clematis montana* var. *rubens* festoon a house wall in late spring.

routine pruning

With the majority of climbers (honeysuckles, jasmines, early flowering clematis, for example) pruning is only necessary to repair winter damage or restore plants to the desired shape.

● **remove any dead or damaged branches,** and carefully tease out and dispose of old and weak stems.

● **tie in loose stems,** bending them away from the vertical.

WHEN TO PRUNE? The basic rules are simple: if the climber flowers in spring, prune straight after flowering; if it flowers in summer or autumn, prune in late winter or early spring.

herbaceous climbers

Herbaceous climbers like the golden hop (*Humulus lupulus* 'Aureus') and perennial peas, such as *Lathyrus rotundifolius*, die back over winter and leave dead stems. If you have not done so already, get rid of dead stems now, before new shoots grow into them. Ideally, they should be cut back to ground level in late winter, but with young plants, it can be helpful to leave the first year's growth to support this year's stems.

mixed climbers

If you are growing a mixture of climbers some may be expanding at the expense of others. Check all the plants now to ensure that growth is under way.

● **cut out any shoots** that threaten less vigorous neighbours but strike the right balance. Avoid spoiling strong growers just to allow space for a weak plant. If any plant is weak and struggling, consider removing it.

early flowering climbers

These are coming to the end of their display and can be pruned now, to produce a good display next winter and spring. Winter jasmine (*Jasminum nudiflorum*) benefits from having all unwanted long growths removed. Trim them back to the main stems to encourage a mass of short, flowering shoots. This treatment also suits: ornamental quince (*Chaenomeles*), *Coronilla valentina*, flowering currant (*Ribes speciosum*), *Forsythia suspensa* and wintersweet (*Chimonanthus*).

Chaenomeles speciosa

taking leaf-bud cuttings of clematis

1 **Remove a whole stem.** Trim the base and discard the soft, fleshy top, cutting just above a pair of leaf buds. You should now have a stem about 5cm (2in) long.

2 **Take a tray** or shallow pot with plenty of drainage holes and fill with a mixture of equal parts perlite or fine grit and soil-less potting compost. Insert each cutting so that the leaf buds at the top are in contact with the compost.

3 **Place the tray** or pot in a propagator or on a windowsill. Inspect the cuttings regularly and immediately remove any that are turning black or rotting. Pot up once rooted.

pruning clematis

This topic is the cause of much unwarranted anxiety. In fact, clematis are seldom harmed, whether left untouched or pruned almost to ground level. The guidelines are these:

● **summer and autumn-flowering clematis** are pruned in winter or early spring.
● **early flowering species** may need attention now, in late spring, or early summer.

Early flowering clematis include *C. alpina* and any clematis that blooms between the shortest day and late spring. Although they perform well without any pruning, if you need to tidy them or to restrict their size, the best time to act is as soon as the flowers are over. Trimming back encourages the plant to make strong growth on which flower buds will form next year. *Clematis montana*, which is in flower now, is more usually pruned in early summer.

pruning Clematis armandii

Unlike most early flowering clematis, the exceptionally vigorous evergreen *Clematis armandii* benefits from drastic treatment, particularly if it has been neglected or is growing in a restricted space.

● Wait until the last flowers have faded. Then cut off all the growth, right back to the trunk. There may not be a single green leaf or stem left when you have finished.
● If the plant is healthy, it will sprout in a couple of weeks. The young stems will be vigorous but extremely brittle. Tie them in carefully as they emerge, using soft garden string and gently bending them to a horizontal position.

● Continue to train the stems as they extend, arranging them so that they cover as much of the wall or fence as possible. On a mature plant, each stem should have grown to around 3m (10ft) by late summer, and a superb display of fragrant white flowers in early spring will be your reward.

propagating clematis

This is the season to propagate late flowering *Clematis viticella* and its hybrids, by taking cuttings or by layering.

cuttings

To take leaf-bud cuttings (see above), select healthy young stems that are beginning to turn woody. Roots will form at the leaf buds, which will start to grow in five to ten weeks.

layering

This is the easiest method of propagating mature clematis (see also page 43) and now is a good time to start the process.

● Take a low-growing stem. On the underside, make a small slanting cut without severing the stem, or simply scrape off the bark.
● Anchor the wounded part in the ground, just below the surface, with a stone or wire staple.
● Within a year, the plant will have grown roots and, as soon as it is dormant, it can be transplanted.

looking ahead . . .

☑ SUMMER Continue to train in new growth of *Clematis armandii*.
☑ Prune *Clematis montana* and its hybrids.
☑ Pot up rooted leaf-bud cuttings of *Clematis viticella* hybrids.

climbers/2
planting and support

Plant herbaceous climbers now to boost vertical displays later in the year. If you provide secure supports and regular attention, your climbers will reward you with a beautiful house wall or boundary.

choosing a climber

Assess your site before you buy a climber, as you need to know what kind of conditions prevail on and around your wall or fence.

- **which direction** does the wall or fence face?
- **how much sun** does it receive?
- **are there overhanging eaves** that might prevent rain from reaching the soil below, and reduce the moisture levels?
- **what is** the soil like?

   The choice of plants will then depend on the aspect and conditions. A north-facing wall is shaded, whereas one facing south is hot and dry. A west-facing wall catches the afternoon or setting sun, which creates gentler conditions than the rising sun warming an east-facing wall, especially in frosty weather. So plant vulnerable or slightly tender species such as summer jasmine (*Jasminum officinale*) and climbing potato vine (*Solanum*) against a west-facing wall, and tougher species like quince and winter jasmine (*Jasminum nudiflorum*) facing east. Mix climbers to give flower and foliage interest over a long period, but make sure they are of similar vigour and have similar pruning requirements.

The soil type is important too, especially if it is limy or chalky, as some plants will not tolerate these alkaline conditions. Sandy soils drain fast and need organic matter added, plus a thick mulch to help to retain moisture, since almost all climbers benefit from a cool, moist root run.

planting climbers

Most climbers need supports and these should be put in place first. Before planting, improve the soil generally by digging in compost or other well-rotted organic matter together with a little bone meal or balanced fertiliser. If you are planting into a specially prepared hole in a paved area, fork the sides and base to make sure there is plenty of space for the roots to run, and that it drains freely.

   An hour or two before you plant, water the climber thoroughly. Then site your planting hole at least 45cm (18in) from the wall; if there is an overhanging roof or gutter, move it farther out to ensure the roots receive plenty of moisture. Plant climbers very slightly deeper than the level of compost in the container. With clematis, plant more deeply so that 8–10cm (3–4in) of the stems are covered. If the top growth is spindly and thin, cut it back hard to a bud at soil level.

   After planting, continue to water the climber at regular intervals until it is established, but do not feed until next year. Once climbers are established, shade their base and therefore their roots with a thick mulch (see page 138), paving slabs or low-growing plants.

planting a climber

1 **Dig a hole** larger and deeper than is needed for the climber's rootball, and tip the bone meal and compost mix into the bottom of the hole. Turn the climber gently out of its pot. If the roots are congested, tease them out.

2 **Place the rootball** in the hole and plant fractionally deeper than the level of compost in the container. Back-fill the hole with soil, firming it down gently with your foot.

3 **Water thoroughly.** If the stems are long enough, tie them to a support. If not, place canes at an angle to encourage young stems to grow towards the fence or wall support.

methods of support

Almost all climbers need to be trained and most need to be tied to a support. Even those that cling by stem rootlets or sucker pads, such as ivy, climbing hydrangea (*H. anomala* subsp. *petiolaris*) or virginia creeper (*Parthenocissus*), will need your help if they are to distribute themselves evenly.

● **horizontal training wires** are the simplest and most effective system. Stretch them taut along the wall or between fence posts, anchoring them at 2m (6ft) intervals with 'vine eyes' (special nails or screws with a hole at one end). Space wires roughly 45cm (18in) apart, with the bottom one this distance above the ground. Use stout galvanised wire, and make sure the anchor points are strong enough to bear the weight of a large climber.

● **trellis is an attractive** alternative to wires. Make sure trellis panels are held clear of the wall or fence so that air can pass freely between plant and structure, and to make tying in easier. Mount panels on wooden battens and secure with long strong screws (see page 126).

● **tie stems loosely to the wires or trellis**, using soft garden string. Plants that cling by tendrils, such as clematis, or twine, like honeysuckle (*Lonicera*), need little more than to have wayward stems secured. Non-clinging plants such as roses and wall shrubs need their stems tied at several points while they are young and flexible.

training climbers

Train climbers, especially flowering kinds, in a fan formation, gently angling the main stems away from the vertical. Training stems like this promotes flowering and ensures the wall or fence is evenly covered all the way down to the ground, rather than merely at the top.

Keep wall shrubs, roses and other climbers that need regular pruning on the outside of the trellis or wires. If the stems extend between support and wall, they are difficult to unravel and will become jammed, sometimes forcing the trellis or vine eyes away from the wall.

Early in the year, the flowers of *Clematis macropetala* bring colour to walls and fences. This climber does well even in a position of cool, semi-shade.

shrubs & trees

Betula utilis

Many spring-flowering species will be in full bloom, but others, their flowers already finished, will need pruning to restore their shape and good looks. As fresh leaves begin to expand on deciduous shrubs, now is a good time to restore overgrown hedges and plant new evergreens and specimen shrubs.

now is the season to . . .

■ **prune shrubs that have flowered already,** and hard-prune shrubs that flower later on new shoots (see right).

■ **regularly water shrubs and trees** planted in early spring, especially on light soils. In dry weather occasionally spray new evergreens with clean water during the evening.

■ **feed young trees and shrubs,** and any you have pruned hard, with a balanced fertiliser; water in if the soil is at all dry.

■ **restore overgrown deciduous hedges** (see Winter) before birds start nesting. Check carefully before starting, and stop work if you find a nest being built.

■ **continue protecting foliage and flower buds** at risk from frost (including many silver and grey shrubs, such as cistus, halimium and romneya) with one or two layers of fleece (see Early Spring); remove as soon as the weather warms up.

■ **check for dead and frost-damaged shoots,** once the risk of frost has passed; prune them back to uninjured wood as a precaution against disease.

■ **tidy and weed** around established trees and shrubs, but make sure you avoid damaging surface roots with over-zealous hoeing or forking.

■ **hand-pull weeds,** or deter them by heavy mulching, around trees and shrubs, such as magnolias, that dislike root disturbance of any kind.

■ **watch out for pests and diseases,** especially aphids and caterpillars, on new soft growth, and mildew in a dry season; remove by hand or treat with appropriate insecticide or fungicide (see page 70).

■ **mulch the warmed soil** during May, to conserve moisture around younger plants, those recently planted and any on very light soils.

■ **deadhead rhododendrons and azaleas** that have finished flowering (see opposite).

■ **plant new evergreens** (see page 42).

■ **propagate bushy shrubs** by layering (see page 43).

■ **take soft-tip cuttings** of shrubs and hedge plants that produce long new growths (see page 43).

and if you have time . . .

■ **prune the stems** of *Buddleja davidii* to varying heights, to produce an attractive tiered display of flowers. Spread the pruning over several weeks to extend the flowering season.

■ **plant bareroot deciduous trees and shrubs** in cooler parts of the country, but only if they are still without leaves. Finish the job as early as possible and be prepared to water them regularly throughout the summer; otherwise wait until early autumn.

■ **plant bamboos,** both as specimen shrubs and for decorative windbreaks. Where space is limited, choose clump-forming species, rather than spreading varieties with potentially invasive runners.

shrub pruning guide

Keep your secateurs sharp and handy, because there is a lot of pruning to do at this time of year. Some of it is cosmetic, but on many species pruning is an essential stimulus to prolific flowering later in the season or next year.

● **prune shrubs that have already flowered,** such as forsythia and flowering currant, immediately after flowering, by completely cutting out a third of the oldest shoots (thicker and darker than the others). Cut them back to ground level or down to a framework of old branches. Lightly trim the rest by cutting off the flowered tips.

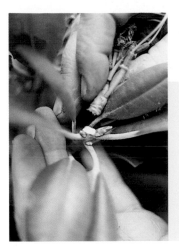

deadheading
Tidy the growth of camellias, magnolias, rhododendrons and azaleas to make room for the new season's shoots. When deadheading, take care not to damage the bud.

● **hard-prune shrubs that flower later** on shoots produced this year, such as hardy fuchsias, *Hydrangea paniculata* and caryopteris: cut all last season's growth either to just above ground level, or to a taller stump if you want a large bush.

● **'stool' ornamental trees** like paulownia, coloured elders and some eucalyptus: that is, cut all stems to just above ground level. These trees produce larger or more decorative leaves when cut back annually to form 'shrubs'.

● **restore grey-leaved shrubs** such as lavender and artemisias to shape. They become leggy and bare at the base if left unpruned. Cut the leafy growth as far back as needed, but stop at least 2–3cm (1in) beyond the older leafless branches. Trim plants again after flowering to encourage bushy growth.

● **prune broad-leaved evergreens** such as laurel and holly to stimulate bright summer foliage and denser growth. Shorten all last year's new shoots by half, using secateurs on large bushes to avoid cutting leaves. Overgrown plants of this kind can be hard-pruned to their original size during April.

● **trim stems of specimen conifers and topiary to shape** with secateurs, but avoid cutting across the sprays of foliage.

Shorten smaller protruding and misplaced shoots to restore shapeliness; larger branches can be tied back in with wire or removed altogether if this does not leave an ugly gap. Where conifers have produced more than one central stem or 'leader', reduce these to the strongest to avoid spoiling the tree's shape. Tip-prune long branches to encourage branching.

hedge care

● **tidy leaves and dead wood** from the base of hedges, and clear weeds. Watch out especially for perennial and twining weeds that can soon infiltrate dense hedges.

● **water newly planted hedges** regularly in dry weather. Concentrate water at the base of each plant rather than giving the hedge an overall sprinkling. Check every two weeks unless rain intervenes.

● **feed young hedges** with a balanced fertiliser at a rate of 125g per m² (4oz per sq yd), distributed evenly around the plants. Older hedges need only half this rate, unless they have been hard-pruned to shape. A mulch of rotted manure or garden compost can replace the spring feed on established hedges.

● **mulch young hedges** liberally with grass mowings in dry weather and on light soils. Spread a mulch 5cm (2in) deep over moist soil and keep topped up as the season progresses.

trimming hedges

You can give formal conifer and other fast-growing hedges, such as privet and lonicera, their first clip of the year now, using shears or a hedge trimmer (see below). Stretch a taut line between two canes and use this guide to ensure accurate cutting and to define the new height.

trimming a privet hedge

1 Clip the sides of the hedge first, working from the bottom up. Gently sweep away the trimmings as you go.

2 Trim the sides to an upright profile or, more traditionally, to a slight batter (an inward lean) so that light can more easily reach the base of the hedge.

3 Clip the top to the string line. Trim a wide hedge in two stages, working to the middle from each side, to ensure a consistent level.

shrubs & trees/2
planting and propagation

Container-grown evergreens are best planted in the spring season as the soil warms up and conditions improve. You can also increase your stock of shrubs and hedge plants using the simple procedures of layering and taking softwood cuttings, which are best done now.

planting new evergreens

Evergreen trees and shrubs can be planted safely during mid and late spring, and this is often preferable in cold regions and on heavy wet soils, where autumn planting can result in root injury or disease. Plants that are root-balled (their roots and surrounding soil wrapped in netting) or bare-rooted should be planted by the beginning of April; container-grown specimens are also best established now before a possibly hot and dry summer season (see below).

Remember that trees and shrubs have a potentially long life in one place, so the planting site needs thorough preparation. Dig the soil down two spade depths, and improve the drainage where necessary. Remove all weeds and weed root fragments over an area of 1m² (10 sq ft) to reduce competition from weeds. For a tree, drive in a short upright support stake, slightly off-centre, before planting.

If planting a container-grown evergreen, water the new plant in its pot and allow to drain. Then remove the pot and carefully tease out some of the roots away from the rootball. Put root-balled plants in position, then cut and remove the netting. After planting any kind of shrub or tree, back-fill the hole with excavated soil and firm the plant in place with your foot. Water thoroughly and cover the area with a thick mulch.

A box hedge is slow growing but makes perfect low edging to a bed if clipped regularly; here, violas form a skirt at its base. Hedge trimmings can be used as a source of soft cuttings to propagate box, privet and lonicera, but they take two to three years to grow into small hedge plants.

Secure a tree to its stake with one or two adjustable tree ties. On exposed sites, it is a good idea to erect a screen of fine mesh or similar windbreak material while the plant is getting established. Place it on the windward side of the plant, to shield it from frost and cold winds.

planting a container-grown conifer

1 Fork plenty of compost or similar well-rotted organic material into the soil, then dig a hole two to three times the width of the plant's rootball.

2 Stand the plant in the hole, keeping the rootball intact, and adjust the planting depth so that the old soil mark on the stem is at surface level.

3 After back-filling the hole with soil, gently shake the tree once or twice to settle the soil around its roots. Then level the soil surface, water and cover the area with a thick organic mulch. Continue to water well in dry weather.

layering bushy shrubs

The lower branches of many shrubs naturally develop roots
where they touch the ground. You can exploit this ability to
produce new plants with little risk of failure, because the
new plant remains attached to its parent until rooted. You
may do this at any time of year, although starting now, when
growth is at its most vigorous, allows a full season's growth
before the new shrub is severed and transplanted in autumn.

• For bushy shrubs such as rosemary, ornamental quince,
cistus, virburnums and rhododendrons, select a healthy,
flexible low shoot that will bend easily to touch the ground
15–20cm (6–8in) near its tip.

• Where it touches, scoop out some of the soil with a trowel
to leave a shallow depression.

• Strip the leaves from the shoot at the point of contact, and
wound the underside to expose some of the inner tissues. Do
this by slicing off a thin layer of bark with a sharp knife, or
by cutting a small slit at an angle to about halfway through,
or simply by twisting the stem.

• Peg the stem down and cover the rooting area with soil.

• Should rooting not occur, carefully re-open the wound,
dust the surfaces with hormone powder and try again. Wait
until spring or the following autumn before detaching the
shoot and moving it to its new home.

taking soft-tip cuttings

In mid to late spring, many shrubs produce long new shoots
that are firm enough for you to take cuttings. Hebe, lavatera,
sage, phlomis and santolina are a few of the many species
easily and quickly propagated like this (see page 63).

watering aid

To assist with watering,
either lay a porous pipe in
the hole, with one end at the
soil surface, or bury a pot
almost to its rim near the
plant as you finish back-
filling. This will ensure that
water reaches right down to
the roots of a newly planted
tree or shrub.

• Trim each shoot to about 5–8cm (2–3in) long, cutting just
below a leaf joint.

• Remove leaves from the lower half of the cutting and pinch
out its soft tip, which can sometimes rot and set up diseases.
If the base of the cutting is firm or starting to look woody, dip
it in hormone powder or liquid to help stimulate rooting.

• Insert the cuttings to just below the lowest leaves in a pot
or tray of cuttings compost or a 50:50 mixture of potting
compost and grit or sharp sand. Make sure the cuttings do
not touch each other.

• Water in well and leave to drain. Stand the pot in a closed
propagator, or cover with a clear plastic bag supported off the
leaves with wire hoops. Keep warm and lightly shaded from
bright sunshine. New, paler top growth and roots appearing
from the base of the pot indicate successful rooting. Cuttings
may then be potted up individually.

layering a shrub

1 Take a young supple stem,
strip off the lower leaves,
and tear the bark slightly. Peg
the stem down in the soil with
a loop of stiff wire.

2 Cover with fine soil or fresh
potting compost.

3 Bend the end of the
pegged stem upwards
and tie it to a vertical cane to
start training the new shrub.
Water well, and keep moist
in dry weather.

alpine gardens

Late spring is the best season for alpine plants, with more in flower now than at any other time of year. During these months, plan new planting schemes and buy plants while you can see their brilliant colours and exquisite forms.

now is the season to . . .

■ **look out for self-sown seedlings,** which are likely to appear now, and take care not to pull them up while weeding. Leave them undisturbed, or transplant any that have popped up in the wrong spot or pot them into small pots to give to friends.

■ **tidy up plants that have flowered,** but leave some spent flowerheads if you want seed or self-sown seedlings.

■ **trim back invasive plants** to prevent them from swamping neighbours. Where necessary, dig out sections of plants.

■ **replenish the grit or gravel mulch** in alpine beds or sinks if it has become buried or scattered.

■ **remove cloches or other forms of protection** from alpines that resent winter wetness. Take cloches off as soon as days noticeably lengthen, otherwise the plants will be tricked into premature growth and made more vulnerable to late frosts.

■ **watch out for weeds** and remove them as soon as they appear; do not allow any to seed, as weeds can be more troublesome on a rock garden than anywhere else.

■ **keep an eye out for pests:** there are few that affect alpines although vine weevils are increasingly common, and most likely to cause problems among primulas, cyclamen and dodecatheon. The tell-tale symptom is sudden wilting. If this occurs, pull up the plant and examine the roots for cream,

comma-shaped grubs. If they are present, consider biological treatment (see page 71). Slugs and snails may trouble young plants while they are small and vulnerable.

■ **prick out alpines raised from seed** sown in early spring into trays or alpine compost, or individually into 8cm (3in) pots.

■ **check cuttings of alpines** taken in early spring and plant them out once they have rooted.

and if you have time . . .

■ **divide oversized plants** once they have finished flowering. (If you are busy postpone this job until early autumn.) Lift the plant with a small fork or trowel and carefully tease it apart into small sections; discard the old central part and replant vigorous outer sections.

building an alpine collection

The majority of alpines enjoy cool, moist but very well-drained soil, and need plenty of sun for their bright flowers. Ideally, this means growing them in a south-facing site away from overhanging trees.

Although many are easy to raise from seed, the fastest way to build a collection of alpines is to buy plants and to divide these on a regular basis, although some, like fairy foxglove (*Erinus alpinus*), will obligingly self-seed. Many, such as dwarf campanulas, cover the ground quickly by means of spreading stems or extending rootstocks. Others, including many saxifrages, develop huge cushions that can be gently broken up and the pieces replanted. Alpines are small enough to be handled easily when in bloom, and few will resent planting or moving at this time of year.

In this rock garden, alpine plants including dianthus and saxifrages enjoy the free-draining conditions of a sloping site.

Good places to grow alpine plants include dry-stone walls, cracks and crevices in paving or walls (see page 131), and gravel or shingle (see page 136). *Haberlea rhodopensis* (right) grows in a gravel niche.

looking ahead...

☑ AUTUMN OR EARLY SPRING Remove any plants that become leggy or untidy and trim or thin the rest.

☑ EARLY SPRING Sow seed of alpines and take cuttings of existing alpines.

sink gardens

The ideal size for an alpine sink garden is approximately 60 x 40cm (24 x 16in) and 20cm (8in) deep. This will allow room for six or seven plants. Choose plants that will flower in different seasons or go for one big bright display that leaves plenty of greenery for the rest of the year. Select a single small shrub or tiny tree (a dwarf conifer or miniature willow, such as *Salix lanata*, for example) to act as a focal point. Water the plants in their containers well, so that they are moist before planting.

Set aside a few small but attractive pieces of rock or large stones. Drill drainage holes in the sink if there is no plug hole, and place a layer of gravel or pieces of terracotta from broken pots in the bottom to make sure that water can escape easily and compost is not washed out.

Fill the sink to the top with a potting compost designed for alpines, then water and allow to settle for a day or two before planting (see below).

COMPOST TIP Make your own free-draining alpine potting compost by blending equal amounts of John Innes No. 2 compost (or a soil-less equivalent) and coarse grit.

rosette-forming alpines to divide now

Divide plants that form cushions of rosettes, such as houseleeks (*Sempervivum*). Gently remove whole rosettes, each with a few roots attached, and replant them in gritty compost.
• *Arabis ferdinandi-coburgi*
• houseleeks • *Saxifraga* x *apiculata* and *S.* 'Tumbling Waters' • *Sedum spathulifolium*

Sempervivum tectorum

flowering plants for an alpine sink

SPRING: *androsaces*, cushion saxifrages, low-growing wallflowers (*Erysimum*), small primulas

SUMMER: alpine pinks, campanulas (especially *C. cochleariifolia*), *Geranium dalmaticum*, *Verbascum* 'Letitia'

AUTUMN: autumn snowflake (*Leucojum autumnale*), *Cyclamen cilicium*, gentians, *Sorbus reducta*

WINTER: snowdrops (*Galanthus nivalis*), winter crocuses

planting an alpine sink

1 **With the plants** still in their pots, arrange them into a miniaturised landscape, placing the largest plant or plants first as a focal point. Also position one or more of the biggest pieces of rock or stones.

2 **Once you are satisfied** with your arrangement, bed the rocks into the compost. Remove the plants from their pots and plant using a trowel. Water in well.

3 **Place the remaining** smaller pieces of rock or stone around the plants. Cover the compost with coarse gravel, 2–3cm (1in) deep. Tuck it carefully round the plants, keeping their leaves free.

water gardens

To maintain the delicate balance of life in your pond, you will need to control rampant water plants and make sure part of the surface is kept clear of water lilies or pond weeds.

Many ponds and pools look their best in late spring, when several water plants are in flower and others are enjoying a surge of new growth.

now is the season to . . .

■ **divide bottom-rooted water plants,** marginal (shallow-water) plants and bog plants that are old or overgrown, to provide young replacements (see opposite).

■ **top up water features regularly;** hot weather in May can cause rapid evaporation.

■ **replenish gravel on baskets** of submerged plants where fish have been foraging.

■ **fix a net across the pond** above the surface of the water, if herons are stealing fish.

■ **clean the pond** only if absolutely necessary; if it is full of tadpoles it is better to wait till autumn.

■ **clear out pond weeds** to keep at least a third of the water surface clear.

■ **move or transplant water plants** while they are in active growth; this will give them a long period to establish in their new surroundings, well before the onset of winter weather.

■ **grow oxygenating plants** from tip cuttings 15cm (6in) long. Tie six to eight cuttings together at the base with a piece of string and plant each bunch, with the string buried, at the bottom of the pond.

■ **plant three small bunches of oxygenating plants** for every square metre of pool (one per sq ft). They absorb minerals and carbon dioxide in the water and are essential to maintain its clarity and quality; choose them according to the scale of your pond as many of these oxygenating plants can be extremely invasive.

■ **include small pieces of floating plants** such as duckweed (*Lemna trisulca*), fairy moss (*Azolla filiculoides*) and frogbit (*Hydrocharis morsus-ranae*), which are also oxygenators. Simply toss them onto the surface (they don't need planting) where they will provide useful shade and prevent the build-up of algae and blanket weed.

■ **plant up new marginal plants,** either bought in or from your own stock. Plant them along the shallow shelf or at the pond edge, in plastic mesh baskets or directly into the soil.

■ **plant deep-water plants** like water lilies in baskets (see page 49).

■ **feed fish liberally** as they become more active, to build up their strength and resistance to disease.

good oxygenating plants
• elodea (*Lagarosiphon*) • frogbit (*Hydrocharis morsus-ranae*)
• hornworts (*Ceratophyllum*) • water violet (*Hottonia palustris*)

dividing water plants

- Lift the plants out of their baskets, or the pond soil. Depending on their size, chop thick-rooted plants into pieces with a knife or sharp spade, or pull them apart with your hands. If large, use two forks back to back.
- Cut plants with creeping rhizomes into 15cm (6in) lengths, each with one or more fat buds.
- Remove any dead or rotting portions with a knife.
- Replant healthy young pieces either directly into the pond soil, or in baskets as shown on page 49.

clearing weeds

Control pond weeds so that at least a third of the water surface is kept clear. This means removing blanket weed and duckweed if they threaten to block out all the light.

- **duckweed** is mainly found growing on still water. Drag out as much as possible with a net and leave it to dry out and die before adding it to the compost heap.

You might need to clear blanket weed several times from late spring into summer. A long-term solution is to fit an ultra-violet filter to your water-circulating system.

- **blanket weed** tends to be a greater problem in new ponds or those recently cleaned. Clear thick layers by dragging out as much as possible by hand. For large amounts or big ponds, use a garden rake; in smaller ponds or where there is a liner, twirl the weed around a stout stick. However, blanket weed often contains beneficial insects and water snails, which feed on the weed, so clearing too much can be self-defeating. Leave the piles of blanket weed by the pond overnight to give insects and snails a chance to crawl back into the water.

testing the water

The health of a pond is finely balanced, and one of the factors that will upset its balance is a change in the relative acidity or alkalinity (the pH) of the water. Simple kits are available to test pH accurately. Readings between 6.5 and 8.5 are satisfactory, but above or below these levels plants and fish will suffer. Where the lime content of the water or soil has added too much alkalinity, making the pH reading too high, suspend a fine mesh bag of peat in the pond to lower the pH. Alternatively, add an appropriate pH-boosting agent to the water to redress the balance.

Check the level of the water surface regularly as pond water can evaporate quickly once the weather warms up. Top it up, from a water butt where possible, using a hosepipe.

water gardens/2

Darmera peltata

pond planting

Late spring marks the beginning of the year for pond plants. As water temperatures begin to rise, the cheerful yellow pondside flowers of marsh marigolds and the lovely pink heads of *Darmera peltata* (above) open, while other plants rush into growth. Now is the time to establish new water plants, either bought in or from your own stock.

To make the care and maintenance of the pond and its plant population as easy as possible, always use rigid plastic-mesh planting baskets to contain water plants. The advantages of using baskets are that they give a greater degree of control over the plants' growing environment and they are easier to lift out of the water, compared with growing the plants *in situ*. You should avoid using wooden or metal containers in water because they may produce toxins that are harmful to fish.

Use loamy garden soil, preferably with a high proportion of clay, or a specially formulated aquatic compost. The soil for water plants should not be enriched with organic matter or fertiliser.

planting marginal plants

Marginals are shallow-water plants that prefer no more than 5–10cm (2–4in) of water covering their roots. They fall into two groups according to their root systems: those with a creeping rootstock, or rhizome, like *Iris laevigata*, and those with fibrous roots, such as pickerel weed (*Pontederia cordata*). Grow both types in baskets. Select a planting basket of a suitable size, and line it with hessian or a geotextile, unless you are using a micro-mesh planting basket. Part-fill with soil or aquatic compost (see opposite), before inserting the plant and firming with more soil. Place the basket on the planting ledge, if there is one, or on brick piles to bring the plants up to the required level.

● **to plant marginal plants with rhizomes** remove dead leaves, trim away any old brown roots with a sharp knife and pack the soil fairly firmly around the roots, leaving the horizontal rootstock exposed.

● **to plant marginal plants with fibrous roots** use a sharp knife to trim off any dead and discoloured leaves and old brown roots, then trim back the healthy roots to about 5–10cm (2–4in), and cut back any large shoots. Plant deeply, with the roots going straight down into the soil and the base of the shoots at soil level.

marginal plants with rhizomes

- arrow arum (*Peltandra sagittifolia*) ● bog arum (*Calla*)
- bogbean (*Menyanthes*)
- corkscrew rush (*Juncus effusus* f. *spiralis*)
- great water plantain (*Alisma plantago-aquatica*) ● *Iris laevigata*
- marsh marigold (*Caltha palustris*)
- sweet flag (*Acorus*)

Caltha palustris

marginal plants with fibrous roots

- candelabra primula (*Primula beesiana*)
- cotton grass (*Eriophorum angustifolium*)
- monkey flower (*Mimulus*)
- pickerel weed (*Pontederia cordata*)

Primula beesiana

planting water lilies in a lined basket

1 **Line the basket** with hessian to stop the compost from spilling out through the mesh, and half-fill with soil or aquatic compost.

2 **Place the water lily** in the centre. Add more soil, packing it firmly around the plant. Fill the basket to within 2–3cm (1in) of the rim. Top up with a layer of coarse gravel to prevent the soil from floating away. Trim off any surplus liner. Water the plant with pond water to settle the soil around the roots.

3 **Once the soil** is saturated, lower the basket into the desired position within the pond.

LINER TIP As an alternative to hessian, use geotextile to line the baskets or use micro-mesh planting baskets.

planting water lilies

Water lilies (*Nymphaea*) are deep-water plants, and require a depth of 45–60cm (18–24in) or more. Before planting or replanting them, trim off any large leaves. (If these are left on they will increase the plant's buoyancy, which may result in it floating free of its container and rising to the pond surface.) To encourage new roots to form quickly, trim back the fibrous roots and cut away any dead or rotting sections of the thick fleshy stem, or rhizome. Once the basket is placed in the water, make sure the shoots reach the surface: this may mean standing the basket temporarily on bricks until the leaves grow, then lowering it gradually over a period of weeks until it sits on the bottom of the pool.

looking ahead . . .

☑ SUMMER Continue to lower baskets of water lilies by removing one brick at a time.

flowering plants
for deeper water
• golden club (*Orontium aquaticum*)
• *Nuphar lutea*
• water fringe (*Nymphoides peltata*)
• water hawthorn (*Aponogeton distachyos*)
• water lilies (*Nymphaea*)

If bubbles rise from the planting basket as it is lowered into the water, hold it steady until it achieves natural buoyancy, otherwise it will tip onto its side and spill the contents.

patios & containers

Seasonal and permanent plants grown in containers and raised beds rely entirely on you for their care. Feed and water regularly from late spring and they will reward you with a cheerful patio display all summer.

now is the season to . . .

■ **plant out half-hardy bedding** plants as soon as the risk of frost has passed, usually late May. You will still find plenty of summer bedding plants in garden centres and other outlets, even though it is too late to order plants by mail or over the Internet.

■ **prepare the soil** in raised beds and patio borders by clearing any weeds and forking in some organic matter, such as rotted manure or mushroom compost. Apply a general fertiliser before planting.

■ **plant annual climbers** in containers or raised beds to bring an extra colourful dimension to the patio. Nasturtiums and sweet peas look charming growing up a wigwam of bamboo canes or rustic poles.

■ **plant some herbs,** not only for kitchen use, but also for their fragrance. Plant them by hot paving – the heat will help to release their aromatic oils. Lavenders, rosemary, sage, marjoram, coriander and basil all grow in hot, dry conditions.

■ **start to think about summer containers** and hanging baskets for a summer patio display (see page 52). Achieve dramatic results by restricting yourself to simple colour schemes, using foliage as well as flowers to keep schemes lively.

■ **plant up pots or raised beds** with summer bedding to provide a colourful splash from July onwards. Or choose unusual flowering perennial plants, like blue agapanthus, and bulbs such as the glorious South African pineapple lily (*Eucomis*).

■ **direct sow hardy annuals** in pots or raised beds (see page 30).

■ **introduce tender shrubs** in large containers. A lemon or pomegranate plant, for example, will provide a wonderful summer display, but must be taken indoors in late autumn.

care of container shrubs

Most evergreens are at their peak of growth and should not be trimmed or pruned until summer.

● **dwarf rhododendrons and camellias** should have their old flowers and seed heads removed (see page 41).

● **early flowering deciduous shrubs** generally benefit from being pruned as soon as flowering is over; remove branches that have flowered to encourage leafy growth in summer and even more flowers next year (see page 40).

● **few topiary specimens** need clipping in late spring, apart from plants that grow rapidly and need several clips a year. Trim privet (*Ligustrum*) and *Lonicera nitida* now, following the original shape. Use small shears, or even scissors, to get the precise outline.

● **give roses** a light feed in late spring and, if you don't object to using chemical sprays, treat to prevent mildew, black spot and aphid attack (see page 70).

PRUNING TIP Do not prune daphnes – they are prone to virus diseases and can get infected at pruning wounds.

Plant up a group of improvised containers after drilling drainage holes. Violas, azaleas and forget-me-nots make a bright display.

feeding

Patio plants get hungry, especially during summer. The more permanent shrubs and trees, in the open ground, will need little by way of plant food, since their roots will be searching for nutrients over a wide area. But plants grown in containers, raised beds, or borders where soil is in any way limited will need feeding regularly from late spring onwards.

Slow-release fertiliser pellets supply food continuously over several months throughout the growing season.

● **liquid feeds** can be given every 7–14 days, when watering, throughout the growing season. Start six weeks after planting, when the fertiliser in the compost will have run out. Use a high-potash feed, like tomato fertiliser, to promote flowers.
● **slow-release fertilisers** provide all the necessary nutrients container plants require for several months or even the whole growing season – see manufacturer's instructions. They release more nutrients as temperature and available moisture increase – just when plants need them most.

FEEDING TIP Avoid over-feeding plants. It makes them grow too lush and they become disease-prone. The results of over-feeding are more of a problem, especially on patios, than plant starvation. Remember that plants manufacture the bulk of their own food from sunlight, water and carbon dioxide in the air; substances absorbed through the roots are merely supplements – essential, but needed only in tiny quantities.

watering

Watering is the single most important task in container gardening. More plants suffer stress through lack of water than from any other cause.
● **water new plants** thoroughly, not only when planted but regularly later, until their root systems are developed.

● **water plants in containers and hanging baskets** daily as summer approaches.
● **check small patio beds** with shallow soil as they dry out fast. Even after rain it is worth checking just below the surface in case the soil is bone dry. A thorough soaking every two weeks in hot, dry weather makes all the difference to the way your patio plants perform over summer.

WATERING TIP The best means of ensuring adequate water supplies for hanging baskets and containers is to fit an automatic watering system (see Summer). These kits need not be complicated and are operated by a time switch, so that watering will still take place if you are away.

Give container-grown plants a good soaking immediately after planting, preferably through a fine rose attachment. Continue watering until the water runs out of the bottom of the pot.

patios & containers/2

creating a summer display

Well-planted pots and hanging baskets will cheer up the patio in summer. Use colourful bedding and plant generously to stage as bright a display as possible.

summer containers

Garden centres have a wide range of bedding and other plants for summer containers. They are often presented in colour groups, so it is easy to choose those that fit a special colour scheme. And why not visit some of the many flower shows and plant fairs that take place at this time of year? You will find a whole range of interesting plants on sale.

● **anchor plants are central to a container,** whether used alone or surrounded by smaller or trailing plants. Fuchsias are a popular choice, but why not try something different, perhaps trained as a standard, such as *Solanum rantonnetii*? Even succulents, like *Aeonium arboreum* and the century plant (*Agave americana*), make fine anchors.

● **trailing or filling plants** to go with the anchors include jolly yellow bidens and cool blue scaevola. New varieties of pelargonium are bred every year, but many older kinds, especially those with aromatic leaves, are just as beautiful and easy to grow.

● **use fragrance, as well as colour.** Heliotrope has a bewitching scent, as do mignonettes (easy annuals), night-scented stocks and sweet peas, especially the older, scented varieties.

● **newly purchased plants** for bedding and containers need to be exposed gradually to cold, windy or excessively wet weather before they go outside. This is known as 'hardening off' (see page 65).

plants for summer containers

anchor plants • *Aeonium arboreum* 'Atropurpureum' • castor oil plant (*Ricinus*) • century plant (*Agave americana*) • daisy bush (*Argyranthemum*), grown as standards • fuchsias • *Solanum rantonnetii* • tree datura (*Brugmansia*)

trailing & filling plants • bacopa • *Bidens ferulifolia* • *Helichrysum petiolare* • laurentia • nasturtiums • pelargoniums • petunias (right) • scaevola

● **water containers daily** from late spring onwards and feed every 7–14 days during the growing season, from six weeks after planting. Use a high-potash feed, such as tomato fertiliser.

hanging baskets

The most attractive baskets are those with plants growing through the sides as well as out of the top. When planting, aim for an almost perfect sphere of foliage and flower.

● **line baskets with natural moss** or with a lining made from coconut-fibre or recycled cardboard. Black plastic is a practical but less attractive alternative.

● **after planting a hanging basket,** wash off any compost that has lodged on the leaves, preferably using rainwater collected in a butt. The plants will take a few days to orientate

planting a summer container

1 Take a large pot, at least 40cm (16in) across the top and with a drainage hole. Fill to roughly two-thirds with soil-less potting compost.

2 Try out the plants in their eventual positions, placing the anchor plant centrally in the container. Then remove the plants and make a hole large enough for the anchor plant's rootball.

3 Place the filling and trailing plants around the 'anchor', encouraging the trailers to grow down over the sides. Add more compost between the plants and gently firm them into position. Water thoroughly.

planting a hanging basket

1 Line a wire mesh basket with moss or an alternative liner. Fill to about a third with soil-less potting compost. Then balance the basket on a bucket or a big pot so that you can work with both hands.

2 Introduce the plants, gently teasing the roots through the sides of the basket and liner. Firm them into the compost. Add more compost and insert more plants, working in layers.

3 Plant the top of the basket last, then firm the plants and water thoroughly.

themselves and will then begin to fill the space around the basket.

● **suspend a hanging basket** from a strong hook well secured to a wall or strong support, and where it is in full light and sheltered from wind. Make sure the basket is easy to reach for watering and that it will not be in your way.

● **for a good display,** hanging baskets require regular feeding and constant watering; in hot weather they may need watering at least twice a day. Mix water-retaining gel into the soil-less compost to reduce the rate at which moisture is lost.

selecting permanent plants

Small shrubs and trees help to give an outdoor seating area a feeling of 'garden', rather than merely an outside room. Those that are evergreen will provide interest all year round and brighten the garden scene in winter. Select the permanent plants in a mixed container first, to create a framework.

trees and shrubs

Choose trees and shrubs that are fairly small or slow growing, because the rooting space is limited. Japanese maples are ideal because they grow at a gentle pace and, provided they have a sheltered, partially shaded spot, are shapely and statuesque. Their autumn colour, winter outline and fresh spring foliage make them great year-rounders, and they grow as well in a roomy container as in open ground.

patio roses

Roses are popular for containers on terraces and patios, but it is important to select those that suit hot, sunny patio conditions.

looking ahead...
☑ SUMMER Continue to feed and water containers and hanging baskets.
☑ Deadhead plants for a continuous display.

● **choose disease-resistant varieties** (check with an up-to-date catalogue).

● **check they will flower** all summer. True patio roses, such as the pink, fragrant Queen Mother, yellow Perestroika or Scarlet Patio, keep on flowering, as long as you remove the dead flowerheads throughout summer.

● **make sure** they do not grow too large.

● **try to choose** varieties for fragrance.

patio climbers

Climbing plants can be grown in containers or in the ground. Vigorous grape vines or wisteria trained on frames or pergolas create a shady canopy in summer, but let in more sunshine when their leaves fall in autumn. Climbing roses, too, can be used in this way, or trained over arches around the edge of the patio. Even small climbing roses, such as the bright coppery-hued Warm Welcome, will grow well in a large container.

The shapely, lime-green flowerheads of euphorbia will brighten the patio in late spring. Being semi-evergreen, this perennial provides interest all year.

lawns

Attention now will influence the appearance of your lawn throughout the summer. Give the lawn a regular spring clean to clear moss, weeds and dead grass, and to encourage strong growth in the future.

now is the season to . . .

■ **control isolated weeds** by spot treating with a liquid or gel weedkiller that is sprayed or brushed onto the leaves.
■ **treat weed-infested lawns** with a combination method (see right).
■ **scarify the lawn** to get rid of thatch.
■ **think about laying a new lawn** (see pages 142–145).
■ **start mowing the lawn** when the grass begins to grow, which is once the soil temperature has risen to 5–7°C (40–45°F).
■ **look out for yellow patches** on your lawn. This may be a sign of 'snow mould' or leatherjacket grubs (see opposite).

weedkiller safety

✓ Read and follow the instructions exactly.
✓ Keep weedkillers locked away from children and pets.
✓ Always wash your hands after using any garden chemicals.
✗ Never mix weedkillers with other garden chemicals.
✗ Never decant weedkillers into unmarked containers.
✗ Never dispose of diluted or undiluted weedkiller down the drain; instead pour it onto a bare patch of soil away from plants. (Once in contact with the soil the chemicals become inactive.)

weed control

In spring the grass grows increasingly fast and so do the weeds. The best time to apply a combined chemical and cultural treatment is in late spring, when the grass is growing vigorously and will not be damaged by the weed-control measures.

Apply a selective hormone weedkiller to the entire lawn. These weedkillers contain chemicals that cause the leaves and stems of weeds to twist, distort and grow upright. The weeds are weakened but are also within reach of the mower blades, making this a combination of chemical and cultural control. If weeds have been allowed to establish in a lawn, it may take several treatments to eradicate them, even to the extent of using different weedkillers on different occasions.

If you prefer not to use chemicals, prise out the weeds individually with an old kitchen knife or a purpose-made tool called a 'grubber'.

A well-maintained lawn forms a fresh green carpet that makes the perfect foil for a colourful border.

dealing with thatch

Over the year small quantities of grass clippings gradually build up in the lawn, even when a collecting box is used. Grass blades die and lie on the soil, as do fragments of moss. If this debris is left it will eventually form a layer of dead material called 'thatch', which often goes unnoticed, hidden by living grasses. The most obvious indicator of thatch is when the lawn feels springy underfoot.

Scarifying, or raking, is the equivalent of giving an established lawn a good scrub and brush up. Use a wire rake to drag out all the thatch, dead grass and dead moss. For large lawns a powered scarifier simplifies this job. Once the debris is removed, air circulates more freely around the grass blades and water can penetrate to the roots.

NEW LAWN TIP Don't scarify a new lawn, even one that has been turfed, because the vigorous action will cause damage.

moss control

To control moss successfully, you must tackle the underlying causes such as shade, compacted soil and poor drainage. Moss can also build up in wet winters on otherwise healthy lawns and if left untreated, it will smother and eventually kill the grass. The use of a lawn sand, that is a combined moss and weedkiller with added fertiliser, saves time and is ideal for the busy gardener. As this product feeds the grass, it will recover quickly and grow over the gaps left by the dead moss.

Choose a day when there is heavy dew so that the chemicals stick to the moss and weed leaves. The moss and other weeds will turn black within five to seven days, but wait until the moss turns brown, which indicates that it is completely dead, before raking. Any patches that return to green should be treated again. Collect and dispose of the dead moss, but not in the compost bin, because the chemical residues will taint its contents.

mowing the lawn

In cold areas, late spring will be the earliest you start cutting your lawn; the heavier the soil, the longer it takes to warm up. In mild areas, where the soil never freezes, you may have mown several times by now. Always begin by giving the shaggy lawn a light trim, with the mower blades on the highest setting. The golden rule is never to reduce the length of the grass by more than a third at a single cut, as this will damage the lawn. Once the grass is under control, progress to a finer, lower cut by adjusting the blades in stages.

pests and diseases

Most lawn problems show up in summer and, even more, in autumn. However, in late spring you may detect yellow circular patches on the lawn.

● **this is the first sign of snow mould,** also known as fusarium patch, which can be troublesome, particularly in wet conditions. Keep it in check by cutting down on applications of high-nitrogen spring fertiliser and spiking the lawn so that moisture does not collect around the base of the grass plants.

● **leatherjacket grubs can also cause yellow patches** on lawns. They feed on grass roots, causing the plants to die. The simplest control is to water the yellow patches and cover them overnight with a sheet of black plastic. In the morning remove the plastic to expose the leatherjackets, which will have come to the surface. Throw bread into the area to attract birds. They will fly in to eat the bread and the grubs.

controlling moss

1 **Scatter lawn sand** evenly over the area, at the rate recommended by the manufacturer.

2 **Use a fan-shaped wire rake** to remove all dead brown moss and debris. Rake from the edges of the area towards the centre to prevent the moss from spreading if any remains alive.

3 **Spiking the lawn** in late spring will help to reduce the incidence of moss by aerating the soil so that grass roots can breathe. Moss is most likely to develop in shady, wet conditions.

fruit

Now that growth is well under way, flowers must be protected from late frost if fruits are to develop. There are various pruning jobs to be done on trees and vines as well as on trained fruit. The second half of spring can bring a foretaste of fruit to come, with strawberries from the greenhouse and small gooseberries thinned from overladen branches.

now is the season to . . .

■ **prune trained fruit trees** such as apples, pears, plums, figs.

■ **thin small fruits** such as apricots and gooseberries, as well as wall-trained fruits.

■ **uncover forced rhubarb** now that open-air supplies are plentiful; remove pots and boxes, and allow forced plants to recover without further picking.

■ **tie in autumn-fruiting raspberry canes** as they develop. Thin them where necessary, keeping only the strongest spaced about 10cm (4in) apart along the wires.

■ **weed mature fruit** and, with a fork, lightly cultivate the surface of the surrounding soil, ready for feeding and mulching.

■ **apply a general or high-potash fertiliser** to bush and cane fruit and trained trees (see opposite).

■ **water new fruit plants** in dry weather at a rate of 25 litres per m² (5 gallons per sq yd) a week, and hoe or pull weeds regularly.

■ **take steps to prevent pests** and diseases making headway by treating at first sight (see page 70).

■ **keep gooseberries watered** and mulched as a precaution against gooseberry mildew, which tends to be much worse in dry conditions.

■ **protect fruit blossom from late frost** with fleece, if hard frost is forecast. This applies to early peach and nectarine fruitlets as well as other small fruit trees and bushes, and wall-trained apples, pears, plums and cherries in flower.

■ **net strawberries** to prevent birds from eating the ripening fruits.

■ **pull out suckers** growing beside raspberries, gooseberries, apples and pears while they are small.

■ **hand-pollinate outdoor peaches,** nectarines and apricots if cold weather is discouraging bees and other pollinating insects; use a soft paintbrush to transfer pollen by gently stroking the centre of each flower. Strawberries under glass may need the same assistance.

Apple blossom
(on 'Cox's Orange Pippin')

fruit cages

• **for an early crop of strawberries outdoors,** cover plants with cloches in cold weather. On warm, sunny days ventilate freely, by removing some or all of the cloches. Water regularly, and feed plants when they start flowering.

• **spread straw or lay mats around strawberries** to keep the fruits clean and dry. Wait to do this until the fruit-bearing stems begin to arch over, as it could prevent the soil from warming up and so delay ripening.

• **mulch raspberries,** using the first few cuts of lawn mowings (provided they haven't been treated with weed or moss killer). Spread a layer of clippings 5–8cm (2–3in) thick on both sides of the rows; alternatively, use garden compost or leaf-mould.

• **check blackcurrants for any overlooked big buds,** conspicuous now as they remain lifeless or produce distorted flowers and leaves. Treat for big bud mite as described on page 71.

• **bees and pollinating insects** can fly through netting cages to pollinate fruit, so there is no need to open the cages specially for this.

pruning

The purpose of pruning now is to improve the health of the fruit plants and ensure maximum cropping later on.

apples and pears

● **remove any surplus new shoots** from trees trained as espaliers, cordons and fans.

● **cut back the ends of branches** on established trained trees and main stems to limit their extent.

● **pinch out flower or fruit clusters** on trees under two years old, to direct energy into growth rather than fruit production.

plums, peaches, nectarines and cherries

Peach blossom is vulnerable to late frost and may need to be protected by horticultural fleece.

● **prune stone fruits** in growth because wounds heal faster than in winter dormancy; this reduces the risk of infection by silver-leaf disease.

● **cut out all dead**, diseased, injured and crossing or overcrowded branches.

● **remove any unwanted** new growth on espalier and fan-trained trees, particularly shoots growing towards the back or front of the tree.

figs

● **hard-prune young trees** to encourage branching; tie in new shoots as they develop.

● **remove any dead or weak shoots** on older trees, and cut off the tips of main branches to stimulate fruiting sideshoots; cut back a few of the old branches to one or two buds, to encourage the formation of some young replacement stems.

grapes

● **cut off the tip from each flowering shoot,** two leaves beyond its first bunch of flowers, and pinch out the tip of any resulting sideshoots after one leaf.

● **tie in the flowering shoots** to training wires.

thinning small fruits

Certain trees and bushes set excessively heavy crops of fruit, which are unlikely to reach good size and quality unless some are removed early.

● **thin trained peaches,** nectarines and apricots, especially those grown under glass, when the fruitlets are the size of hazelnuts. Reduce each cluster to a single fruit, and thin out the rest so that the fruitlets are spaced about 8–10cm (3–4in) apart along the branches.

● **thin gooseberries** now (see below).

● **trained apples and pears** benefit from similar treatment towards the end of May.

feeding bush and trained fruits

Once plants have started growing, usually in April, use a general-purpose or high-potash feed in powdered or granular form, and sprinkle it over the soil area shaded by the stems or branches.

● **for bush or cane fruit,** apply powdered or granular feed at a rate of 70g (2oz) per plant.

● **for trained fruit trees,** apply at a rate of 100g per m² (3oz per sq yd).

● **in dry weather,** water in the fertiliser.

● **two or three weeks later** spread a generous mulch of garden compost or well-rotted manure over thoroughly moist, weed-free soil.

thinning gooseberries

1 Thin gooseberries when they are roughly the size of grapes.

2 Leave the fruits or fruit clusters 5–8cm (2–3in) apart, and use the thinnings for cooking or to make jam.

there is still time to:

● **plant perpetual strawberries** and autumn-fruiting raspberries for crops this year.

● **prune blueberries** and cut down old canes of autumn raspberries, but do this before new growth is well advanced.

● **sow alpine strawberry seeds** under glass or outdoors, if conditions are warm.

● **train and tie in the new fruiting canes** of blackberries, hybrid berries and other brambles, fanning them out in their cropping positions.

vegetables

As the weather starts to warm up, soil preparation begins in earnest. A warm, drying soil is ideal for working a seedbed to a fine tilth and for sowing hardier vegetables outdoors. It is a hectic time for the gardener, but work done now will have a major impact on the success of summer cropping.

now is the season to . . .

■ **sow hardier vegetables outdoors** once the soil has warmed to a minimum temperature of 7–7.5°C (44–45°F). (See Winter for planning.)

■ **sow many of the cabbage family outdoors,** including cauliflowers, kale, kohl rabi and sprouting broccoli, all of which mature much later in the year. Choose different varieties to give a continuity of supply: cauliflowers, for example, can be autumn-maturing (early to late autumn), winter-maturing (late winter through to early spring) and spring-maturing (early spring until early summer the following year).

■ **sow root vegetables outdoors** (see page 60). Dig down two spade depths to allow for deeper root penetration, which will give better quality vegetables.

■ **begin successional sowings** of quick-maturing crops such as lettuce and radish, and crops that you don't want maturing all at once, such as peas and dwarf beans (see opposite).

■ **sow runner beans,** which like a warmed soil, later rather than earlier, in double rows. Position supports as soon as the seedlings emerge, as bean seedlings grow rapidly.

■ **plant maincrop potatoes** 10cm (4in) deep (see page 61).

■ **plant out autumn and winter-maturing** brussels sprouts.

■ **plant out bulb onions** and onion sets (see page 61).

■ **make regular patrols** through the vegetable patch with a sharp hoe to keep weeds in check.

■ **mulch perennial crops,** such as rhubarb or artichokes, with well-rotted organic matter to help suppress weeds and retain moisture.

■ **water regularly:** it is important to give the young plants as much water as they need to keep them growing steadily.

■ **look out for signs of potential pests** such as slug damage or early aphid infestation (see page 71). Pests are more easily dealt with if spotted early.

■ **protect the cabbage family** from flea beetle and cabbage root fly damage by covering with fleece or fitting 'collars' round individual plants.

■ **harvest asparagus shoots** ('spears') in established beds, once they are about 15cm (6in) high. Slice the stem 2–3cm (1in) below soil level.

■ **keep harvesting the flowering shoots** of sprouting broccoli so that more are produced.

and if you have time . . .

■ **start a long-term planting** of asparagus (it takes five years to produce spears). Set the crowns in trenches 10cm (4in) deep, 30cm (12in) apart, with 45cm (18in) between the crowns.

Get peas off to a flying start in cold areas by sowing in a length of plastic guttering filled with seed compost. Slide the 'instant' row of peas into a shallow trench outdoors when weather conditions allow.

sowing quick-maturing crops

Many vegetables grow quickly and mature all at once, so sowing little and often – or successional sowing – is the best way to maintain a regular supply.

● **sow peas, spinach, spinach beet and dwarf beans** (also known as french, string or kidney beans); make successional sowings every three weeks. Sow beans in double rows.

● **sow lettuces and radishes** every two to three weeks. You can sow quick-growing salad crops such as lettuce, rocket and radishes between rows of slow growers such as parsnips, for efficient use of space; this is known as intercropping.

● **sow salad onions** at three to four-week intervals, thinly in 7–8cm (3in) wide bands, to avoid the need for thinning. Harvest them about seven weeks after sowing.

recommended cultivars

PEAS (EARLY) • 'Daybreak' • 'Fortune' • 'Kelvedon Wonder'

PEAS (MAINCROP) • 'Bikini' • 'Cavalier' • 'Rondo'

DWARF BEANS • 'Aramis' • 'Masal' • 'Purple Teepee'

RUNNER BEANS • 'Lady Di' • 'Red Rum' • 'White Lady'

SPINACH (SUMMER) • 'America' • 'Trinidad'

SALAD ONIONS • 'Ishikuro' • 'Summer Isle' • 'White Lisbon'

LETTUCE • 'Beatrico' • 'Freckles' • 'Miluna' • 'Revolution'

RADISH • 'Cherry Belle' • 'French Breakfast' • 'Juliette'

Know when the soil is ready: if weed seeds are germinating, then the soil should have warmed enough to prepare a seedbed for hardier vegetable seeds.

sowing sweetcorn

1 Sow seeds of sweetcorn individually in biodegradable peat pots in a heated greenhouse.

2 Peat pots must not be allowed to dry out, so stand them in a tray of water, which is slowly taken up from the bottom. When in the ground, the roots will grow through the base.

sowing beans

Sow beans directly into the ground, 2–3cm (1in) deep and 15cm (6in) apart.

vegetables/2

Rows of vegetable seedlings (above) are a rewarding sight in late spring. Thinning them leaves space for the remaining young plants to develop.

Thin carrot seedlings under fleece (right), protected from the low-flying pest, carrot root fly. The cultivar 'Fly Away' has lower levels of the chemical that attracts carrot root fly.

growing root crops

Many root crops that mature well into the second half of the year can be sown outdoors now: beetroot, carrot, parsnip, swede and turnip. The timing of sowing is a bit of a balancing act: beetroot, for example, if sown too early, may 'bolt', producing premature seed.

● **beetroot** Space seeds 15cm (6in) apart with 15cm (6in) between rows, to grow medium-sized, nicely rounded beets.

● **maincrop carrots** Sow in shallow seed drills, only 1cm (½in) deep. Sow thinly, 5cm (2in) apart in rows 15cm (6in) apart, to reduce the need for thinning out and reduce risk of carrot root fly. Water the drills immediately after sowing if the soil is dry; do not overwater, as the plants would then produce too much leaf and the roots would split, especially if watered heavily after a dry period.

● **parsnips** Sow in rows or in blocks 10cm (4in) apart with 10cm (4in) between rows, to prevent the roots from becoming too large and misshapen; the longer the growing season, the larger they grow. Do not grow close to carrots as they both attract carrot root fly.

recommended cultivars

BEETROOT • 'Bolthardy' • 'Chioggia Pink' • 'Red Ace'
CARROTS (MAINCROP) • 'Bertan' • 'Fly Away' • 'Parmex'
PARSNIPS • 'Avonresister' • 'Gladiator' • 'White Gem'
POTATOES (MAINCROP) • 'Desirée' • 'Nadine' • 'Romano'
ONION SETS • 'Giant Fen Globe' • 'Sturon' • 'Stuttgart Giant'

growing potatoes and onions

Potatoes and onions like a soil that is fertile but not too rich, otherwise leaf growth is encouraged at the expense of roots. The storage life of the roots will also be reduced.

potatoes

There are two main types of potato: earlies and maincrop. Earlies are planted in early spring and need only 14–15 weeks in the ground to produce tender 'new' potatoes for immediate use. These are the potatoes to grow in a small garden because they take up less space and for a shorter time. Maincrop potatoes have a longer growing season (about 20 weeks) and need more space, but they produce heavier yields, which also store well.

● **earlies** Earth up early potatoes to protect new shoots from late frosts. Once the threat of frost has passed, continue to earth up when the tops (haulms) of early potatoes are about 25cm (10in) high. Draw up the soil to cover the bottom 12–13cm (5in) of the stems so that tubers form on the buried sideshoots.

● **maincrop** Plant maincrop potatoes now. Space them 40cm (16in) apart with 75cm (2ft 6in) between the rows. Grow them apart from other crops, if possible, as they take up a lot of space above ground, with their abundant leafy growth, as well as below ground.

onions

Onions may be planted as seed or sets. It is a race against time to get enough growth on the plant before the bulbs start to swell after midsummer's day. Hand-weed carefully to avoid disturbing their shallow roots.

● **bulb onions** Seeds sown in early spring can be planted out now that the soil is warmer, burying the bulbs just below the soil surface. A spacing of 25–30cm (10–12in) apart and 25–30cm (10–12in) between the rows is ideal, but they must be kept well-watered until they have established.

● **onion sets** Plant out these 'mini-plants' now, 15cm (6in) apart, with 15cm (6in) between rows, and 1cm (½in) deep to give medium-sized, nicely rounded bulbs. If possible, select smaller sets as they are less likely to 'bolt'. 'Golden Ball' is a good cultivar that tolerates later planting.

tender crops

If you wait for the soil to warm up before sowing tender crops, the plants will just produce leafy growth and little or no crop, so they must be started off under protection. Most also hate root disturbance, so sow them in individual small pots. Plants that start growing in a greenhouse or polythene tunnel or on a kitchen windowsill must have two to three weeks of hardening off before being transplanted into the garden soil (for gradual acclimatisation to outdoor growing conditions, see page 65). If you buy your young plants from a garden centre or nursery, they should have already been hardened off, but it is worth checking.

● **aubergines, peppers and tomatoes** can be moved outside to grow successfully when the soil temperature reaches 10°C (50°F).

● **courgettes, marrows and squashes** can all be grown outside, but generally tend to do better in a coldframe or polythene tunnel. They prefer high humidity and may suffer from mildew if grown outside in dry conditions. Transplant them with minimum root disturbance, as even slight damage to the roots can result in the roots rotting and, eventually, in the loss of the plant.

● **young plants of sweetcorn** should be about 15–20cm (6–8in) high before they are planted out. Transplant them in their moist peat pots into square or rectangular blocks (as they are pollinated by wind), with the plants spaced 35cm (14in) apart, with 35cm (14in) between rows.

Pinch out the tops of broad beans once in full flower as a way of controlling blackfly without using chemicals.

harvesting now

- asparagus
- early carrots
- early turnips
- lettuce (overwintered and seedling)
- radishes
- spinach
- spring cabbage (left)
- spring or salad onions
- sprouting broccoli

herbs

The herb garden is full of promise at this time of year, as fresh aromatic leaves unfurl and young plants replace the old. Start to gather the first fragrant tips from established herbs, but also continue sowing, planting and propagating for later harvest.

Herbs such as rosemary, mint, basil, sage and bay revel in the good drainage and extra attention they receive in containers.

herbs **suitable for containers**
- basil • bay • chives • curry plant • french tarragon
- lemongrass • marjoram • oregano • parsley • rosemary (small plants) • sage (small plants) • salad burnet • thyme

herbs **to raise from soft-tip cuttings**
- bay • french tarragon • germander • lemon verbena
- sage • thyme

now is the season to . . .

■ **trim young woody herbs**, such as sage and artemisias, to keep them dense and shapely.

■ **clip mature sage, rosemary and santolina** hard, but not into the old wood. Cut out completely any damaged, straggly or misplaced shoots.

■ **lightly shear over thyme plants** to remove bare stems.

■ **thin early sowings of salad** and other annual herbs to 10cm (4in) apart, then water to settle the disturbed seedlings.

■ **pot up strong seedlings** in 10cm (4in) pots for planting in containers or standing on the kitchen windowsill.

■ **think of planting a herb hedge** as an edging (see opposite).

■ **plant out mint and tarragon** forced from dormant roots under glass in late winter and pot-grown herbs to use out of season.

■ **plant up your own seedlings** and home-raised plants in pots and troughs where garden space is limited.

■ **top-dress herbs in large containers** by replacing the top 2–5cm (1–2in) of soil with fresh potting compost.

■ **harden off cuttings** rooted and potted up in late summer last year under glass, and plant out in permanent positions.

■ **take cuttings** of shrubby herbs like bay, rosemary and santolina using sideshoots pulled off with a short 'heel' of woody tissue from the main stem.

■ **take soft-tip cuttings** of sage and tarragon (see opposite).

■ **harvest herbs** while they are young by pinching off their growing tips. This encourages larger, bushier plants.

■ **in exposed positions, support angelica** and other tall herbs before they are damaged by spring winds.

■ **harvest sweet woodruff** when the tiny white flowers appear, a sign that you can start cutting and drying flowering stems at their most aromatic for use in tonics and tisanes.

■ **crumble leftover dried herbs from last season** as fresh herbs become available; scatter them over newly sown flower and vegetable seeds to confuse soil pests.

and if you have time . . .

■ **divide perennial clump-forming herbs**, but keep transplants watered in dry weather.

■ **prepare new herb beds** for sowing and planting.

■ **sow essential herbs** under glass; many, such as basil and parsley, germinate faster as the weather warms up.

planting herb hedges

Small aromatic evergreens like box, lavender, germander and semi-evergreen hyssop have traditionally been used to make low hedges for edging or sheltering herb borders and creating divisions or intricate knots in more formal gardens. Evergreen herbs are best planted in April or in early autumn, when pot-grown plants will establish quickly.

● Choose small, bushy plants as these settle in faster than larger specimens. Water them well an hour or two before planting.

● Mark the line of the hedge. Use a garden line or string pulled taut for straight edges; for curves, lay a hosepipe on the ground or sprinkle a sand trail.

Small-leaved box, which can be tightly clipped, makes an ideal low edging for a herb or vegetable bed.

● Dig or fork over a 30cm (12in) wide trench along the line. Break up the excavated soil, and mix in a little bone meal and garden compost to improve the texture.

● Knock the plants from their pots, and plant them about 23–25cm (9-10in) apart along the row, with the top of the rootballs at ground level. Carefully firm the soil around each plant.

● Water in the plants and lightly trim their shoot tips to encourage early branching.

propagation

Many perennial herbs can be propagated now. This will ensure young, more vigorous replacements for ageing plants.

● **layer thyme, sage and rosemary** (see page 43). Gently pull down a low, strong-growing branch to touch the ground at least 8cm (3in) from its tip, scoop out a small hole and fill with moist potting compost. Peg the stem down just below the surface with a stone or bent wire, mound more compost over the pegged area and leave until autumn.

● **take multiple layers from old rosemary** and other tall woody plants like lavender by bending all the bare, leggy stems to the ground and pegging them down as described above.

● **root the stems by 'dropping'** the whole plant. 'Dropping' means digging up an old woody plant with a sizable rootball and excavating the hole 30cm (12in) deeper. Replant at the lower level and mound soil around the emerging stems to increase the potential rooting area. Leave until autumn.

● **sow short-lived annual herbs** such as chervil, coriander and dill to provide pickings later in the year. Sow under glass in April and plant out in late May after hardening off (see page 65).

Plant invasive herbs such as mint inside a plastic bag filled with soil and lower it into a hole in the ground. This will prevent the roots from spreading.

taking soft-tip cuttings

1 **Propagate sage plants** by taking 'softwood' cuttings from the tips of young shoots. Trim a small piece of healthy stem just below a leaf joint and remove the bottom pair of leaves.

2 **Insert cuttings into pots** of sharp sand and leave them in a mini propagator or on a windowsill out of direct sunlight until they take root.

looking ahead . . .

☑ LATE SUMMER Take semi-ripe cuttings of herbs.
☑ AUTUMN Check if layered and 'dropped' plants have rooted and are ready to be cut free from the parent plant.
☑ WINTER Pot up roots of mint and tarragon under glass.

the greenhouse

Greenhouse plants are completely dependent on you for their welfare. During April and May there is a change of emphasis from keeping plants warm and safe from frost, to protecting them from sudden and extreme heat, as well as a marked increase in watering.

now is the season to . . .

■ **increase ventilation** in the greenhouse as temperatures rise by day and, later on, at night.

■ **shield plants from hot sunshine,** to protect their leaves from drying and scorching (see below).

Damping down the greenhouse floor and benches reduces the temperature because energy is used up evaporating the water. It also increases humidity, which helps plants by reducing the amount of moisture lost through their leaves.

■ **increase humidity** by soaking, or 'damping down', the greenhouse floor and benches with a watering can or hose whenever you water.

■ **water and feed plants regularly;** it becomes critical at this time of year.

■ **mulch greenhouse beds** with well-rotted organic matter or composted bark, to prevent the soil from drying out quickly. Mulch the compost in large pots with gravel or shingle to help keep plant roots moist.

■ **prepare plants for outdoor conditions:** all plants grown under glass, especially half-hardy kinds, must be accustomed to cooler temperatures, or hardened off, before being planted in the garden (see opposite).

■ **prick out seedlings** sown earlier in the year as soon as they are large enough to handle; keep shaded with newspaper in sunny weather until they are growing vigorously.

■ **pot up especially large seedlings** such as sunflowers and chrysanthemums individually, and move them on to the next pot size when their roots reach the sides.

■ **pot up mail-order plants** as they arrive and stand in a well-lit position, but keep separate from other plants for a few days, in case they are carrying pests or diseases. Transfer seedlings and plug plants to trays or small pots as soon as possible.

■ **watch out for the first signs of aphids** on the soft growth of fuchsias, carnations and other bedding plants, and also vine weevil damage on many pot plants (see page 71).

■ **lightly spray the underside of leaves with water** in hot weather, to deter red spider mites from getting established.

■ **inspect woody-stemmed plants** such as grape vines and greenhouse fruits for scale insects.

and if you have time . . .

■ **take soft-tip cuttings** (see page 63), using short sideshoots and growing tips of: tender perennials (coleus, fuchsias, pelargoniums, marguerites, heliotropes and dahlias), flowering shrubs (hydrangeas, brooms and azaleas) and woody herbs (lemon verbena or sage).

■ **take leaf cuttings** from begonias and streptocarpus (see Summer).

controlling temperature

There are several ways of keeping a greenhouse cool and moist, and you may need to use them all together in really hot weather. Smell the air when you open the greenhouse doors. A good growing atmosphere is moist and earthy, whereas low humidity smells dry and dusty.

● **when using shade paint,** always shade the outside of the glass. Shading the inside keeps out sunlight without reducing the temperature (see picture, opposite).

● **open ventilators** when temperatures rise much above 13°C (55°F) during the day; if possible open them wider on the lee of the greenhouse to prevent draughts from the windy side.

● **by the end of May** vents may need to be left open a little throughout the night.

● **leave the door open** in very warm, still conditions.

● **improve the flow of cool air** by adding louvred panels to the greenhouse sides.

● **think about installing automatic window openers,** adjusted to open once a chosen temperature is reached, to save time and worry about temperature fluctuation.

FROST TIP If an unseasonable cold frosty night should threaten, place a covering of newspaper or fleece over seedlings and tender plants, and remove it in the morning.

shading plants from hot sun

Bright sunshine will quickly scorch young seedlings, dry out compost and reduce humidity to levels at which plants struggle to grow healthily. Provide shade from April onwards with a special shade paint that becomes transparent in wet

weather. Wash the greenhouse glass before applying a first, light coat to the outside of the glass with a roller, brush or spray. Follow with a denser second coat in late May.

Alternatively, cover the greenhouse roof with shade netting, sold in various densities, or fit adjustable blinds, which can be operated by hand or controlled automatically.

VENTILATION TIP Most greenhouses are inadequately ventilated, so consider adding more roof vents if it is difficult to keep cool. Ideally the total area of roof vents should equal 15–20 per cent of the ground area of the greenhouse.

getting plants ready for the garden

The best way to acclimatise plants to outdoor conditions (harden off) is to transfer them to a coldframe and keep the lid closed for a week; if frost threatens, cover the frame overnight with a blanket or old mats. Start ventilating the frame on mild days by raising the lid a little; gradually open it farther until it is left off completely after two to three weeks, when plants will be fully acclimatised.

An alternative is to stand plants outdoors on warm days, out of the wind, and bring them back in at night for the first two weeks. Leave them out for a few nights in succession before finally transplanting them into open ground.

watering greenhouse plants

Leafy, tropical and actively growing species require more water than cool or dry-climate plants, such as desert cacti and alpines. All plants are likely to need more in hot or windy weather than when conditions are dull, cool or humid.

- **check established pot plants** at least once daily: they will need more water as the days become warmer.
- **water first thing** in the morning or late in the afternoon. Always avoid wetting the foliage in bright sunlight, otherwise it could scorch.
- **keep water at greenhouse temperature** in a tank if there is room. Alternatively, fill a couple of cans with mains water and leave them in the greenhouse overnight to warm up.
- **stand pots** of young seedlings and very dry plants in a tray of water to soak up as much as they require, then allow them to drain (right).

the greenhouse/2
planting and propagation

There is a lively bustle under glass as a steady flow of plants moves from propagation to planting stage. Crops sown in early spring will need potting on or moving to growing bags and their training started. And there is a range of food plants that can still be sown now to crop this summer.

Greenhouse cucumbers can be trained on vertical strings as single cordons. On traditional varieties it is important to distinguish between male and female flowers as you need to remove the males.

planting greenhouse crops

Start planting tomatoes, cucumbers, peppers, aubergines and melons, sown in early spring, during April, but be prepared to protect them with fleece or newspapers until later in May if frosty nights are forecast. You need to:

● **prepare and water growing bags,** and stand in position in the greenhouse for a few days to warm up before planting.

● **plant tomatoes** only when they have formed their first flowering truss.

● **plant cucumbers and melons** when three or four leaves have grown above the first pair.

● **water plants well beforehand,** then plant them 38–45cm (15–18in) apart in moist growing bags or 25cm (10in) pots, or direct in the greenhouse border.

● **water them into place,** using a diluted liquid feed.

feeding new plants

Most compost mixtures include fertilisers that are sufficient for about six weeks' growth (some contain slow-release fertiliser that lasts for several months), but after that you will need to feed plants regularly.

● **feeding is the most efficient way** to supply extra nutrients. Dilute concentrated organic or inorganic feeds according to instructions and water pots and trays once or twice a week. Use tomato fertiliser because it is cheap and will encourage fruit production. Most liquid greenhouse fertilisers can also be given as foliar feeds, useful for watering or spraying on cuttings, plants with small root systems and those recovering from disease treatment.

training greenhouse plants

Unless you are growing dwarf or bush varieties of tomato, regular training is essential to limit plant growth and maximise cropping.

● **train modern self-pollinating all-female cucumber plants,** which fruit on the main stem, like cordon tomatoes (see opposite). The traditional kinds should have their sideshoots tied laterally to a net suspended vertically from overhead wires. Remove all flowers without a tiny cucumber at their base; these are male flowers, and pollination results in bitter fruit. Pinch off the tip of each sideshoot two leaves beyond a developing fruit.

● **train melons on nets** in the same way as cucumbers, or let them spread over the border as ground cover, under tomato or cucumber plants. Pinch out the growing tip after five leaves have formed, to encourage sideshoots. Be prepared to hand-pollinate female flowers using male blooms.

propagating by seed

The following flowers and vegetables can be raised from seed in late spring.

● **cinerarias and greenhouse primulas** (*Primula obconica*, *P. sinensis* and *P. x kewensis*): grow in pots for early indoor colour from late winter.

● **late flowering annuals** like china asters, chrysanthemums and zinnias.

● **fast-growing half-hardy annuals,** such as marigolds (*Tagetes*), for bedding out in summer.

● **runner beans,** french beans, outdoor cucumbers, sweetcorn, courgettes and squashes: sow seeds individually in small pots or specially formulated root trainers about six weeks before the last expected frosts.

● **cucumbers and melons** for growing in an unheated greenhouse or coldframe.

● **biennials and perennials,** if you have no space for an outdoor nursery bed.

there is still time to . . .

● **sow a late crop of dwarf broad beans** in small pots for planting outdoors in early summer. They will crop before runner and french beans.

Regal pelargoniums are among the plants that can be successfully raised from soft-tip cuttings taken now (see page 63) or in late summer for overwintering in the greenhouse.

training tomatoes

1 When growing tomatoes in a greenhouse border as single-stemmed cordons, anchor the string beneath the rootball when planting and attach it to a stong overhead wire or the top of the greenhouse roof.
TIP If growing plants in a growing bag, loop the string under the bag instead.

2 Tie the stems to the strings as they grow, or simply twist the string round the stem. (You can also use canes.)

3 Don't forget to snap off all sideshoots from the base of the leaves when they are about 2–5cm (1–2in) long.

What you do in the garden in late spring will determine the success of the remaining seasons. Even though this is the busiest season of the year, make time to sit and refresh yourself with the loveliness of spring flowers and new foliage.

late spring checklist

Use this checklist to make sure you have not overlooked any important seasonal jobs.

● **make sure indoor sowings** of summer bedding and early vegetables are up to date. During May you can continue outdoors, adding biennials and successional crops to your sowing list.

● **prick out seedlings** under glass as soon as they are large enough to handle, and thin or transplant outdoor sowings before they become overcrowded.

● **start a weed control routine,** by hand-pulling, hoeing or spraying as appropriate.

● **water and ventilate the greenhouse** freely, but keep an eye on the possibility of night frosts.

● **support taller flowers** before winds spoil their shape.

● **water outdoor plants** regularly in dry weather, and mulch to conserve soil moisture.

Harden off plants ready to go out in the open garden, and feed any that are left waiting beyond their transplanting date.

● **plant up hanging baskets** and other seasonal containers, but do not leave tender plants outdoors until frosts are past.

● **finish planting herbaceous perennials,** root-balled conifers and bareroot deciduous shrubs early in April, then concentrate on planting container-grown evergreens until early May.

● **finish hard–pruning** and restoring shrubs and hedges as soon as possible; begin pruning spring shrubs as their flowers fade.

● **start regular mowing** and hedge-trimming when growth is long enough.

● **feed established plants** of all kinds, and water according to need in dry weather.

● **tidy and plant up ponds,** and start feeding fish when they become active.

Hedges can be trimmed to shape as soon as growth is long enough. Here, hellebores, white narcissi and tulips flower at the base of evergreen hedges clipped into geometric shapes.

- **look for early signs of pests** and diseases, especially on fruit.
- **clean, deadhead and repot houseplants**, increase watering as growth revives, and feed if necessary.
- **rest or discard** winter and spring-flowering conservatory plants such as cyclamen, freesias and arum lilies. Feed and plant out forced spring bulbs after flowering.

Rake gravel drives and paths, and spot-treat any perennial weeds with systemic herbicide on a still, warm day. Brush down steps, paved paths, decking and patio surfaces, and treat them with an algicide if they are green and slippery.

tidying the garden

Keeping the garden tidy is not simply cosmetic. Even the wildest natural garden needs maintenance from time to time, to prevent unwanted or more robust plants from taking over, and to discourage pests and disease. Formal gardens need more routine tidying, and you must decide how much orderliness is appropriate or manageable.

- **clear away dead topgrowth** in borders left for plant protection or to help wildlife (see Autumn), down to ground level. Pull up spring bedding, discard or compost.
- **when clearing spring bedding** such as forget-me-nots, shake the seed heads under mature fruit trees and flowering shrubs, and hope for a colourful display next spring.
- **fork lightly over beds and borders** to remove weeds and self-sown seedlings. This will also break up any surface crust and expose soil pests to foraging birds. Fork in decaying mulches, and lightly loosen newer mulches that might be effective for another season so that rain can penetrate. Take care not to damage plant roots.
- **collect up fallen branches**, twigs and leaves left over from autumn. Clear all prunings and hedge-trimming debris, and dead material from frost-damaged and injured plants. Provided they are not diseased, these can be shredded and added to a compost heap.

get ready for watering

Be prepared to water more frequently as spring progresses. Sowings may fail and new plants quickly suffer until their roots are fully established, so target vulnerable plants in dry weather, especially if hot sun is reinforced with drying winds.

feeding routines

After winter and early spring rains, soils will be depleted, and many plants benefit from feeding now when they are actively growing.

- **give spring-flowering bulbs** a single feed of general fertiliser when their flowers fade, to help them with food storage for next season.
- **give acid-loving plants** such as rhododendrons, azaleas, camellias, pieris, heathers (*Erica*) and tree heathers (*E. arborea*) a dressing of special ericaceous fertiliser.
- **give a general granular feed** to all other shrubs, fruit, herbaceous perennials, and hedges, especially those cut back hard to restore their shape.

Erica arborea

Treat these feeds as a spring tonic to supplement long-term food supplies from dressings of well-rotted manure or garden compost forked in or applied as a mulch.

The priorities for watering are new and recently moved plants, seeds and seedlings, leafy vegetables and plants in flower. These have the greatest need for consistently moist conditions to ensure steady growth.

- **check over all watering equipment** before it is needed.
- **test hosepipes** and couplings for leaks.
- **clean out water butts**, pipework and guttering.
- **ensure that all sprinklers and soaker hoses** are in proper working order.

continuing plant protection

Spring is the most fickle season, with sharp frosts and sudden cold spells, as well as very warm sunshine. Even May can spring surprises on unprepared gardeners.

- **do not hurry to unwrap pots and containers** insulated last year against frost (see Autumn).
- **keep cloches and fleece handy** to cover outdoor sowings and recent transplants.
- **remember to harden off young plants** raised outdoors under glass or plastic in the same way as greenhouse plants (see page 65), to fully acclimatise them before planting them in their flowering positions.

the healthy garden/2

aiming for positive health

Spring is a critical time for plants, not least because warmer conditions favour the spread of common pests, such as greenfly, and diseases that have survived the winter as dormant spores. Striving for a totally problem-free garden is unrealistic because pests and diseases are always arriving from outside. It is more practical to accept a permanent low level of infection, and to prevent pests and diseases from getting out of hand with a few sensible precautions.

Vigorous, well-grown plants with plenty of space to develop naturally are more likely to withstand disorders than overcrowded, starved and dry plants, so encourage the good health of your plants by satisfying their needs:
- **water them** before they are too dry.
- **feed adequately** to sustain steady growth.
- **reduce competition** from weeds.
- **keep the garden tidy:** clear away dead plants, check soil acidity and drainage, and avoid over-feeding as precautions against diseases.

dealing with pests

Learn to identify the common pests and to distinguish them from gardeners' allies such as ladybirds, lacewings, centipedes, hoverflies and ground beetles and their larval, immature forms. Some pests, such as froghoppers ('cuckoo spit'), are simply a nuisance and may be ignored, whereas others like the beautiful lily beetle can be a serious threat.

When problems do occur, try to use physical and specific biological controls or sprays, rather than general insecticides that kill a wide range of insects. Larger pests like beetles, caterpillars and snails, for example, can be picked off by hand, while forceful spraying with water will deter red spider mites and dislodge other pests such as greenfly.
- **grow pest or disease-resistant** varieties.
- **mingle flowers** with vegetables to hide those that are vulnerable to attack.
- **physical barriers** such as fleece can protect brassicas from caterpillars and carrots from root flies.
- **use netting** over fruit to deter birds.
- **grow flat-headed flowers** such as achilleas, asters, marigolds and sedums to attract insect predators.
- **use traps** to catch fruit moths, slugs and flying greenhouse pests.

If you do spray, remember that contact insecticides such as derris are effective but short-lived, whereas systemic chemicals are absorbed and remain in the plant for several days, which can delay the harvesting of vegetables and fruit.

Position a comfortable seat, or just an upturned bucket, where you tend to work most – planning and dreaming are as important as busy activity in a well-tended garden.

A red admiral butterfly feeds on a flat-headed sedum flower.

weed patrol

Controlling weeds is a necessary task at any season, but especially now when they tend to appear almost anywhere, racing to gain a head start on competitors. Dormant seeds in freshly disturbed soil germinate quickly.

- **identify weeds carefully** when tidying beds and borders, as useful flower, shrub and tree seedlings often start appearing now, especially after a cold winter.
- **hoe bare ground regularly** to prevent weeds from getting beyond the seedling stage – this is particularly important in vegetable beds, since many weeds host the same pests and diseases as cultivated crops.
- **mulch wherever possible** to smother and suppress weed germination as your soil warms up. Pull larger weeds by hand, but stubborn perennial species and those growing in gravel, paths and other hard surfaces may need spot treatment with a systemic herbicide to prevent regrowth.
- **keep rough and still uncultivated areas** under control by shearing or rotary-mowing weeds before they can flower and seed themselves.

fruit pests

Fruits are susceptible to a number of pests and ailments, often at very specific times during spring. If you are following a chemical spray routine, these are the critical stages for specific fruit. Do not spray when flowers are open.

- **strawberries** Spray insecticide from April until harvest, against aphids.
- **raspberries** Use a systemic fungicide in April to prevent fungal diseases.
- **gooseberries** Spray with fungicide against mildew, when flowers first open and again when berries are visible. Treat against caterpillars in May with insecticide.
- **blackcurrants** Control big bud mites by spraying insecticide when flower buds resemble miniature bunches of grapes, and again a month later.
- **apples and pears** Use a combined insecticide and fungicide while flower buds are green, and again when they show colour, to treat most common problems.
- **plums and cherries** Spray insecticide at green bud stage to control aphids and fruit grubs.

Cabbage white caterpillars are a constant threat to cabbages and other brassicas.

seasonal threats

- **powdery mildew** This disease of leaves and shoots in overcrowded and dry conditions shows as a greyish white coating. Avoid by pruning and spacing plants to admit plenty of air, water plants well in dry weather, and remove any affected growth such as white, distorted shoots on apples or dying forget-me-not leaves.
- **aphids** These affect many plants and start building up populations in mid and late spring. Disperse with water, spray with insecticide, or encourage natural predators by feeding garden birds and attracting beneficial insects.

- **caterpillars** Various kinds appear on plants as soon as moths and butterflies are on the wing. Look under leaves for egg clusters, which can be crushed with finger and thumb; remove caterpillars whenever you notice them.

Aphids cluster on a rose bud.

- **slugs and snails** These all-year pests are particularly active in spring, feeding voraciously on young growth and seedlings. You can try various remedies: collect them on damp evenings for disposal; trap them under large leaves such as rhubarb laid on the ground; use proprietary beer traps; discourage them with barriers of grit or crushed eggshells; encourage frogs, toads and thrushes; or, as a last resort, use slug pellets sparingly, but hide these from birds and hedgehogs.
- **vine weevils** Both adult weevils and their underground grubs are a continuous threat to pot-grown plants and open ground plants such as bergenias and strawberries, but they are particularly active now. Few chemicals are effective, so water pots with biological controls based on parasitic nematodes, and keep the soil regularly cultivated round outdoor plants to expose the grubs to birds.

The sharp yellows and intense greens of early spring are now joined by gentler hues – the pinks, soft mauves and whites of cherry blossom and lilac, the wine or rose-pink of crab apple blooms – and the hotter, more strident tones of tulips, to give a vast palette of colour. With exceptions such as euphorbias, early columbines and honesty, most biennials and perennials have yet to bloom, but spring-flowering clematis are in their full glory on walls and fences, and gem-like alpine auriculas and saxifrages stud rock gardens or alpine sinks. Queens of the late spring floral display, however, are the stunning rhododendrons and azaleas.

Euphorbia x *martinii*

plant selector

perennials

Although a few are evergreen, most durable non-woody plants are herbaceous, that is they die down in winter and re-emerge in spring. Plant when dormant, in autumn or early spring.

purple, blue and violet

1 Aquilegia 'Hensol Harebell'
Columbine

The ferny leaves are a beautiful feature of this easy perennial, with purplish tints in early spring and more stormy tones as they die down. Spurred blue flowers poised above the leafy clump succeed one another into summer. Self-seeds freely but may not reproduce itself identically. Hardy.
Height: 75cm (2ft 6in) **Spread:** 30cm (12in)
Site: Partial shade, sun. Fertile and well-drained soil, preferably moist
Use: Sunny or lightly shaded border, woodland garden
Good companions: *Chaenomeles speciosa* 'Moerloosei', *Delphinium grandiflorum* 'Blue Butterfly', *Lunaria annua*, *Viola cornuta* Alba Group

2 Brunnera macrophylla

The blue of the 'forget-me-not' flowers is immediately appealing. The large heart-shaped leaves are less coarse in the white-variegated and spotted kinds, notably 'Langtrees', with aluminium splashes. Hardy.
Height: 45cm (18in) **Spread:** 60cm (2ft)
Site: Partial shade. Humus-rich and moist but well-drained soil
Use: Shady border, woodland garden, ground cover
Good companions: *Erythronium dens-canis*, *Helleborus orientalis*, *Hosta sieboldiana* var. *elegans*, *Primula vulgaris*

3 Geranium phaeum
Dusky cranesbill, Mourning widow

In late spring and early summer the nodding purple-black flowers, with prettily swept-back silky petals, strike a sombre note in shaded parts of the garden. This easy plant often self-seeds. The white-flowered 'Album' form lights up dark corners. Hardy.

Height: 75cm (2ft 6in) **Spread:** 45cm (18in)
Site: Shade, partial shade. Reasonably fertile and well-drained soil
Use: Shady border, woodland garden
Good companions: *Helleborus foetidus*, *Iris foetidissima*, *Meconopsis cambrica*, *Polygonatum* x *hybridum*

4 Geranium sylvaticum 'Mayflower'
Wood cranesbill

Above a base of fingered leaves, masses of purple to violet-blue flowers open over several weeks in spring and early summer. The mixture of a close range of colours is attractive, but the pure white of 'Album' is also lovely. Hardy.
Height: 75cm (2ft 6in) **Spread:** 60cm (2ft)
Site: Partial shade, sun. Moist but well-drained soil
Use: Sunny or lightly shaded border
Good companions: *Campanula lactiflora*, *Hemerocallis lilioasphodelus*, *Paeonia mlokosewitschii*, *Smilacina racemosa*

5 Iris 'Demon'
Dwarf bearded iris

A compact free-flowering iris with fragrant flowers of deep blue-purple, shading to velvety brown-purple around the gold-tipped beard. Hardy.
General care: Do not allow other plants to overshadow the roots (rhizomes). Divide these every three years.
Height: 30cm (12in) **Spread:** 15cm (6in)
Site: Sun. Light and well-drained soil. Does well on lime

Use: Front of sunny border, raised bed, rock garden
Good companions: *Artemisia schmidtiana* 'Nana', *Dianthus alpinus* 'Joan's Blood', *Sedum* 'Herbstfreude'

6 Iris 'Rare Edition'
Intermediate bearded iris

A sturdy stem carries eye-catching flowers clear of the stiff grey-green leaf fans. The erect petals (standards) are violet-purple speckled with white. The slightly drooping outer petals (falls), with pale bluish beards, are white edged with purple. Hardy.
General care: Do not allow other plants to overshadow the roots (rhizomes). Divide these every three years.
Height: 60cm (2ft) **Spread:** 25cm (10in)
Site: Sun. Fertile and well-drained soil. Does well on lime
Use: Raised bed, rock garden, sunny border
Good companions: *Cytisus* x *kewensis*, *Hebe cupressoides* 'Boughton Dome', *Pulsatilla vulgaris*

Good companions: *Asplenium scolopendrium, Dicentra formosa alba, Hosta* 'Francee', *Polygonatum* x *hybridum*

7 Lathyrus vernus
Spring vetchling
From mid-spring this bushy plant, dense with divided leaves, is covered with tight sprays of purple pea flowers, nicely varied with tints of crimson and blue. In summer, when flowering has finished, the foliage dies down. Hardy.
Height and spread: 30cm (12in)
Site: Sun. Well-drained, even poor, stony soil
Use: Gravel garden, sunny border
Good companions: *Allium cristophii, Cistus* 'Silver Pink', *Erysimum* 'Bowles' Mauve', *Gladiolus communis* subsp. *byzantinus*

8 Omphalodes cappadocica
Navelwort
Sprays of white-eyed blue flowers hover over the dense cover of slightly hairy oval leaves. 'Cherry Ingram' has larger deep blue flowers. Hardy.
Height: 25cm (10in) **Spread:** 45cm (18in)
Site: Partial shade. Humus-rich and moist soil
Use: Ground cover, shady border, woodland garden
Good companions: *Convallaria majalis, Dicentra* 'Luxuriant', *Rubus* 'Benenden', *Viburnum carlesii* 'Aurora'

9 Pulmonaria 'Mawson's Blue'
Lungwort
For those who find the spotted leaves of some lungworts unattractive, this has plain dark green foliage and flowers of purplish blue. Hardy.
Height: 40cm (16in) **Spread:** 45cm (18in)
Site: Partial shade. Fertile, humus-rich and moist but well-drained soil
Use: Ground cover, shady border, wild garden, woodland garden

10 Trillium erectum
Birth root, Stinking benjamin
The nodding flowers, borne above the foliage, have their parts arranged in threes, the reddish purple petals curving back at the tips. The rich green leaves are also arranged in threes. Hardy.
Height: 50cm (20in) **Spread:** 30cm (12in)
Site: Partial shade, shade. Humus-rich and moist but well-drained soil
Use: Lightly shaded border, woodland garden
Good companions: *Arisaema candidissimum, Dryopteris affinis, Mahonia japonica, Uvularia grandiflora*

11 Viola riviniana Purpurea Group
Dog violet, Wood violet
In this dark form, purplish green leaves make a sombrely effective base for the violet-purple flowers. Very attractive as an underplanting, but runs too freely to mix with choice plants. Hardy.
Height: 10cm (4in) **Spread:** 40cm (16in)
Site: Partial shade, sun. Fertile and moist but well-drained soil
Use: Ground cover, wild garden, woodland garden
Good companions: *Ajuga reptans, Galanthus nivalis, Milium effusum* 'Aureum'

12 Viola sororia 'Freckles'
Sister violet, Woolly blue violet
The appeal of this violet lies in the heavy purple speckling on the white or pale blue flowers. Hardy.
Height: 10cm (4in) **Spread:** 20cm (8in)
Site: Partial shade. Fertile and moist but well-drained soil
Use: Lightly shaded border, underplanting for shrubs, woodland garden
Good companions: *Brunnera macrophylla, Corydalis flexuosa, Dicentra* 'Langtrees', *Dryopteris erythrosora*

purple, blue and violet (continued)

1 Ajuga reptans 'Purple Torch'
Bugle

Bugles are low creeping plants with spoon-shaped evergreen leaves that overlap to make dense ground cover. Most bear spikes of blue flowers in late spring and early summer and some, such as 'Burgundy Glow', have colourful variegated leaves. The misleadingly named 'Purple Torch' form is plain leaved and produces dense spikes of pinkish or mauve flowers. Hardy.
Height: 15cm (6in) **Spread:** 1m (3ft)
Site: Partial shade. Moist but well-drained soil
Use: Ground cover, woodland garden
Good companions: *Convallaria majalis*, *Epimedium* x *youngianum* 'Niveum', *Heuchera cylindrica* 'Greenfinch'

pink and mauve

2 Cardamine pratensis 'Flore Pleno'
Cuckoo flower, Lady's smock

The wild plant, found in damp ground over much of the Northern Hemisphere, has single flowers that are white to purple. An easy and much better plant for the garden is this double form, with spires of mauve-pink flowers rising from dark green, deeply cut leaves. Hardy.
Height: 45cm (18in) **Spread:** 30cm (12in)
Site: Partial shade, shade. Fertile and moist soil
Use: Pond side, shady border, woodland garden
Good companions: *Astilbe* x *arendsii* 'Irrlicht', *Hosta* 'Ginko Craig', *Ranunculus aconitifolius* 'Flore Pleno'

3 Dicentra spectabilis
Bleeding heart

A cottage garden favourite but an elegant plant in any setting, partly because of its attractively cut light green leaves. From an open clump stems arch out, loaded with white-tipped pink lockets. The vigorous white-flowered 'Alba' form is equally beautiful. The foliage dies down in summer. Hardy.
General care: Plant in a sheltered position because the stems are fragile, as are the roots.
Height: 1.2m (4ft) **Spread:** 50cm (20in)
Site: Partial shade, sun. Fertile and moist but well-drained soil
Use: Sunny or lightly shaded border
Good companions: *Clematis alpina* 'Frances Rivis', *Lunaria annua* 'Alba Variegata', *Tulipa* 'Spring Green'

4 Geranium macrorrhizum 'Ingwersen's Variety'
Cranesbill

A semi-evergreen coloniser with pleasantly aromatic leaves that give random touches of autumn colour. All the forms make attractive and effective ground cover. This form has soft mauve-pink flowers. For a stronger effect use 'Bevan's Variety', with

crimson-purple flowers. 'Album' is palest pink with deeper pink touches. Hardy.
Height: 50cm (20in) **Spread:** 60cm (2ft)
Site: Partial shade, sun. Reasonably fertile and well-drained soil
Use: Ground cover, mixed border
Good companions: *Dicentra* 'Luxuriant', *Geranium* x *magnificum*, *Viola cornuta*

5 x Heucherella tiarelloides
A low dense cover of evergreen leaves is topped by spires of tiny flowers, which create a salmon-pink haze lasting into summer. Hardy.
Height and spread: 45cm (18in)
Site: Partial shade, sun, shade. Lime-free, moist but well-drained soil
Use: Ground cover, shady or sunny border, woodland garden
Good companions: *Arum italicum* subsp. *italicum* 'Marmoratum', *Exochorda* x *macrantha* 'The Bride', *Hydrangea quercifolia*

6 Meconopsis quintuplinervia
Harebell poppy

The dark green of the leaves is lightened by rusty or golden bristles. The mauve-blue poppies, darker at the base, dance lightly on hairy stems. Hardy.
Height: 45cm (18in) **Spread:** 30cm (12in)
Site: Partial shade. Lime-free, humus-rich and moist but well-drained soil
Use: Peat bed, woodland garden
Good companions: *Enkianthus campanulatus*, *Fothergilla major* Monticola Group, *Rhododendron* 'Bow Bells'

7 Polemonium 'Lambrook Mauve'
Jacob's ladder

Sprays of bell flowers, which are a silky and delicate mauve, continue into early summer. The

arrangement of paired leaflets has given the polemoniums their common name. Hardy.
Height and spread: 45cm (18in)
Site: Sun, partial shade. Fertile and moist but well-drained soil
Use: Sunny or lightly shaded border
Good companions: *Ajuga reptans* 'Purple Torch', *Aquilegia vulgaris* 'Nivea', *Geranium sylvaticum* 'Mayflower'

8 Primula sieboldii

Heads of pink or purple flowers, with notched petals and a white eye, stand above hairy pale green leaves. An easy plant to grow in moist acid soil. Hardy.
Height: 30cm (12in) **Spread:** 45cm (18in)
Site: Partial shade. Lime-free, moist and humus-rich soil
Use: Pond and stream side, shady border, woodland garden
Good companions: *Matteuccia struthiopteris*, *Primula japonica* 'Postford White'

9 Tellima grandiflora 'Purpurteppich'
Fringe cups

Swaying slender stems carry little cup-shaped flowers that are green with a pink rim. The attractively scalloped leaves mature to red-purple. Hardy.
Height: 60cm (2ft) **Spread:** 30cm (12in)
Site: Partial shade, sun. Moist but well-drained soil
Use: Ground cover, shady or sunny border, woodland garden
Good companions: *Geranium psilostemon*, x *Heucherella tiarelloides*, *Philadelphus coronarius* 'Aureus'

bronze and maroon

10 Dryopteris erythrosora
Buckler fern

The young glossy fronds are red-bronze, then mature to dark green. Tattered remnants sometimes survive the winter but this fern is usually deciduous. Plant in a sheltered position. Hardy.
Height: 60cm (2ft) **Spread:** 40cm (16in)
Site: Partial shade. Humus-rich and moist soil
Use: Shady border, woodland garden
Good companions: *Epimedium* x *warleyense* 'Orangekönigin', *Filipendula ulmaria* 'Aurea', *Tiarella cordifolia*

11 Iris 'Holden Clough'
Beardless iris

The yellow flowers are so heavily veined with purple that the overall effect is of rich bronzy maroon. The ribbed leaves often last through the winter. Hardy.
Height: 75cm (2ft 6in) **Spread:** 15cm (6in)
Site: Sun, partial shade. Moist but well-drained soil
Use: Pond and stream side, sunny border
Good companions: *Astrantia major* subsp. *involucrata* 'Shaggy', *Miscanthus sinensis* 'Zebrinus'

12 Podophyllum hexandrum

The white or pale pink cup-shaped flowers have a crystalline beauty as they peep out from the plant's large leaves, which are lobed and handsomely mottled with maroon. The flowering season extends into summer. The ornamental yellowish fruit that follow are highly toxic. Hardy.
Height: 50cm (20in) **Spread:** 1.2m (4ft)
Site: Partial shade, shade. Humus-rich and moist but well-drained soil
Use: Shady border, woodland garden
Good companions: *Dryopteris affinis*, *Hosta undulata* var. *univittata*, *Smilacina racemosa*

PLANT SELECTOR

red and russet

1 Dicentra 'Luxuriant'
Hummocks of ferny fresh green leaves are topped by sprays of red locket-shaped flowers. The season continues into early summer. Hardy.
Height: 30cm (12in) **Spread:** 45cm (18in)
Site: Partial shade. Fertile and moist but well-drained soil
Use: Ground cover, shady border, woodland garden
Good companions: *Erythronium dens-canis*, *Helleborus orientalis*, *Pulmonaria saccharata* Argentea Group

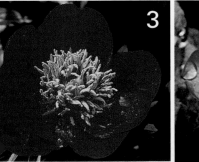

2 Epimedium x rubrum
Barrenwort, Bishop's mitre
The new leaflets retain copper-red tints for several weeks before turning light green. The foliage, often with splashes of bright coral in autumn, lasts through the winter. In early spring there are sprays of white-spurred crimson flowers. Hardy.
General care: In winter cut away old leaves so that flowers can be seen when they emerge.
Height and spread: 30cm (12in)
Site: Partial shade. Moist but well-drained soil
Use: Ground cover, shady border, woodland garden
Good companions: *Brunnera macrophylla*, *Corylopsis pauciflora*, *Dicentra formosa alba*, *Lunaria rediviva*

3 Paeonia peregrina
Peony
The scarlet satin petals of the single blooms cup yellow stamens. The flowering season extends into early summer, and the glossy cut leaves remain an attractive deep green throughout the summer. Hardy.
Height and spread: 60cm (2ft)
Site: Sun, partial shade. Fertile and moist but well-drained soil
Use: Sunny or lightly shaded border
Good companions: *Delphinium* Belladonna Group 'Atlantis', *Iris pallida* 'Argentea Variegata', *Veronica gentianoides*

4 Primula 'Wanda'
Primrose
The radiating leaves, often evergreen, are tinged with purple, complementing the wine-red flowers, which are brightened by a yellow eye. The flowers frequently open early and continue for weeks. Hardy.
Height: 15cm (6in) **Spread:** 30cm (12in)
Site: Partial shade, sun. Humus-rich and moist but well-drained soil
Use: Sunny or shady border, woodland garden
Good companions: *Anemone blanda*, *Galanthus nivalis*, *Scilla siberica*

yellow and orange

5 Doronicum orientale 'Magnificum'
Leopard's bane
An abundance of yellow daisy flowerheads, up to 5cm (2in) across, make this a cheerful plant to follow on from the yellow-flowered daffodils. Its roots colonise ground but not aggressively. Hardy.
Height: 50cm (20in) **Spread:** 1m (3ft)
Site: Partial shade, sun. Fertile and moist but well-drained soil
Use: Lightly shaded border, sunny border, woodland garden
Good companions: *Alchemilla mollis*, *Euphorbia polychroma*, *Lunaria annua*

6 Epimedium x versicolor 'Sulphureum'
Barrenwort, Bishop's mitre
The foliage, tinted red-bronze in spring and autumn, is retained through winter. In spring there are prettily spurred yellow flowers. Hardy.
General care: In winter cut away old leaves so that flowers can be seen when they emerge in spring
Height: 30cm (12in) **Spread:** 1m (3ft)
Site: Partial shade, sun. Moist but well-drained soil
Use: Ground cover, sunny or shady border, woodland garden
Good companions: *Doronicum orientale* 'Magnificum', *Euphorbia griffithii* 'Fireglow', *Geranium* 'Johnson's Blue'

7 Epimedium x warleyense 'Orangekönigin'
Barrenwort, Bishop's mitre
The foliage has lovely coppery tints in spring. The flowers, produced in pretty sprays, are an unusual combination of yellow and orange-brown. Hardy.
General care: In winter cut away old leaves so that flowers can be seen when they emerge in spring.
Height: 50cm (20in) **Spread:** 75cm (2ft 6in)
Site: Partial shade. Moist but well-drained soil
Use: Shady border, woodland garden
Good companions: *Hosta* 'Gold Standard', *Milium effusum* 'Aureum', *Waldsteinia ternata*

8 Euphorbia amygdaloides 'Purpurea'
Milkweed, Wood spurge
The new shoots are eye-catching beetroot-red and gradually turn purplish green. The long-lasting bracts (the petal-like parts around the tiny flowers) are pale yellow, becoming greener with age. Contact with the milky sap may cause a skin reaction. Hardy.
Height and spread: 45cm (18in)
Site: Partial shade. Humus-rich and well-drained but preferably moist soil
Use: Ground cover, shady border, woodland garden
Good companions: *Arum italicum* subsp. *italicum* 'Marmoratum', *Heuchera cylindrica* 'Greenfinch', *Vinca minor* 'La Grave'

9 Euphorbia polychroma
Milkweed, Spurge
The flowers themselves are tiny and inconspicuous, but the bracts surrounding them are a vibrant yellow shading to lime-green. The effect, which lasts well into summer, is of a compact dome studded with arresting flowers. Contact with the milky sap may cause a skin reaction. Hardy.
Height and spread: 45cm (18in)
Site: Sun, partial shade. Well-drained, preferably moist soil
Use: Raised bed, rock garden, sunny or partially shaded border

Good companions: *Allium hollandicum* 'Purple Sensation', *Choisya ternata*, *Iris* 'Jane Phillips', *Tulipa* 'West Point'

10 Filipendula ulmaria 'Aurea'
Meadowsweet, Queen of the meadows
The wrinkled and divided leaves pass through different shades of yellow before turning light green in summer. They scorch in full sun. Hardy.
General care: Remove flowers as they appear to prevent self-seeding.
Height: 75cm (2ft 6in) **Spread:** 60cm (2ft)
Site: Partial shade. Fertile, moist, even boggy soil
Use: Bog garden, pond and stream side, shady border
Good companions: *Astilbe* 'Professor van der Wielen', *Euphorbia griffithii* 'Fireglow', *Rodgersia podophylla*, *Trollius europaeus*

11 Hosta fortunei var. albopicta
Plantain lily
Tightly scrolled leaves unfold to reveal a yellow tongue surrounded by an irregular edge of pale green. By midsummer, when the mauve flowers open, the leaves are two-tone green. Hardy.
Height: 45cm (18in) **Spread:** 1m (3ft)
Site: Partial shade. Fertile, moist, well-drained soil
Use: Ground cover, bog garden, pond and stream side, shady border
Good companions: *Astrantia major* subsp. *involucrata* 'Shaggy', *Kirengeshoma palmata*, *Matteuccia struthiopteris*

12 Meconopsis cambrica
Welsh poppy
Appealing yellow or orange flowers, held trembling above ferny leaves, continue to appear throughout summer. Self-seeds generously. Hardy.
Height: 45cm (18in) **Spread:** 25cm (10in)
Site: Partial shade. Lime-free, moist and humus-rich soil
Use: Shady border, wild garden, woodland garden
Good companions: *Alchemilla mollis*, *Rhododendron luteum*, *Stachyurus praecox*

13 Milium effusum 'Aureum'
Bowles' golden grass, Golden wood millet
Bright yellow ribbon leaves in spring and early

summer are joined by shimmering sprays of little golden flowers at the start of summer. Hardy.
Height: 60cm (2ft) **Spread:** 30cm (12in)
Site: Partial shade, sun. Humus-rich and moist but well-drained soil
Use: Lightly shaded or sunny border, woodland garden
Good companions: *Geranium sylvaticum* 'Mayflower', *Hosta fortunei* var. *albopicta*, *Viola riviniana* Purpurea Group

14 Paeonia mlokosewitschii
Caucasian peony, Mollie-the-witch
The lemon-yellow single flowers are soon over but the foliage is of great beauty. The seed pods split in autumn to reveal scarlet and black. Hardy.
Height and spread: 75cm (2ft 6in)
Site: Sun. Fertile and well-drained soil
Use: Sunny border
Good companions: *Allium* 'Globemaster', *Iris* 'Jane Phillips', *Rosa xanthina* 'Canary Bird', *Sisyrinchium striatum* 'Aunt May'

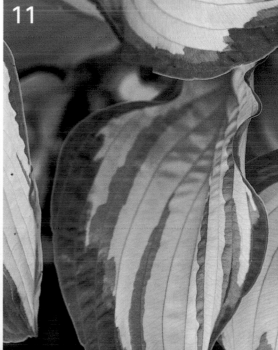

yellow and orange (continued)

1 Uvularia grandiflora
Bellwort, Large merrybells
The drooping leaves and hanging yellow bells,
with prettily twisted petals, give an impression of
elegant somnolence. Hardy.
Height: 75cm (2ft 6in) **Spread:** 30cm (12in)
Site: Partial shade, shade. Humus-rich and moist
but well-drained soil
Use: Shady border, woodland garden
Good companions: *Meconopsis quintuplinervia,
Tiarella cordifolia, Trillium erectum*

2 Valeriana phu 'Aurea'
Valerian
This form would not be grown just for the small
white flowers in midsummer, but the bright clear
yellow of the young leaves makes it a valued
foliage plant for several weeks in spring. As the
foliage matures it turns lime-green and eventually
loses its yellow tint. Hardy.

Height: 1m (3ft) **Spread:** 60cm (2ft)
Site: Sun. Well-drained, preferably moist soil
Use: Bedding, sunny border
Good companions: *Fuchsia magellanica* 'Versicolor', *Hyacinthus orientalis* 'Ostara', *Myosotis sylvatica* 'Royal Blue'

3 Waldsteinia ternata

This low-growing evergreen makes a dense and glossy carpet that shows off the sprays of bright yellow flowers into early summer. Hardy.
Height: 10cm (4in) **Spread:** 60cm (2ft)

Site: Partial shade, sun. Reasonably fertile and well-drained, preferably moist soil
Use: Ground cover, wild garden, woodland garden
Good companions: *Euphorbia griffithii* 'Fireglow', *Helleborus argutifolius*, *Paeonia delavayi* var. *ludlowii*, *Pleioblastus auricomus*

cream and white

4 Anemone sylvestris
Snowdrop anemone

Rapid coloniser with deeply cut leaves above which dangle white flowers with a yellow boss. The white fluff that follows contains the seeds. Contact with the sap may produce a skin reaction. Hardy.
Height and spread: 45cm (18in)
Site: Partial shade, sun. Humus-rich and well-drained soil
Use: Underplanting for shrubs, wild garden, woodland garden
Good companions: *Colchicum speciosum* 'Album', *Exochorda* x *macrantha* 'The Bride', *Osmanthus delavayi*, *Viburnum opulus* 'Roseum'

5 Anthericum liliago
St bernard's lily

An easy plant to grow with grey-green grassy leaves and erect spires of starry white flowers. The flowering season continues into early summer. Good for cutting. Often self-seeds but is rarely troublesome. Hardy.
Height: 75cm (2ft 6in) **Spread:** 30cm (12in)
Site: Sun. Well-drained, preferably moist soil
Use: Sunny border, wild flower garden
Good companions: *Agapanthus* 'Lilliput', *Geranium renardii*, *Veronica spicata* 'Heidekind'

6 Aquilegia vulgaris 'Nivea'
Columbine, Granny's bonnet

The short-spurred flowers of the common columbine are usually in shades of violet, plum or pink. All are worth growing but are outclassed by this white-flowered form in which the beautiful ferny leaves are grey-green. The season spans late spring and early summer. Hardy.
Height: 1m (3ft) **Spread:** 45cm (18in)
Site: Partial shade, sun. Fertile and moist but well-drained soil
Use: Sunny or partially shaded border, woodland garden
Good companions: *Lilium martagon* var. *album*, *Paeonia lactiflora* 'Bowl of Beauty', *Thalictrum aquilegiifolium* 'Thundercloud'

7 Asphodelus albus
Asphodel

The narrow, keeled leaves make an untidy base for spires of starry flowers. Their whiteness is warmed by the pink veins that run down the centre of each petal. Hardy.
Height: 1m (3ft) **Spread:** 30cm (12in)
Site: Sun. Well-drained, even stony, dry soil
Use: Gravel garden, sunny border, wildflower garden
Good companions: *Allium cristophii*, *Artemisia ludoviciana* 'Valerie Finnis', *Cistus ladanifer*, *Ruta graveolens* 'Jackman's Blue'

8 Bergenia 'Beethoven'
Elephant's ears

This is an easy plant, with large and leathery evergreen leaves making impressive clumps; unlike the leaves of some bergenias, these are not noted for taking on strong colours in autumn and winter. Instead of the familiar magenta-pink and purple, the flowers here are white surrounded by a red or pink calyx (the outer ring of parts at the base of each flower). Hardy.
Height and spread: 45cm (18in)
Site: Sun, partial shade. Well-drained, preferably moist soil
Use: Gravel garden, ground cover, sunny or partially shaded border
Good companions: *Buddleja* 'Lochinch', *Eryngium* x *tripartitum*, *Iris* 'Pearly Dawn', *Lavandula* x *intermedia* Dutch Group

9 Convallaria majalis
Lily-of-the-valley

Where it is happy, this plant makes vigorous and fast-spreading ground cover, but it can fail to thrive where expected. The paired leaves are almost oval, with veins running lengthwise. At the centre nestle little sprays of dangling bells, which are waxy, white and fragrant. Hardy.
Height: 20cm (8in) **Spread:** 30cm (12in)
Site: Partial shade, sun. Fertile, humus-rich and moist but well-drained soil
Use: Ground cover, wild garden, woodland garden
Good companions: *Epimedium* x *youngianum* 'Niveum', *Hydrangea* 'Preziosa', *Syringa vulgaris* 'Madame Lemoine', *Weigela* 'Victoria'

10 Corydalis ochroleuca

Although delicate-looking, this is a great survivor and self-seeder. It can be too vigorous for a rock garden but is completely at home lodged in a wall. Above the ferny, light green leaves, short stems bear showers of curiously curved spurred flowers with yellow throats. Hardy.
Height and spread: 30cm (12in)
Site: Partial shade, sun. Fertile and well-drained soil
Use: Underplanting for shrubs, wild garden, woodland garden
Good companions: *Dryopteris affinis*, *Euphorbia amygdaloides* 'Purpurea', *Gentiana asclepiadea*

11 Dicentra 'Langtrees'

The hybrid dicentras combine finely cut foliage and pretty dangling flowers, which are produced over weeks in late spring and early summer. The leaves of 'Langtrees' are silvery blue-green and the flowers are white, tinged with pink. Hardy.
Height: 30cm (12in) **Spread:** 45cm (18in)
Site: Partial shade. Humus-rich and moist but well-drained soil
Use: Edging for lightly shaded border, woodland garden, underplanting for shrubs
Good companions: *Ajuga reptans* 'Purple Torch', *Aquilegia* 'Hensol Harebell', *Brunnera macrophylla*, *Geranium macrorrhizum* 'Ingwersen's Variety'

12 Disporum sessile 'Variegatum'
Fairy bells

The fresh green tapered leaves, irregularly streaked white, are as ornamental as the white tubular flowers, tipped with green, that hang beneath them. The black berries that follow usually go unnoticed. Hardy.
Height and spread: 60cm (2ft)
Site: Partial shade. Humus-rich and moist but well-drained soil
Use: Shady border, peat bed, woodland garden
Good companions: *Helleborus orientalis*, *Hosta* 'Royal Standard', *Trillium grandiflorum*, *Uvularia grandiflora*

cream and white (continued)

1 Epimedium x youngianum 'Niveum'
Barrenwort, Bishop's mitre

Above the foliage, which when young is suffused with soft shades of coppery brown, float little sprays of white flowers. Other lovely forms include 'Merlin', which has purplish flowers. Hardy.
Height: 25cm (10in) **Spread:** 30cm (12in)
Site: Partial shade. Moist but well-drained soil
Use: Ground cover, shady border, woodland garden
Good companions: *Dicentra* 'Langtrees', *Omphalodes cappadocica*

2 Hosta undulata var. univittata
The amount of white in the centre of the twisted leaves varies greatly from plant to plant. There are mauve flowers in summer. Hardy.
Height: 45cm (18in) **Spread:** 75cm (2ft 6in)
Site: Partial shade. Humus-rich and moist but well-drained soil
Use: Ground cover, bog garden, pond and stream side, shady border
Good companions: *Aquilegia* McKana Group, *Polemonium* 'Lambrook Mauve', *Tiarella wherryi*

3 Lunaria rediviva
Perennial honesty

The sweetly scented bunched flowers are faintly tinted with mauve and last until early summer. Elliptic papery seedpods follow. Hardy.
Height: 75cm (2ft 6in) **Spread:** 30cm (12in)
Site: Partial shade, sun. Moist but well-drained soil
Use: Sunny or shady border, wild garden, woodland garden
Good companions: *Geranium sylvaticum* 'Mayflower', *Hyacinthoides non-scripta*, *Prunus avium* 'Plena'

4 Paeonia lactiflora 'White Wings'
Peony

In this single-flowered scented variety, ruffled petals form creamy white cups around golden stamens. In autumn the glossy green leaves take on warm tints. Hardy.
Height: 75cm (2ft 6in) **Spread:** 1m (3ft)
Site: Sun, partial shade. Fertile and well-drained soil
Use: Sunny or lightly shaded border
Good companions: *Iris* 'Florentina', *Lilium regale*, *Rosa* 'Louise Odier', *Veronica gentianoides*

5 Polygonatum x hybridum
Solomon's seal

This is elegant and easy to grow among shrubs. Veined leaves lie along arching stems, from which dangle green-tipped ivory bells. Inedible blue-black fruits follow. All parts of this plant may be harmful if eaten. Hardy.
Height: 1.2m (4ft) **Spread:** 45cm (18in)
Site: Partial shade, shade. Humus-rich and moist but well-drained soil
Use: Shady border, wild garden, woodland garden
Good companions: *Helleborus foetidus*, *Hosta* 'Royal Standard', *Pachysandra terminalis*

6 Primula japonica 'Postford White'
Japanese primrose

Whorls of white flowers, each with a yellow or reddish centre, are carried on a sturdy stem above a rosette of pale green leaves. Hardy.
Height and spread: 45cm (18in)
Site: Partial shade, sun. Lime-free, humus-rich and moist soil
Use: Bog garden, pond and stream side, moist border
Good companions: *Cardamine pratensis* 'Flore Pleno', *Hosta sieboldiana* var. *elegans*, *Rheum palmatum* 'Atrosanguineum', *Rodgersia pinnata* 'Superba'

7 Ranunculus aconitifolius 'Flore Pleno'
Fair maids of France, Fair maids of Kent, White bachelor's buttons

At the base of the plant are fingered leaves with jagged edges. The stems above are almost leafless but carry many white, double button flowers. They are long lasting and their season extends into summer. Contact with the sap may cause skin reactions. Hardy.
Height: 60cm (2ft) **Spread:** 45cm (18in)
Site: Sun, partial shade. Fertile, humus-rich and well-drained soil
Use: Sunny or lightly shaded damp border, woodland garden
Good companions: *Astilbe* x *arendsii* 'Irrlicht', *Iris sibirica* 'Ego', *Zantedeschia aethiopica* 'Crowborough'

8 Smilacina racemosa
False Solomon's seal, False spikenard

Stems, with strongly veined leaves, are topped by tapered tufts of densely packed greenish white or cream flowers that are sweetly scented. Hardy.
Height: 1m (3ft) **Spread:** 60cm (2ft)
Site: Partial shade, shade. Lime-free, humus-rich and moist but well-drained soil
Use: Shady border, woodland garden
Good companions: *Cornus kousa* var. *chinensis*, *Disanthus cercidifolius*, *Meconopsis betonicifolia*, *Trillium grandiflorum*

9 Tiarella cordifolia
Foam flower

Spreading by surface runners, this easy colonising plant makes a dense cover of pale green leaves. The creamy froth of small starry flowers is carried on spikes and lasts into summer. Hardy.

Height: 25cm (10in) **Spread:** 30cm (12in)
Site: Partial shade, shade. Humus-rich and moist but well-drained soil
Use: Ground cover, shady border, woodland garden
Good companions: *Hydrangea paniculata* 'Unique', *Omphalodes cappadocica*, *Spiraea* 'Arguta'

silver and grey

10 Iris 'Florentina'
Orris root

Pale grey flowers are warmed by purple tints and yellow beards. Combined with fans of grey-green leaves, they give a silvery effect in the garden. Sweetly scented. Hardy.

General care: Do not allow other plants to overshadow the roots (rhizomes). Divide these every three years
Height: 75cm (2ft 6in) **Spread:** 45cm (18in)
Site: Sun. Fertile and well-drained soil. Does well on lime
Use: Sunny border
Good companions: *Allium hollandicum* 'Purple Sensation', *Aubrieta* 'Greencourt Purple', *Clematis alpina* 'Frances Rivis'

green

11 Dryopteris affinis
Golden male fern

The green of the unfurling fronds contrasts with the golden-brown midribs. The mature fronds are dark green and often last through winter. Hardy.
Height and spread: 1m (3ft)
Site: Partial shade, shade, sun. Humus-rich and moist soil
Use: Bog garden, pond and stream side, shady border, wild garden, woodland garden
Good companions: *Fargesia murieliae*, *Lobelia* 'Queen Victoria', *Primula florindae*

12 Euphorbia x martinii
Milkweed, Spurge

Evergreen and shrubby, the reddish stems and grey-green leaves form a dome-shaped clump topped by lime-green flowerheads. Each small flower-like cup is lit by a red eye. Hardy.
Height and spread: 1m (3ft)
Site: Sun, partial shade. Well drained soil
Use: Gravel garden, sunny or lightly shaded border, wild garden
Good companions: *Buddleja davidii* 'Black Knight', *Cytisus* x *praecox* 'Allgold', *Onopordum acanthium*, *Stipa gigantea*

13 Iris 'Green Spot'
Dwarf bearded iris

A sturdy iris with lightly scented flowers in white and pale green. The outer petals (falls) are nearly horizontal, each printed with a green spot. Hardy.
General care: Do not allow other plants to overshadow the roots (rhizomes). Divide these every three years.
Height: 25cm (10in) **Spread:** 20cm (8in)
Site: Sun. Fertile and well-drained soil. Good on lime
Use: Raised bed, rock garden, sunny border
Good companions: *Campanula carpatica*, *Crocus imperati* subsp. *imperati* 'De Jager', *Cytisus* x *beanii*, *Lavandula angustifolia* 'Nana Alba'

annuals & biennials

Most of the short-lived plants that brighten beds and containers
in spring are biennials sown the previous summer. Many annuals are
sown in spring for summer displays.

purple, blue and violet

1 Myosotis sylvatica 'Royal Blue'
Forget-me-not

Although forget-me-nots have tiny flowers, the
numerous sprays create a haze of colour, usually
blue, from late spring to early summer. The taller
kinds, such as this richly coloured selection, create
an airy effect. In the dwarf Ball and Victoria Series
the colour range covers blue, pink and white. These
easily grown biennials self-seed freely. Hardy.
General care: Sow seed outdoors in early
summer and plant out in autumn.
Height: 30cm (12in) **Spread:** 15cm (6in)
Site: Partial shade, sun. Moist but well-drained soil
Compost: Soil-based (John Innes No. 2) or soil-less
Use: Container, sunny or partially shaded border,
wild garden, woodland garden
Good companions: *Hyacinthus orientalis* 'Carnegie',
Primula 'Guinevere', *Tulipa* 'Estella Rijnveld'

2 Viola Sorbet Series
Winter-flowering pansy

Despite being called winter-flowering pansies, the
numerous strains of these invaluable plants often
reach their peak in spring. The Sorbet Series has
small flowers, usually bicoloured and in shades of
purple, blue, mauve, yellow and cream. Hardy.
General care: Sow seed outdoors in summer and
plant out in autumn. Deadhead regularly.
Height: 15cm (6in) **Spread:** 30cm (12in)
Site: Sun, partial shade. Fertile, humus-rich and
moist but well-drained soil
Compost: Soil-based (John Innes No. 2) or soil-less
Use: Bedding, container, raised bed, sunny or
lightly shaded border

Good companions: *Crocus vernus* subsp.
albiflorus 'Purpureus Grandiflorus', *Hyacinthus
orientalis* 'Carnegie', *Iris histrioides* 'Major', *Tulipa*
'Queen of Night'

pink and mauve

3 Bellis perennis
Daisy

These double versions of the lawn weed have
larger flowerheads in pink, white or red, and they
bloom over a long season. The Pomponette
Series has neat button flowers. The Habanera
Series has shaggier ones. Perennials usually
grown as biennials. Hardy.
General care: Sow seed outdoors in early
summer and plant out in early autumn.
Height: 10–20cm (4–8in) **Spread:** 15cm (6in)
Site: Sun, partial shade. Moist but well-drained soil
Compost: Soil-based (John Innes No. 2) or soil-less
Use: Bedding, container, edging, sunny or
shady border
Good companions: *Chionodoxa luciliae*, *Primula*
'Wanda', *Tulipa* 'Estella Rijnveld', *Tulipa* 'Mount
Tacoma'

4 Iberis umbellata Fairy Series
Candytuft

An easy annual producing a low mound of narrow
leaves that is almost hidden by clusters of small
scented flowers. In this mixture the colours are
pink and purple shades with some white. Hardy.
General care: For flowers from late spring to late
summer, sow seed *in situ* in autumn and two or
three times between early spring and early summer.
Height: 20cm (8in) **Spread:** 25cm (10in)
Site: Sun. Well-drained, even poor soil. Good
on lime
Compost: Soil-based (John Innes No. 2) or soil-less
Use: Bedding, container, front of sunny border,
raised bed
Good companions: *Clarkia amoena* Satin Series,
Consolida ajacis Imperial Series, *Nigella damascena*
'Miss Jekyll Sky Blue', *Tulipa* 'Heart's Delight'

5 Primula 'Guinevere'
Polyanthus

Red-tinged stems rising from a base of bronzed,
purple-veined leaves carry bunched purplish pink
flowers with a yellow eye. Short-lived evergreen
perennial often grown as a biennial. Hardy.
General care: Sow seed outdoors in early
summer and plant out in early autumn. Divide
plants after flowering or in autumn
Height: 20cm (8in) **Spread:** 25cm (10in)
Site: Partial shade, sun. Humus-rich and moist soil,
preferably acid
Compost: Soil-based (John Innes No. 2) or soil-less
Use: Bedding, container, raised bed, lightly
shaded border
Good companions: *Bellis perennis* Pomponette
Series, *Primula vulgaris* 'Alba Plena', *Puschkinia
scilloides* var. *libanotica*, *Scilla siberica*
'Spring Beauty'

bronze and maroon

6 Primula Gold-laced Group
Polyanthus

Stems rising from rough leaves support a posy of
four to eight jaunty flowers. The mahogany-red

petals are set around a yellow centre and outlined in yellow. Short-lived semi-evergreen perennials often grown as biennials. Hardy.
General care: Sow seed outdoors in early summer and plant out in autumn. Divide plants after flowering or in autumn
Height: 25cm (10in) **Spread:** 30cm (12in)
Site: Partial shade. Fertile and moist but well-drained soil
Compost: Soil-based (John Innes No. 2) or soil-less
Use: Bedding, container, greenhouse or conservatory, shady border
Good companions: *Muscari armeniacum*, *Narcissus* 'February Gold', *Tulipa* 'Queen of Night'

red and russet

7 Erysimum cheiri 'Fire King'
Wallflower

Upright stems carry velvety, sweetly scented flowers. This selection is vibrant orange-red, but mixtures such as Fair Lady Series include plants with cream, pink, purple or red flowers. Short-lived perennials invariably grown as biennials. Hardy.
General care: Sow seed outdoors in late spring or early summer and plant out in mid-autumn.
Height: 60cm (2ft) **Spread:** 30cm (12in)
Site: Sun. Well-drained soil, preferably limy
Compost: Soil-based (John Innes No. 2) or soil-less
Use: Bedding, container, sunny border
Good companions: *Euphorbia griffithii* 'Fireglow', *Lupinus* 'Chandelier', *Rosa xanthina* 'Canary Bird', *Tulipa* 'West Point'

8 Primula Cowichan Garnet Group
Polyanthus

In the Cowichan strain of polyanthus the leaves are usually tinted bronze and the well-proportioned flowers are in rich and varied colours. The Garnet Group flowers are the colour of old wine. Although often treated as biennials, these short-lived perennials can be maintained by division. Hardy.
General care: Sow seed outdoors in early summer and plant out in autumn. Divide plants after flowering or in autumn.

Height: 25cm (10in) **Spread:** 30cm (12in)
Site: Partial shade, sun. Fertile and moist but well-drained soil
Compost: Soil-based (John Innes No. 2) or soil-less
Use: Bedding, container, greenhouse or conservatory, shady border
Good companions: *Hyacinthus orientalis* 'Carnegie', *Myosotis sylvatica* 'Royal Blue', *Primula vulgaris*, *Veronica peduncularis* 'Georgia Blue'

yellow and orange

9 Erysimum cheiri 'Golden Gem'
Wallflower

Dense trusses of four-petalled flowers provide a bright yellow display over several weeks. Compact evergreen perennial grown as a biennial. Hardy.
General care: Sow seed outdoors in late spring or early summer and plant out in mid-autumn.
Height and spread: 15cm (6in)
Site: Sun. Well-drained soil, preferably limy
Compost: Soil-based (John Innes No. 2) or soil-less
Use: Bedding, container, raised bed, sunny border
Good companions: *Ceanothus thyrsiflorus* var. *repens*, *Jasminum nudiflorum*, *Muscari armeniacum*, *Narcissus* 'Jack Snipe'

10 Erysimum cheiri 'Orange Bedder'
Wallflower

The free-flowering Bedder Series are short-growing wallflowers suited to bedding schemes, often sold as a mixture in shades of yellow, orange and scarlet. The colour of 'Orange Bedder' is intense. Perennial almost invariably grown as a biennial. Hardy.
General care: Sow seed outdoors in late spring or early summer and plant out in mid-autumn.
Height: 25cm (10in) **Spread:** 30cm (12in)
Site: Sun. Well-drained soil. Good on lime
Compost: Soil-based (John Innes No. 2) or soil-less
Use: Bedding, container, raised bed, sunny border
Good companions: *Lupinus* 'Chandelier', *Nepeta* 'Six Hills Giant', *Rosa* 'Golden Wings'

cream and white

11 Erysimum cheiri 'Ivory White'
Wallflower

The fragrant four-petalled flowers are creamy white. Short-lived perennial almost invariably grown as a biennial. Hardy.
General care: Sow seed outdoors in late spring or early summer and plant out in mid-autumn
Height: 60cm (2ft) **Spread:** 30cm (12in)
Site: Sun. Well-drained soil, preferably limy
Compost: Preferably soil-based
Use: Bedding, container, sunny border
Good companions: *Cytisus* x *praecox* 'Allgold', *Iris* 'Demon', *Tulipa* 'Generaal de Wet', *Tulipa* 'Spring Green'

12 Lunaria annua 'Alba Variegata'
Honesty, Satin flower

The pink-purple spires of honesty are followed by long-lasting mica-like seed discs. In this white-flowered form the leaves have a white variegation. Freely self-seeding biennial. Hardy.
General care: Sow seed outdoors in late spring or early summer and plant out in autumn.
Height: 1m (3ft) **Spread:** 30cm (12in)
Site: Partial shade, sun. Moist but well-drained soil
Use: Lightly shaded border, wild garden, woodland garden
Good companions: *Aquilegia* 'Hensol Harebell', *Hyacinthoides non-scripta*, *Prunus* 'Shirofugen'

bulbs

Much spring colour is provided by bulbs, a group of perennials with underground food storage organs that are described technically as true bulbs, corms, tubers or rhizomes.

purple, blue and violet

1 Fritillaria meleagris
Snake's head fritillary

The leaves are narrow and the stems slender, so when grown in grass the purple or greenish white chequered flowers seem to float. Hardy.

General care: Plant in autumn with the top of the bulb about 8cm (3in) deep.

Height: 30cm (12in) **Spread:** 8cm (3in)

Site: Sun, partial shade. Humus-rich and moisture-retentive soil

Compost: Soil-based (John Innes No. 2) with added leaf-mould

Use: Border, container, damp meadow, rock garden

Good companions: *Camassia leichtlinii* subsp. *suksdorfii* Caerulea Group, *Crocus speciosus*, *Narcissus bulbocodium* var. *conspicuus*

2 Hyacinthoides non-scripta
English bluebell

This spreads freely in its ideal setting of dappled shade under deciduous trees. The leaves are glossy dark green and the tubular bells, usually violet-blue but sometimes white or pink, are carried on a stem that bends at the tip. The larger-flowered Spanish bluebell (*Hyacinthoides hispanica*) tolerates sun and drier conditions. Hardy.

General care: Plant in autumn, with the top of the bulb about 10cm (4in) deep.

Height: 30cm (12in) **Spread:** 10cm (4in)

Site: Partial shade. Humus-rich, moist but well-drained soil

Use: Underplanting for shrubs, wild garden, woodland garden

Good companions: *Davidia involucrata*, *Magnolia* x *soulangeana*, *Rhododendron* 'Loderi King George'

3 Hyacinthus orientalis 'Ostara'
Hyacinth

Densely packed flowers make a stocky violet-blue column above the deep green leaves. Hardy.

General care: Plant in autumn with the top of the bulb about 10cm (4in) deep.

Height: 25cm (10in) **Spread:** 10cm (4in)

Site: Sun, partial shade. Fertile, well-drained soil

Compost: Soil-based (John Innes No. 2) or soil-less

Use: Formal bedding, container, raised bed, sunny or lightly shaded border

Good companions: *Erysimum* x *allioni*, *Fritillaria imperialis* 'Rubra'

4 Muscari armeniacum
Grape hyacinth

Tapered spikes of bright blue bells, white at the constricted rim, stand erect above linear leaves. This robust and easy bulb increases freely by seed and by division, and is best used for massed effect and not for mixing with choice plants. Hardy.

General care: Plant in autumn with the top of the bulb about 10cm (4in) deep.

Height: 20cm (8in) **Spread:** 10cm (4in)

Site: Sun, partial shade. Moist, well-drained soil

Use: Underplanting for shrubs, wild garden, woodland garden

Good companions: *Magnolia* 'Elizabeth', *Magnolia soulangeana*, *Malus floribunda*

pink and mauve

5 Erythronium dens-canis
European dog's-tooth violet

Nodding flowers, with upturned petals, are poised over maroon-mottled leaves. The flower colour varies from purplish pink to white. 'Pink Perfection' and the darker 'Rose Beauty' are two excellent pink selections. The botanical and common names derive from the tooth-like shape of the corm. Hardy.

General care: Plant in late summer with the top of the corm about 10cm (4in) deep.

Height: 15cm (6in) **Spread:** 20cm (8in)

Site: Partial shade. Fertile, humus-rich and moist but well-drained soil

Use: Rock garden, underplanting for shrubs, woodland garden

Good companions: *Acer palmatum* var. *dissectum* Dissectum Viride Group, *Anemone nemorosa* 'Royal Blue', *Cyclamen hederifolium*

6 Oxalis adenophylla
Shamrock, Sorrel

Neatly pleated leaflets are packed together to make a small grey-green cushion. Furled buds open in late spring and early summer to five-petalled flowers that are near white but have pink veining, centres and tips. Hardy.

General care: Plant in autumn, with the top of the rhizome (the bulb-like root) just below the surface of the soil.

Height and spread: 10cm (4in)

Site: Sun. Gritty and well-drained soil

Use: Paving, raised bed, rock garden

Good companions: *Daphne cneorum* 'Eximia', *Dianthus alpinus* 'Joan's Blood', *Geranium cinereum* 'Ballerina'

7 Erythronium californicum 'White Beauty'
Dog's-tooth violet

A fine form of one of the easiest of the North American species. The leaves are generally lightly mottled or marbled, and round the centre of each creamy-white flower is a rust-coloured ring. Hardy.

General care: Plant in late summer with the top of the corm about 10cm (4in) deep.

Height: 30cm (12in) **Spread:** 15cm (6in)

Site: Partial shade. Fertile, humus-rich and moist but well-drained soil

Use: Rock garden, underplanting for shrubs, woodland garden

Good companions: *Anemone blanda*, *Arum italicum* subsp. *italicum marmoratum*, *Galanthus elwesii*, *Primula vulgaris*

8 Hyacinthus orientalis 'Carnegie'
Hyacinth

Pure white single flowers, waxy and powerfully scented, are densely packed in a short spike. Hardy.

General care: Plant in autumn with the top of the bulb about 10cm (4in) deep.

Height: 25cm (10in) **Spread:** 10cm (4in)

Site: Sun, partial shade. Fertile and well-drained soil

Compost: Soil-based (John Innes No. 2) or soil-less

Use: Formal bedding, container, raised bed, sunny or lightly shaded border

Good companions: *Bellis perennis* Pomponette Series, *Corydalis flexuosa*, *Crocus vernus* 'Jeanne d'Arc', *Hedera helix* 'Adam'

9 Leucojum aestivum 'Gravetye Giant'
Summer snowflake

This has rich green linear leaves and the drooping white bells are neatly tipped with green. Hardy.

General care: Plant in autumn with the top of the bulb about 10cm (4in) deep.

Height: 75cm (2ft 6in) **Spread:** 20cm (8in)

Site: Sun, partial shade. Humus-rich and moist soil

Use: Moist border, pondside and streamside

Good companions: *Cardamine pratensis* 'Flore Pleno', *Primula japonica* 'Postford White', *Salix hastata* 'Wehrhahnii'

10 Muscari botryoides 'Album'
Grape hyacinth

Spikes of small white flowers, with constricted rims, rise through the narrow leaves. Some grape hyacinths increase too rapidly to trust them in a rock garden, but this spreads more slowly. Hardy.

General care: Plant in autumn with the top of the bulb about 8cm (3in) deep. Lift and divide congested clumps after leaves have died down.

Height: 15cm (6in) **Spread:** 5cm (2in)

Site: Sun. Moist but well-drained soil

Compost: Soil-based (John Innes No. 2) or soil-less

Use: Container, raised bed, rock garden

Good companions: *Armeria juniperifolia*, *Crocus chrysanthus* 'Cream Beauty', *Iris* 'Joyce', *Phlox subulata* 'McDaniel's Cushion'

11 Narcissus 'Actaea'
Poeticus daffodil

The tiny, yellow and red-rimmed cup is surrounded by glistening white petals. This and the slightly later-flowering old pheasant's eye (*N. poeticus* var. *recurvus*), with swept back flowers, can extend the spring bulb season into early summer. Hardy.

General care: Plant in autumn with the top of the bulb about 10cm (4in) deep.

Height: 45cm (18in) **Spread:** 15cm (6in)

Site: Sun. Reasonably fertile and moist soil

Use: Sunny border, damp meadow

Good companions: *Camassia leichtlinii* subsp. *suksdorfii* Caerulea Group, *Fritillaria meleagris*, *Narcissus cyclamineus*

12 Ornithogalum nutans
Star-of-Bethlehem

The colour scheme is cool and restrained. The sprays of white stars have green stripes on the underside of the petals and the leaves are silvered down the centre. Where conditions suit it, this multiplies too freely to include in borders and rock gardens. Hardy.

General care: Plant in autumn with the top of the bulb about 10cm (4in) deep.

Height: 40cm (16in) **Spread:** 10cm (4in)

Site: Partial shade, sun. Well-drained and reasonably moist soil

Use: Underplanting for shrubs, wild garden, woodland garden

Good companions: *Colchicum* 'Rosy Dawn', *Geranium sylvaticum* 'Album', *Lilium martagon* var. *album*

tulips

Tulips are colourful hardy bulbs for formal spring bedding and containers. Plant them in autumn, 10–15cm (4–6in) deep, in fertile, well-drained soil in sun. In containers use a soil-based (John Innes No. 2) compost.

1 Tulipa 'Spring Green'
A late-flowering Viridiflora tulip, this has flowers that are green or a combination of green and another colour.
Height: 40cm (16in) **Spread:** 10cm (4in)
Good companions: *Buxus sempervirens*, *Primula auricula* 'Osbourne Green'

2 Tulipa 'Mount Tacoma'
Although less elegant than single late-flowering white tulips such as the lily-flowered 'White Triumphator', this double late tulip produces long-lasting flowers of dazzling purity.
Height: 40cm (16in) **Spread:** 10cm (4in)
Good companions: *Syringa vulgaris* 'Katherine Havemeyer', *Tulipa* 'Queen of Night'

3 Tulipa 'West Point'
The single lemon-yellow flowers of this lily-flowered tulip have a waisted goblet shape with elegantly curved tips.
Height: 50cm (20in) **Spread:** 10cm (4in)
Good companions: *Bellis perennis* Pomponette Series, *Primula* 'Guinevere'

4 Tulipa 'Queen of Night'
The sheeny flowers of this single late tulip are an exceptionally dark purple-maroon.
Height: 60cm (2ft) **Spread:** 10cm (4in)
Good companions: *Erysimum* 'Ivory White', *Malus* x *moerlandsii* 'Profusion', *Philadelphus coronarius* 'Aureus'

5 Tulipa 'Estella Rijnveld'
In this parrot tulip, the green-tinged buds have fringed petals and open to an extravagant swirl of white and red.
Height: 60cm (2ft) **Spread:** 10cm (4in)

Good companions: *Bellis perennis* Pomponette Series, *Hyacinthus orientalis* 'Carnegie', *Primula* 'Guinevere'

6 Tulipa 'Red Wing'
The shredded edge of the petals in this Fringed Group tulip gives each vivid red flower a distinctive outline.
Height: 50cm (20in) **Spread:** 10cm (4in)
Good companions: *Bellis perennis* Habanera Series, *Hyacinthus orientalis* 'Ostara', *Primula* Cowichan Garnet Group

7 Tulipa 'Fancy Frills'
A pale fringe encrusts petals that are rich pink with a near-white central blaze.
Height: 45cm (18in) **Spread:** 10cm (4in)
Good companions: *Hyacinthus orientalis* 'Carnegie', *Myosotis sylvatica* 'Royal Blue', *Tulipa* 'Queen of Night'

8 Tulipa 'Shirley'
The ivory-white petals of this Triumph Group tulip (surrounding Late Group tulips) are lightly streaked and edged with purple.
Height: 60cm (2ft) **Spread:** 10cm (4in)
Good companions: *Erysimum cheiri* 'Ivory White', *Tulipa* 'Mount Tacoma'

9 Tulipa saxatilis Bakeri Group 'Lilac Wonder'
In warm sun, the mauve-pink petals of this Species tulip open to reveal a lemon-yellow base. Suitable for a rock garden.
Height: 20cm (8in) **Spread:** 8cm (3in)
Good companions: *Aubrieta* 'Doctor Mules', *Muscari botryoides* 'Album', *Phlox subulata* 'McDaniel's Cushion'

1

2

3

4

climbers

Trained on architectural structures or other plants, climbers add a vertical dimension to the garden. Many begin flowering in spring and supply welcome early colour. Plant climbers in the dormant season.

purple, blue and violet

1 Clematis alpina 'Frances Rivis'
Alpine clematis

A selection of the slender deciduous species (see 11, opposite) with large, deep blue flowers. Plant with the base in shade. Hardy.
General care: Prune lightly after flowering.
Height: 3m (10ft) **Spread:** 1.5m (5ft)
Site: Sun, partial shade. Fertile, humus-rich and well-drained soil. Good on lime
Compost: Soil-based (John Innes No. 3)
Use: Container, shrub climber, training on tripod, wall
Good companions: Buddleja crispa, Paeonia mlokosewitschii, Rosa xanthina 'Canary Bird'

2 Clematis 'Helsingborg'
Alpina Group clematis

This slender deciduous clematis has nodding blue-purple flowers with long, elegant outer petal-like sepals. Plant with the base in shade. Hardy.
General care: Prune lightly after flowering
Height: 3m (10ft) **Spread:** 1.5m (5ft)
Site: Sun, partial shade. Fertile, humus-rich and well-drained soil. Does well on lime
Compost: Soil-based (John Innes No. 3)
Use: Container, shrub climber, training on tripod, wall
Good companions: Choisya ternata, Hyacinthus orientalis 'Carnegie', Tulipa 'Queen of Night'

3 Clematis macropetala
Clematis

A slender deciduous clematis with violet-blue flowers that have a paler centre filled with petal-like stamens. Ornamental fluffy seed heads follow. Plant with the base in shade. Hardy.
General care: Prune lightly after flowering.
Height: 3m (10ft) **Spread:** 1.5m (5ft)
Site: Sun, partial shade. Fertile, humus-rich and well-drained soil. Good on lime
Compost: Soil-based (John Innes No. 3)
Use: Container, shrub climber, training on tripod, wall
Good companions: Geranium sylvaticum 'Mayflower', Iris 'Jane Phillips', Narcissus 'Peeping Tom', Tulipa 'West Point'

pink and mauve

4 Clematis armandii 'Apple Blossom'
Clematis

Thought by many to be the best evergreen clematis, this needs a sheltered position on a warm wall. The glossy leaves provide good year-round cover and are bronze-green when young. The flowers, borne in mid-spring, are white flushed with pink. 'Snowdrift' has white flowers. Plant with the base in shade. Not fully hardy.
General care: Prune immediately after flowering.
Height and spread: 6m (20ft)
Site: Sun. Fertile, humus-rich and moist but well-drained soil. Good on lime
Use: Warm wall
Good companions: Cynara cardunculus, Passiflora caerulea, Rosa 'Reine des Violettes', Vitis vinifera 'Purpurea'

5 Clematis macropetala 'Markham's Pink'
Clematis

Bright pink and free-flowering cultivar of the deciduous species Clematis macropetala (see 3, above). Plant with the base in shade. Hardy.
General care: Prune lightly after flowering.
Height: 3m (10ft) **Spread:** 1.5m (5ft)
Site: Sun, partial shade. Fertile, humus-rich and well-drained soil. Does well on lime
Compost: Soil-based (John Innes No. 3)
Use: Container, shrub climber, training on tripod, wall
Good companions: Clematis 'Huldine', Digitalis purpurea, Nepeta 'Six Hills Giant'

6 Clematis montana var. rubens 'Elizabeth'
Clematis

The deciduous species is very vigorous, producing masses of white flowers in late spring and early summer. This variety, one of several selections in shades of pink, has purplish foliage and the large scented flowers are pale pink. Plant with the base in shade. Hardy.
General care: Prune immediately after flowering.
Height: 10m (30ft) **Spread:** 5m (15ft)
Site: Sun, partial shade. Fertile, humus-rich and moist but well-drained soil
Use: Pergola, trellis, tree climber, wall
Good companions: Campanula lactiflora, Lilium regale, Paeonia lactiflora 'Festiva Maxima', Rosa 'Bobbie James'

7 Wisteria sinensis
Chinese wisteria

Very vigorous deciduous climber with attractive large leaves that are divided into many leaflets. Most of the fragrant pea flowers in the trailing sprays open at the same time so that their mauve-blue makes a strong but elegant impression. By pruning it is possible to maintain plants at almost any size. Hardy.
General care: Prune in late summer and again in winter.
Height: 15m (50ft) **Spread:** 6m (20ft)
Site: Sun. Moist but well-drained soil, preferably lime-free
Use: Pergola, trained standard, tree climber, wall
Good companions: Clematis montana var. rubens 'Elizabeth', Paeonia lactiflora 'Bowl of Beauty', Rosa 'Madame Alfred Carrière', Rosa 'Madame Grégoire Staechelin'

yellow and orange

8 Rosa banksiae 'Lutea'
Yellow banksian rose

Vigorous semi-evergreen rose with slender, almost thornless stems. It takes a few years to settle and needs a sheltered position, but an established plant provides a beautiful display of small, double yellow flowers before the main rose season is under way. Lightly scented. Not fully hardy.
General care: Prune lightly every two or three years, only removing a few of the oldest stems.
Height: 12m (40ft) **Spread:** 6m (20ft)
Site: Sun. Fertile, moist but well-drained soil
Use: Warm wall
Good companions: Campsis x tagliabuana 'Madame Galen', Clematis 'Perle d'Azur', Paeonia delavayi var. ludlowii

9 Rosa 'Gloire de Dijon'
Old glory rose

This stiff-stemmed climber starts flowering early and continues over a long season. The fragrant double flowers are buff rather than yellow and have apricot tints. Hardy.
General care: Prune lightly between late autumn and early spring.
Height: 3m (10ft) **Spread:** 1.5m (5ft)
Site: Sun. Fertile, moist but well-drained soil
Use: Sunny wall or screen

Good companions: *Clematis* 'Gipsy Queen', *Clematis* 'Perle d'Azur', *Cleome hassleriana*, *Lilium regale*

10 Rosa 'Maigold'
Climbing hybrid Scots briar rose

Stiff-stemmed and thorny rose with glossy leaves and scented, semi-double, copper-yellow flowers. The display in late spring and early summer is generous but in autumn it is sparse. Can be grown as a free-standing shrub. Hardy.
General care: Prune lightly between late autumn and early spring.
Height: 4m (12ft) **Spread:** 2m (6ft)
Site: Sun. Fertile and moist but well-drained soil
Use: Specimen shrub, well-lit wall or screen
Good companions: *Allium hollandicum* 'Purple Sensation', *Clematis* 'Royal Velours', *Solanum crispum* 'Glasnevin'

cream and white

11 Clematis alpina subsp. sibirica 'White Moth'
Alpine clematis

The species is a slender deciduous climber, which often starts producing its blue flowers in early spring. The moth-like form of this late-flowering white version is due to the double petals. Very suitable for a courtyard or small garden. Plant with the base in shade. Hardy.
General care: Prune lightly after flowering.
Height: 3m (10ft) **Spread:** 1.5m (5ft)
Site: Sun, partial shade. Fertile, humus-rich and well-drained soil. Good on lime
Compost: Soil-based (John Innes No. 3)
Use: Container, shrub climber, training on tripod, wall
Good companions: *Aquilegia vulgaris* 'Nivea', *Clematis alpina* 'Frances Rivis', *Dicentra spectabilis* 'Alba', *Tulipa* 'Estella Rijnveld'

12 Wisteria sinensis 'Alba'
Chinese wisteria

This form of the vigorous *Wisteria sinensis* (see 7, opposite) has powerfully scented white flowers. Hardy.
General care: Prune in late summer and again in winter to control size.
Height: 15m (50ft) **Spread:** 6m (20ft)
Site: Sun. Moist but well-drained soil, preferably free of lime
Use: Pergola, trained standard, tree climber, wall
Good companions: *Clematis montana* var. *rubens* 'Elizabeth', *Clematis* 'Perle d'Azur', *Rosa* 'Gloire de Dijon'

shrubs & trees

Shrubs and small trees have durable frameworks of woody branches. Blossom and tints of new foliage make many conspicuously attractive in spring. Plant in the dormant season – in autumn or early spring.

purple, blue and violet

1 Ceanothus 'Puget Blue'
/California lilac/
The dense framework of branches and dark leaves of this evergreen shrub is almost hidden in the second half of spring by the rounded heads of small deep blue flowers. Suitable for training against a warm wall. Not fully hardy.
Height and spread: 3m (10ft)
Site: Sun. Well-drained soil
Use: Sunny sheltered border, wall shrub
Good companions: *Actinidia kolomikta*, *Myrtus communis* subsp. *tarentina*, *Solanum laxum* 'Album' (syn. *S. jasminoides* 'Album')

2 Ceanothus thyrsiflorus var. repens
Creeping blueblossom
This low-growing evergreen shrub makes a dark green mound that is covered in late spring and early summer with rounded heads of mid-blue flowers. Hardy.
Height: 1m (3ft) **Spread:** 2.5m (8ft)
Site: Sun. Well-drained soil
Use: Gravel garden, large rock garden, raised bed, sunny border
Good companions: *Artemisia absinthum* 'Valerie Finnis', *Gaura lindheimeri*, *Rosa glauca*, *Verbena bonariensis*

pink and mauve

3 Acer palmatum 'Corallinum'
Japanese maple
One of several Japanese maples, this slow-growing deciduous shrub has brilliant pink foliage in spring. In summer the deeply cut leaves are pale green but usually colour crimson and scarlet in autumn, most vividly on acid soil. Hardy but requires a sheltered position.
Height and spread: 1.2m (4ft)
Site: Partial shade. Humus-rich and moist but well-drained soil, preferably lime-free
Use: Shady border
Good companions: *Enkianthus campanulatus*, *Erythronium dens-canis*, *Rhododendron* 'Cilpinense', *Trillium erectum*

4 Acer pseudoplatanus 'Brilliantissimum'
Sycamore
In spring the young leaves of this slow-growing deciduous tree are an astonishing shade of shrimp pink. As they mature they turn yellow, then later green. Hardy.
Height and spread: 6m (20ft)
Site: Sun. Reasonably fertile and moist but well-drained soil
Use: Canopy in mixed planting, specimen tree
Good companions: *Euonymus alatus*, *Quercus coccinea* 'Splendens', *Taxus baccata* 'Fastigiata'

5 Cercis siliquastrum
Judas tree
This deciduous tree or large shrub bears clusters of bright purple-pink pea flowers on the bare stems or bursting from the trunk. The heart or kidney-shaped leaves are blue-green. Hardy.
Height and spread: 10m (33ft)
Site: Sun. Reasonably fertile and well-drained soil
Use: Canopy in mixed planting, specimen tree
Good companions: *Acanthus mollis* Latifolius Group, *Buddleja alternifolia*, *Cistus ladanifer*, *Helleborus argutifolius*

6 Cornus florida 'Cherokee Chief'
Flowering dogwood
Large petal-like bracts surround the tiny flowers of this deciduous tree or shrub. These are generally white or pink, strongly veined and often twisted, but in this selection they are vivid dark pink. Inedible red fruit follow. The leaves colour well in autumn. Hardy.

Height and spread: 6m (20ft)
Site: Sun. Reasonably fertile and well-drained soil, preferably lime-free
Use: Canopy in mixed planting, specimen tree or shrub, woodland garden
Good companions: *Choisya ternata*, *Cotoneaster frigidus* 'Cornubia', *Euonymus europaeus* 'Red Cascade'

7 Crataegus laevigata 'Paul's Scarlet'
May, Midland thorn

The species, of which this is a selection, and the hawthorn (*Crataegus monogyna*) are thorny deciduous trees of rounded outline that bear masses of pink or white flowers followed by inedible red fruits (haws). They are often used for country hedges, but are also attractive and easily grown trees for the smaller garden. This example carries a profusion of red double flowers. Hardy.
Height and spread: 8m (25ft)
Site: Sun, partial shade. Well-drained soil
Use: Canopy in mixed planting, specimen tree
Good companions: *Malus floribunda*, *Prunus laurocerasus* 'Otto Luyken', *Sarcococca hookeriana* var. *digyna*, *Sorbus* 'Joseph Rock'

8 Deutzia x elegantissima 'Rosealind'

The deutzias are mainly easy-going deciduous shrubs. They are covered with pink or white starry flowers in late spring or early summer. The pink flowers of 'Rosealind' are carried on arching stems and bridge the two seasons. Hardy.
General care: Prune immediately after flowering.
Height and spread: 1.5m (5ft)
Site: Sun, partial shade. Reasonably fertile and well-drained soil
Use: Sunny or lightly shaded border, underplanting for shrubs and trees
Good companions: *Exochorda* x *macrantha* 'The Bride', *Osmanthus delavayi*, *Viburnum opulus* 'Compactum'

9 Enkianthus campanulatus

The leaves of this tree-like shrub turn brilliant red before falling in autumn. The flowers in spring are of a subdued and delicate beauty. Red veining gives a pink tinge to the creamy bell-shaped blooms, which hang in pretty clusters. Hardy.
Height: 3m (10ft) **Spread:** 2.5m (8ft)
Site: Sun, partial shade. Lime-free, humus-rich and moist but well-drained soil
Use: Canopy in mixed planting, woodland garden
Good companions: *Fothergilla major* Monticola Group, *Hamamelis* x *intermedia* 'Pallida', *Rhododendron luteum*

10 Magnolia x soulangeana
Magnolia

A very large deciduous shrub or small tree, this produces a sensational display of chalice-shaped flowers, which open in mid-spring. The magnolia usually seen has cream flowers flushed purplish pink, but all the named white and purple-flowered forms are worth growing. Hardy.
Height and spread: 6m (20ft)
Site: Sun. Humus-rich and moist but well-drained soil, preferably lime-free
Use: Canopy in mixed planting, specimen tree or shrub, woodland garden
Good companions: *Bergenia* 'Beethoven', *Muscari armeniacum*, *Narcissus* 'Jenny'

11 Malus floribunda
Japanese crab apple

With a dense head of arching branches, this small deciduous tree is suitable for a small to medium garden. Crimson buds open to pale pink or white flowers, which are followed by small red-and-yellow apples. Hardy.
Height and spread: 8m (25ft)
Site: Sun, partial shade. Reasonably fertile, well-drained soil
Use: Canopy in mixed planting, specimen tree
Good companions: *Anemone blanda*, *Narcissus* 'Jack Snipe', *Spiraea* 'Arguta'

12 Malus x moerlandsii 'Profusion'
Crab apple

Round-headed tree with copper-red young leaves, which mature to bronze-red. In late spring there is a burst of thickly clustered, dark purplish pink flowers. Small red-purple apples follow. Hardy.
Height and spread: 10m (33ft)
Site: Sun. Fertile and moist but well-drained soil
Use: Canopy in mixed planting, specimen tree
Good companions: *Anemone* x *hybrida* 'Honorine Jobert', *Bergenia cordifolia* 'Purpurea', *Narcissus* 'February Gold'

13 Paeonia suffruticosa
Moutan, Tree peony

Despite their common name, tree peonies are deciduous shrubs. The framework of branches is somewhat stiff and awkward, but the leaves are attractively cut and the flowers are breathtaking. There are many magnificent cultivars in shades of pink as well as red, purple and white. Hardy.
General care: Protect young growth from frost.
Height and spread: 2m (6ft)
Site: Sun, partial shade. Fertile, humus-rich and moist but well-drained soil
Use: Sunny or lightly shaded border
Good companions: *Aquilegia* 'Hensol Harebell', *Campanula persicifolia*, *Rosa* 'Nevada'

pink and mauve (continued)

1 Prunus 'Kanzan'
Ornamental cherry

Although this deciduous tree is less graceful than many ornamental cherries, the upward-sweeping branches make it a useful avenue tree where space is limited. The young leaves are copper-red and the double flowers purplish pink. Hardy.

Height: 10m (33ft) **Spread:** 6m (20ft)
Site: Sun. Well-drained soil, preferably with a trace of lime
Use: Avenue, specimen tree
Good companions: *Crocus speciosus*, *Crocus tommasinianus*, *Scilla siberica* 'Spring Beauty'

2 Prunus 'Shirofugen'
Ornamental cherry

This broad-headed and vigorous deciduous tree brings the ornamental cherry season to a magnificent conclusion. Thickly clustered double white flowers open from purple-pink buds to coincide with the copper-red phase of the young leaves. As the long-stalked flowers fade they revert to purple-pink. Leaves usually colour orange-red in autumn. Hardy.

Height: 8m (25ft) **Spread:** 10m (33ft)
Site: Sun, partial shade. Moist, well-drained soil
Use: Canopy in mixed planting, specimen tree, woodland garden
Good companions: *Anemone nemorosa* 'Royal Blue', *Galanthus elwesii*, *Hyacinthoides non-scripta*

3 Syringa vulgaris 'Katherine Havemeyer'
Lilac

The numerous large-flowered forms of the common lilac are easy deciduous shrubs. They are a glorious feature of spring, when the dense heads of single or double fragrant flowers are borne in profusion. The flowers of 'Katherine Havemeyer' are mauve-pink and double. Hardy.

General care: Deadhead after flowering and remove growth sprouting from the base (suckers).
Height and spread: 6m (20ft)
Site: Sun, partial shade. Reasonably fertile and well-drained soil
Use: Sunny or lightly shaded border
Good companions: *Iris* 'Florentina', *Iris* 'Jane Phillips', *Rosa xanthina* 'Canary Bird'

4 Viburnum carlesii 'Aurora'
Viburnum

One of several forms of a deciduous shrub noted for the delicious fragrance of its waxy flowers, which are pink or red in bud and white or pink on opening. In this case the rounded heads are red and the open flowers pink. The downy leaves, copper tinted when young, may take on purplish or crimson tones in autumn. Hardy.

Height and spread: 2m (6ft)

Site: Sun, partial shade. Moist well-drained soil
Use: Sunny or lightly shaded border
Good companions: *Geranium psilostemon*, *Hydrangea quercifolia*, *Viburnum* x *bodnantense* 'Dawn'

5 Viburnum opulus 'Roseum'
Guelder rose, Snowball tree

The guelder rose, of which this is a form, is an attractive shrub with maple-like leaves, heads of white flowers and translucent red berries that glisten among the richly coloured autumn leaves. 'Roseum' produces no berries, the flowers being sterile, but these age to pink. Hardy.

Height and spread: 4m (12ft)
Site: Sun, partial shade. Moist but well-drained soil
Use: Sunny or lightly shaded border, wild garden, woodland garden
Good companions: *Digitalis purpurea*, *Fuchsia magellanica* 'Versicolor', *Lunaria annua*

red and russet

6 Camellia japonica 'Bob Hope'
Camellia

The common camellia, an evergreen shrub with glossy dark leaves, is the parent of hundreds of cultivars with flowers in a colour range that includes white, red and all shades of pink. Many flower in early spring but the season extends over many weeks. 'Bob Hope' is compact and bears large, semi-double bright red flowers of peony form. Plant in a sheltered position to protect buds and flowers from cold winds and frosts. Hardy.

Height: 3m (10ft) **Spread:** 2.5m (8ft)
Site: Partial shade. Lime-free, humus-rich and moist but well-drained soil
Compost: Soil-based and lime-free (ericaceous)
Use: Container, greenhouse or conservatory, shady border, underplanting for trees
Good companions: *Eucryphia* x *nymansensis* 'Nymansay', *Rhododendron* 'Bow Bells', *Rhododendron* 'Loderi King George'

7 Paeonia suffruticosa 'Hana-daijin'
Moutan, Tree peony

The flowers of tree peonies cover a range of sumptuous colours (see 13, page 93). 'Hana-daijin' bears double flowers with waved petals enclosing a golden centre. Hardy.

General care: Protect young growth from frost.
Height and spread: 2m (6ft)
Site: Sun, partial shade. Fertile, humus-rich and moist but well-drained soil

Use: Sunny or lightly shaded border
Good companions: *Aquilegia* 'Hensol Harebell', *Campanula persicifolia*, *Geranium psilostemon*, *Rosa* 'Nevada'

8 Photinia x fraseri 'Red Robin'

The small white flowers of this evergreen shrub count for little, but new growth is brilliant red and makes a striking garden feature in spring and early summer before the leaves turn glossy green. Can be used as an attractive alternative to *Pieris* 'Forest Flame' where there is chalk in the soil. Plant in a sheltered position. Not fully hardy.

Height and spread: 5m (15ft)
Site: Sun, partial shade. Fertile, moist but well-drained soil
Use: Sunny or lightly shaded border, underplanting for trees
Good companions: *Epimedium* x *youngianum* 'Niveum', *Helleborus orientalis*, *Pulmonaria* 'Mawson's Blue'

9 Pieris 'Forest Flame'

In spring drooping sprays of fragrant white flowers are a lovely feature of this evergreen shrub, but more eye-catching is the brilliant red of its young growth, which turns pink then greenish white and finally green. Plant in a sheltered position. Not fully hardy.

Height: 3m (10ft) **Spread:** 2m (6ft)
Site: Sun, partial shade. Lime-free, humus-rich and moist but well-drained soil
Use: Sunny or lightly shaded border, underplanting for trees
Good companions: *Acer japonicum* 'Vitifolium', *Rhododendron* 'Britannia'

yellow and orange

10 Berberis darwinii
Barberry

Drooping clusters of small bright orange flowers make this evergreen shrub conspicuous in spring. In autumn there are blue-black berries among the glossy spine-tipped leaves. Hardy.

Height and spread: 3m (10ft)
Site: Sun, partial shade. Well-drained soil
Use: Sunny or lightly shaded border
Good companions: *Cytisus* x *praecox* 'Allgold', *Geranium phaeum*, *Potentilla fruticosa* 'Tangerine'

11 **Berberis x stenophylla**
Barberry

The numerous arching branches of this vigorous evergreen shrub bear fragrant orange-yellow flowers in spring. Generally a light crop of blue-black berries follows. The leaves are prickly. Hardy.

Height: 3m (10ft) **Spread:** 5m (15ft)
Site: Sun, partial shade. Well-drained soil
Use: Informal hedge, sunny or lightly shaded bed
Good companions: *Berberis thunbergii* 'Atropurpurea Nana', *Cotinus* 'Flame', *Syringa vulgaris* 'Katherine Havemeyer'

12 **Cytisus x kewensis**
Broom

This low, spreading deciduous shrub is best sited where the arching stems, laden in spring with creamy-yellow pea flowers, can hang down. Hardy.

Height: 30cm (12in) **Spread:** 2m (6ft)
Site: Sun. Well-drained soil
Use: Bank, large rock garden, raised bed
Good companions: *Euonymus alatus* 'Compactus', *Euphorbia characias* subsp. *wulfenii*, *Pinus sylvestris* 'Beuvronensis'

1 Cytisus x praecox 'Allgold'
Broom

The arching stems of this dense and bushy deciduous shrub are closely set with deep yellow pea flowers. Their scent is strong and acrid. Short-lived, but good as a filler. Hardy.

Height and spread: 1.5m (5ft)

Site: Sun. Well-drained soil

Use: Gravel garden, sunny border

Good companions: *Artemisia ludoviciana* 'Valerie Finnis', *Stachys byzantina* 'Silver Carpet', *Verbascum* Cotswold Group 'Gainsborough'

2 Kerria japonica 'Pleniflora'
Jew's mantle

This easy deciduous shrub has slender, glossy green stems that are attractive in winter. Its high season, though, is spring, when the bush carries numerous rich yellow double flowers. Hardy.

General care: Cut out old stems immediately after flowering.

Height and spread: 3m (10ft)

Site: Sun, partial shade. Well-drained soil

Use: Sunny or lightly shaded border, underplanting for deciduous trees

Good companions: *Forsythia* x *intermedia* 'Lynwood', *Fritillaria imperialis*, *Narcissus* 'Peeping Tom'

3 Laburnum × watereri 'Vossii'
Golden rain

This small deciduous tree is often trained on a pergola, a method of growing that shows off the numerous cascades of yellow flowers, which can be up to 60cm (2ft) long. The flowering season extends into early summer. All parts of the plant are highly toxic. Hardy.

Height and spread: 8m (25ft)
Site: Sun. Fertile and well-drained soil
Use: Canopy for mixed planting, pergola, specimen tree
Good companions: *Allium hollandicum* 'Purple Sensation', *Myosotis sylvatica*, *Tulipa* 'Generaal de Wet', *Wisteria sinensis*

12

4 Magnolia 'Elizabeth'
Magnolia

This conical deciduous tree bears fragrant light yellow flowers, up to 20cm (8in) across, over several weeks in spring. Their cup shape and erect stance are particularly conspicuous on the bare branches before the large leaves unfurl. These open bronze and later change to dark green. Hardy.

Height: 10m (33ft) **Spread:** 6m (20ft)
Site: Sun, partial shade. Humus-rich and moist but well-drained soil, preferably lime-free
Use: Canopy in mixed planting, specimen tree
Good companions: *Acer palmatum* 'Sango-kaku', *Hamamelis* × *intermedia* 'Pallida', *Narcissus* 'February Gold'

5 Paeonia delavayi var. ludlowii
Tree peony

The large, deeply cut, bright green leaves of this deciduous shrub make it worth growing for its foliage alone. The yellow cup-shaped flowers, 13cm (5in) across, open as the leaves are developing, and their season extends into early summer. Hardy.

Height and spread: 2.5m (8ft)
Site: Sun, partial shade. Fertile, humus-rich and moist but well-drained soil
Use: Sunny or lightly shaded border
Good companions: *Brunnera macrophylla*, *Helleborus orientalis*, *Lilium regale*, *Viburnum plicatum* 'Mariesii'

6 Philadelphus coronarius 'Aureus'
Mock orange

There are fragrant single white flowers in late spring and early summer, but this deciduous shrub is grown mainly for the sunny effect of its bright yellow young leaves. By mid-summer these have lost their fresh radiance. Hardy.

Height: 2.5m (8ft) **Spread:** 2m (6ft)
Site: Partial shade. Well-drained soil
Use: Lightly shaded border
Good companions: *Choisya ternata*, *Cotinus* 'Grace', *Euonymus alatus* 'Compactus'

7 Pleioblastus auricomus
Bamboo

This upright evergreen bamboo is grown for its bright foliage. Hollow purplish canes carry blade-like leaves that are yellow streaked with green. The clumps spread but without posing a threat. Hardy.

General care: To promote the growth of fresh leaves, cut the canes down in autumn.
Height: 1.2m (4ft) **Spread:** 1.5m (5ft)
Site: Sun. Humus-rich and moist but well-drained soil
Compost: Soil-based
Use: Container, sunny border, wild garden
Good companions: *Epimedium* × *versicolor* 'Sulphureum', *Milium effusum* 'Aureum', *Paeonia delavayi* var. *ludlowii*

8 Rosa xanthina 'Canary Bird'
Shrub rose

The clear yellow of the small single flowers makes a cheerful start to the long rose season. The blooms have a musky scent and are borne freely along arching stems. The ferny grey-green leaves are attractive throughout summer, and there are odd flowers as a reminder of the generous spring display. Hardy.

Height and spread: 3m (10ft)
Site: Sun. Reasonably fertile and moist but well-drained soil
Use: Specimen shrub, sunny border
Good companions: *Aquilegia* McKana Group, *Iris* 'Jane Phillips', *Rosa* 'Golden Wings'

9 Salix lanata
Woolly willow

This shrubby deciduous willow makes a grey rounded bush. The dark green leaves are covered with silvery wool. Hairy catkins that are yellow with pollen and 5–8cm (2–3in) long sit among the young leaves. Hardy.

Height: 1m (3ft) **Spread:** 1.5m (5ft)
Site: Sun. Moist but well-drained soil
Use: Large rock garden, raised bed, sunny border
Good companions: *Corydalis flexuosa*, *Crocus speciosus*, *Crocus tommasinianus*

cream and white

10 Choisya ternata
Mexican orange blossom

A compact evergreen shrub, this has glossy aromatic leaves and numerous clusters of scented white flowers in late spring. After the main season, the shrub may flower sporadically, often with a little burst in autumn. It is usually seen at its best in a sheltered town garden. Hardy.

Height and spread: 2.5m (8ft)
Site: Sun, partial shade. Well-drained soil
Use: Sunny or shady border, mixed trees and shrubs
Good companions: *Ceanothus thyrsiflorus* var. *repens*, *Cistus ladanifer*, *Melianthus major*, *Wisteria sinensis*

11 Davidia involucrata
Dove tree, Ghost tree, Handkerchief tree

When in flower, this conical deciduous tree seems to be decked with freshly laundered handkerchiefs. The small flowers are clustered in rounded heads, but each cluster is surrounded by a pair, unequal in size, of white leaf-like bracts. Hardy.

Height: 15m (50ft) **Spread:** 10m (33ft)
Site: Sun, partial shade. Fertile and moist but well-drained soil
Use: Canopy in mixed planting, specimen tree, woodland garden
Good companions: *Cornus alba* 'Elegantissima', *Geranium sylvaticum* 'Mayflower', *Hydrangea* 'Preziosa', *Hydrangea quercifolia*

12 Erica arborea var. alpina
Tree heath

This somewhat formless evergreen shrub with needle-like leaves is dramatically transformed in spring when tight conical sprays are covered with small grey-white flowers that have the fragrance of honey. Hardy.

Height: 2m (6ft) **Spread:** 1m (3ft)
Site: Sun. Lime-free and moist but well-drained soil
Use: Heather garden, large rock garden, sunny border
Good companions: *Calluna vulgaris* 'Peter Sparkes', *Erica carnea* 'King George', *Ledum groenlandicum*

cream and white (continued)

1 Exochorda x macrantha 'The Bride'
Pearl bush

This deciduous shrub produces a mound of pliant arching stems, which are garlanded with white flowers. Excellent with late spring bulbs. Hardy.
General care: Cut out about a fifth of the old stems after flowering.
Height: 2m (6ft) **Spread:** 3m (10ft)
Site: Sun, partial shade. Moist but well-drained soil
Use: Sunny or lightly shaded border
Good companions: *Magnolia* x *soulangeana*, *Tulipa* 'Queen of Night', *Tulipa* 'Spring Green'

2 Fothergilla major Monticola Group

The fragrant bottlebrush flowers, usually white but sometimes tinged pink, are the spring feature of this deciduous shrub. In autumn the leaves turn brilliant shades of yellow, orange and red. Hardy.
Height: 2.5m (8ft) **Spread:** 2m (6ft)
Site: Sun, partial shade. Lime-free, humus-rich and moist but well-drained soil
Use: Sunny or lightly shaded border, woodland garden
Good companions: *Acer japonicum* 'Vitifolium', *Meconopsis betonicifolia*, *Rhododendron* 'Bow Bells'

3 Halesia carolina
Silver bell, Snowdrop tree

This deciduous shrub or spreading small tree starts to flower before the leaves are fully developed. Numerous small clusters of white bells hang from the slender branches in late spring and are followed by inedible four-winged fruits. Plant in a position sheltered from cold winds. Hardy.
Height: 6m (20ft) **Spread:** 8m (25ft)
Site: Sun, partial shade. Lime-free, humus-rich and moist but well-drained soil
Use: Canopy in mixed planting, woodland garden
Good companions: *Acer griseum*, *Hamamelis* x *intermedia* 'Pallida', *Rhododendron* 'Loderi King George'

4 Ledum groenlandicum
Labrador tree

A rounded bush of dark aromatic leaves, this low evergreen shrub is studded with flat heads of small white flowers. Shoots and the undersides of the leaves are covered with a rusty felt. Hardy.
Height: 1m (3ft) **Spread:** 1.2m (4ft)

Site: Sun, partial shade. Lime-free, humus-rich and moist but well-drained soil
Use: Heather garden
Good companions: *Calluna vulgaris* 'Darkness', *Erica carnea* 'Springwood White', *Gaultheria mucronata* 'Bell's Seedling'

5 Magnolia denudata
Lily tree, Yulan

Provided the fragrant flowers are not spoilt by late frosts, this deciduous shrub or small tree is one of the great delights of spring. The dome of bare branches is liberally covered with upright white blooms. Plant in a sheltered position. Hardy.
Height and spread: 8m (25ft)
Site: Sun. Moist but well-drained soil, preferably lime-free
Use: Canopy in mixed planting, specimen shrub or tree
Good companions: *Narcissus* 'Dove Wings', *Primula* 'Guinevere', *Scilla siberica*

6 Magnolia x kewensis 'Wada's Memory'
Magnolia

The fragrant white flowers of this deciduous small tree or shrub are borne on bare stems. They are large, up to 13cm (5in) across, with fluttering limp petals. The leaves are bronze tinted on opening but later turn dark green, and are aromatic when bruised. Hardy.
Height: 10m (33ft) **Spread:** 6m (20ft)
Site: Sun. Humus-rich and moist but well-drained soil, preferably lime-free
Use: Canopy in mixed planting, specimen tree
Good companions: *Camellia* 'Cornish Snow', *Erythronium californicum* 'White Beauty', *Erythronium dens-canis*, *Eucryphia* x *nymansensis* 'Nymansay'

flower. Erect candles, composed of numerous small fragrant flowers, are produced in spring and early summer and occasionally in autumn. Hardy.
Height: 1m (3ft) **Spread:** 1.5m (5ft)
Site: Sun, partial shade. Moist but well-drained soil, preferably lime-free
Compost: Soil-based with added organic matter
Use: Container, informal hedge, sunny or shaded border, underplanting for trees
Good companions: *Cercidiphyllum japonicum, Hydrangea macrophylla* 'Blue Wave', *Mahonia japonica*

10 Prunus 'Shôgetsu'
Ornamental cherry
A good choice for a small to medium garden, this small but rather flat-topped deciduous tree bears numerous clusters of pink buds that open to frilly double white flowers. The foliage usually shows orange and red tints in autumn. Hardy.
Height: 5m (15ft) **Spread:** 8m (25ft)
Site: Sun, partial shade. Moist but well-drained soil
Use: Canopy in mixed planting, specimen tree, woodland garden
Good companions: *Anemone blanda, Colchicum speciosum* 'Album', *Primula vulgaris*

11 Prunus 'Ukon'
Ornamental cherry
The leaves of this spreading deciduous tree are bronze tinted when they open in mid-spring. Their colour goes well with the greenish cream of the semi-double flower clusters. Attractive red-brown foliage in autumn. Hardy.
Height and spread: 8m (25ft)
Site: Sun. Moist but well-drained soil
Use: Canopy in mixed planting, specimen tree, woodland garden
Good companions: *Arum italicum* subsp. *italicum* 'Marmoratum', *Epimedium* x *warleyense* 'Orangekönigin', *Helleborus argutifolius*

12 Rubus 'Benenden'
Related to the blackberry, this thornless deciduous shrub has attractive lobed leaves. Glistening white flowers, each one 5cm (2in) across with a boss of yellow stamens, open along arching stems. Hardy.
General care: Prune after flowering.
Height and spread: 3m (10ft)
Site: Sun, partial shade. Well-drained soil
Use: Sunny or lightly shaded border, wild garden, woodland garden
Good companions: *Forsythia* x *intermedia* 'Lynwood', *Hydrangea aspera* Villosa Group, *Lonicera* x *purpusii* 'Winter Beauty'

7 Osmanthus delavayi
Slow-growing evergreen shrub with small glossy dark green leaves that show off the pure white of the neat tubular flowers. The sweet scent is delicious in the garden and indoors. Hardy.
General care: For a compact shape, prune immediately after flowering.
Height: 4m (12ft) **Spread:** 2.5m (8ft)
Site: Sun, partial shade. Reasonably moist but well-drained soil
Use: Sunny or lightly shaded border, underplanting for deciduous trees
Good companions: *Bergenia* 'Beethoven', *Muscari armeniacum, Sorbus cashmiriana*

8 Prunus avium 'Plena'
Gean, Wild cherry
A somewhat pyramidal deciduous tree, this form of the European species has a fissured trunk banded with peeling red-brown bark. In spring the branches are loaded with drooping clusters of double white flowers. In autumn the leaves turn crimson. Hardy.
Height: 12m (40ft) **Spread:** 10m (33ft)
Site: Sun. Moist but well-drained soil
Use: Canopy in mixed planting, specimen tree, woodland garden
Good companions: *Cyclamen hederifolium, Galanthus nivalis, Helleborus orientalis*

9 Prunus laurocerasus 'Otto Luyken'
Cherry laurel, Laurel
The glossy evergreen foliage of the cherry laurels makes them valuable year-round shrubs and hedging plants. This compact form has narrow lustrous leaves and is one of the most effective in

cream and white (continued)

1 Sorbus aria 'Lutescens'
Whitebeam

The whitebeam is a columnar, compact deciduous tree. The leaves are an attractive grey-green colour when young, and later turn dark green on the upper surface and grey-white and downy on the underside. White spring flowers are followed by clusters of inedible spherical berries, which ripen to scarlet as the foliage turns gold and russet in autumn. 'Lutescens' is outstanding in spring because of the creamy whiteness of the young leaves. Hardy.
Height: 10m (33ft) **Spread:** 8m (25ft)
Site: Sun. Well-drained soil. Good on chalk
Use: Canopy in mixed planting, specimen tree, woodland garden
Good companions: *Philadelphus* 'Belle Etoile', *Prunus* 'Taihaku', *Syringa vulgaris* 'Katherine Havemeyer'

2 Spiraea 'Arguta'
Bridal wreath, Foam of May

In spring numerous clusters of small white flowers are borne along the whole length of the slender arching branches of this dense deciduous shrub. The toothed narrow leaves are bright green. Hardy.
Height and spread: 2.5m (8ft)
Site: Sun. Fertile and moist but well-drained soil
Use: Sunny border
Good companions: *Abelia schumannii*, *Osmanthus delavayi*, *Ribes sanguineum* 'Pulborough Scarlet', *Rosa* 'Céleste'

3 Syringa vulgaris 'Madame Lemoine'
Lilac

Like *Syringa vulgaris* 'Katherine Havemeyer' (see page 94), this is a double form of the popular deciduous shrub, but here the fragrant flowers are creamy yellow in bud and pure white on opening. Hardy.
General care: Deadhead after flowering and remove suckers (growth sprouting from the base).
Height and spread: 6m (20ft)
Site: Sun, partial shade. Reasonably fertile and well-drained soil
Use: Sunny or lightly shaded border
Good companions: *Buddleja* 'Lochinch', *Cynara cardunculus*, *Rosa glauca*

4 Viburnum plicatum 'Mariesii'
Japanese snowball tree

The spreading branches of this deciduous shrub are arranged in tiers. The bush is already in leaf when the white flowers open in flat-topped heads – small fertile flowers surrounded by large sterile flowers on the outside. The display lasts into early summer. The foliage often colours richly in autumn. Hardy.
Height: 3m (10ft) **Spread:** 4m (12ft)
Site: Sun, partial shade. Moist but well-drained soil
Use: Sunny or lightly shaded border, woodland garden
Good companions: *Campanula lactiflora*, *Chaenomeles* x *superba* 'Knap Hill Scarlet', *Geranium sylvaticum* 'Mayflower'

5 Xanthoceras sorbifolium

This large upright deciduous shrub has bright green leaves composed of many sharply toothed leaflets. The starry white flowers, with a yellow to bright red eye, are borne on upright stems. Best in a hot position and suitable for training against a warm wall. Hardy.
Height: 4m (12ft) **Spread:** 3m (10ft)
Site: Sun. Fertile and well-drained soil
Use: Sunny border, wall shrub
Good companions: *Ceanothus* 'Puget Blue', *Clematis alpina* 'Frances Rivis', *Clematis* 'Bill MacKenzie'

green

6 Acer palmatum var. dissectum Dissectum Viride Group
Japanese maple

The Japanese maples are deciduous shrubs and small trees. They are remarkable for the range of leaf shape and size among the various cultivars as well as for the brilliant colours many assume in autumn. Some are slow-growing mound-forming shrubs, with leaves divided into five or more lobes that are cut right to the base. The Dissectum Viride Group have finely divided leaves that are bright green in spring, then plainer in summer before colouring well in autumn, most vividly on acid soil. Plant in a sheltered position. Hardy.
Height: 2m (6ft) **Spread:** 3m (10ft)
Site: Partial shade. Humus-rich and moist but well-drained soil, preferably lime-free
Use: Shady border, underplanting for trees
Good companions: *Cercidiphyllum japonicum*, *Erythronium californicum* 'White Beauty', *Rhododendron* 'Loderi King George'

rhododendrons

Rhododendrons, which include azaleas, are ornamental shrubs that need neutral to acid soil or an ericaceous compost. Those selected here are all hardy and flower in late spring to early summer.

1 Rhododendron 'Loderi King George'

Large, evergreen and rounded. Huge trusses of scented white flowers open from pink buds.

Height and spread: 4m (12ft)

Good companions: *Camellia japonica* 'Elegans', *Kalmia latifolia* 'Ostbo Red'

2 Rhododendron 'Dopey'

Compact and evergreen, with many trusses of scarlet flowers marked with brown.

Height and spread: 2m (6ft)

Good companions: *Acer palmatum* var. *dissectum* Dissectum Viride Group, *Camellia japonica* 'Bob Hope', *Rhododendron* 'Britannia'

3 Rhododendron 'Strawberry Ice'

Deciduous azalea. Dark-veined pale pink blooms with a yellow-marked throat open from deep pink buds. Suitable for full sun.

Height and spread: 2m (6ft)

Good companions: *Cornus florida* 'Cherokee Chief', *Halesia carolina*, *Rhododendron* 'Vanessa Pastel'

4 Rhododendron 'Lionel's Triumph'

Large-leaved and evergreen with trusses of soft yellow flowers that are pink in bud.

Height and spread: 4m (12ft)

Good companions: *Disanthus cercidifolius*, *Magnolia* 'Elizabeth'

5 Rhododendron macabeanum

Evergreen shrub with huge leaves. Cream or yellow purple-blotched flowers in mid-spring.

Height: 12m (40ft) **Spread:** 6m (20ft)

Good companions: *Eucryphia* x *nymansensis*

'Nymansay', *Hamamelis* x *intermedia* 'Jelena', *Magnolia* 'Elizabeth'

6 Rhododendron 'Vuyk's Scarlet'

Small-leaved and dwarf evergreen azalea. Vivid red flowers. Suitable for full sun.

Height: 75cm (2ft 6in) **Spread:** 1.2m (4ft)

Good companions: *Erica arborea* var. *alpina*, *Ledum groenlandicum*, *Pieris* 'Forest Flame'

7 Rhododendron 'Bow Bells'

Compact and evergreen, with copper-tinted young leaves and pink flowers.

Height and spread: 2m (6ft)

Good companions: *Acer palmatum* 'Corallinum', *Camellia* x *williamsii* 'Donation', *Fothergilla major* Monticola Group

8 Rhododendron 'Golden Torch'

On this compact evergreen shrub pink buds open to peachy-yellow flowers.

Height and spread: 1.5m (5ft)

Good companions: *Acer palmatum* 'Corallinum', *Fothergilla major* Monticola Group, *Hamamelis* x *intermedia* 'Pallida'

9 Rhododendron 'Palestrina'

Small-leaved evergreen azalea. Clusters of two or three white flowers that are pale green in the throat.

Height and spread: 1.2m (4ft)

Good companions: *Camellia* 'Donation', *Kalmia latifolia* 'Ostbo Red'

alpines

Most small perennials and shrubs that thrive in well-drained conditions do not need to be grown in a special rock garden. Many flower in spring and early summer. Plant in mild weather between autumn and early spring.

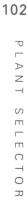

purple, blue and violet

1 Gentiana acaulis
Trumpet gentian

The sensational deep blue of the trumpets, which have green spotting in the throat, make this one of the most celebrated of all alpine plants. Its flowering can be unpredictable. Hardy.

Height: 8cm (3in) **Spread:** 45cm (18in)
Site: Sun. Moist but gritty and well-drained soil
Compost: Soil-based (John Innes No. 1) with added grit and leaf-mould
Use: Alpine house, raised bed, rock garden, scree, trough
Good companions: *Hebe cupressoides* 'Boughton Dome', *Iris histriodes* 'Major', *Narcissus* 'Jack Snipe'

2 Gentiana verna
Spring gentian, Star gentian

The starry flowers are small but their deep azure colour makes a strong impression. This evergreen perennial tends to be short-lived, so it is worth bringing on young plants as replacements. Hardy.

Height: 8cm (3in) **Spread:** 15cm (6in)
Site: Sun. Moist but well-drained and gritty soil
Compost: Soil-based (John Innes No. 1) with added grit and leaf-mould
Use: Alpine house, raised bed, rock garden, scree, trough
Good companions: *Daphne cneorum* 'Eximia', *Muscari botryoides* 'Album'

3 Primula marginata 'Kesselring's Variety'
Primula

The species is an evergreen or semi-evergreen perennial forming rosettes of jagged leaves with silvery margins. The stems are covered with a white mealy powder and carry clusters of lightly scented mauve-blue flowers with a powdery white eye. This selection is richly coloured. Best planted in crevices and protected from excess wet. Hardy.

Height: 15cm (6in) **Spread:** 30cm (12in)
Site: Partial shade. Moist but well-drained and gritty soil
Compost: Soil-based (John Innes No. 1) with added leaf-mould and grit
Use: Alpine house, dry wall, raised bed, rock garden
Good companions: *Alchemilla conjuncta*, *Geranium cinereum* 'Ballerina'

4 Pulsatilla vulgaris
Pasque flower

This tactile perennial produces a tuft of finely cut leaves that are very hairy when young, and from which rise nodding buds of silky hairiness. The purple or mauve flowers have golden stamens. In summer there are silky seed heads. Hardy.

Height: 25cm (10in) **Spread:** 30cm (12in)
Site: Sun. Fertile and well-drained soil
Use: Front of border, raised bed, rock garden, scree
Good companions: *Armeria maritima* 'Dusseldorfer Stölz', *Crocus imperati* subsp. *imperati* 'De Jager', *Gypsophila repens* 'Rosa Schönheit'

pink and mauve

5 Aethionema 'Warley Rose'
Stone cress

This evergreen or semi-evergreen shrubby perennial is easy to grow. It produces broad spikes of densely clustered rich pink flowers in quantity. Hardy.

Height: 15cm (6in) **Spread:** 30cm (12in)
Site: Sun. Well-drained soil. Good on lime
Use: Dry wall, paving, raised bed, rock garden, scree
Good companions: *Aubrieta* 'Greencourt Purple', *Dianthus deltoides* 'Leuchtfunk', *Silene schafta*

6 Armeria juniperifolia
Sea pink, Thrift

Pink flowers huddle over the small evergreen hummock of narrow rather sharp-tipped leaves. The flowers are richly coloured in the form 'Bevan's Variety'. Hardy.

Height: 8cm (3in) **Spread:** 15cm (6in)
Site: Sun. Well-drained and gritty soil
Compost: Soil-based (John Innes No. 1) with added grit
Use: Paving, raised bed, rock garden, scree, trough

Good companions: *Artemisia schmidtiana* 'Nana', *Lavandula angustifolia* 'Nana Alba', *Raoulia australis* Lutescens Group

7 Aubrieta hybrids
Aubrieta

Mat-forming aubrietas are evergreen perennials. In spring they are covered with four-petalled, sometimes double flowers in mauve, pink, purple or red. 'Rose Queen' has pink flowers; 'Greencourt Purple' is purple. Hardy.

General care: To keep plants compact, trim after flowering in early summer.
Height: 5cm (2in) **Spread:** 60cm (2ft)
Site: Sun. Well-drained soil. Good on lime
Use: Front of border, paving, raised bed, rock garden, sunny bank
Good companions: *Aurinia saxatilis* 'Citrina', *Campanula garganica*, *Iberis sempervirens* 'Weisser Zwerg'

8 Daphne cneorum 'Eximia'
Garland flower

The daphnes, which are noted for the superlative fragrance of their small flowers, tend to be temperamental. This sprawling evergreen shrub, the most rewarding of the dwarf daphnes, dislikes

root disturbance, so start with a young pot-grown specimen. The starry pink flowers are borne profusely in late spring and early summer. Hardy.
Height: 20cm (8in) **Spread:** 1m (3ft)
Site: Sun, partial shade. Humus-rich and well-drained soil
Use: Dry wall, front of border, raised bed, rock garden, scree
Good companions: *Diascia barberae* 'Ruby Field', *Gypsophila repens* 'Rosa Schönheit', *Tulipa clusiana*

9 Penstemon 'Six Hills'

Several shrubby and sub-shrubby evergreen penstemons are low growing and bear masses of funnel-shaped flowers. This hybrid makes a small bush of grey-green leaves. It produces mauve flowers in late spring and early summer. Hardy.
Height: 15cm (6in) **Spread:** 25cm (10in)
Site: Sun. Well-drained and gritty soil
Use: Paving, raised bed, rock garden, scree
Good companions: *Armeria juniperifolia*, *Artemisia schmidtiana* 'Nana', *Crocus sieberi* 'Hubert Edelsten', *Geranium cinerium* subsp. *subcaulescens*

10 Phlox douglasii 'Boothman's Variety'
Phlox

The species is a shrubby evergreen perennial that makes a bright green mat of narrow leaves. In late spring and early summer saucer-shaped mauve or pink flowers almost hide the foliage. The mauve flowers of this cultivar have a dark eye. Other cultivars have white or crimson flowers. Hardy.
Height: 15cm (6in) **Spread:** 45cm (18in)
Site: Sun. Fertile and well-drained soil
Use: Dry wall, paving, raised bed, rock garden
Good companions: *Convolvulus sabatius*, *Rhodanthemum hosmariense*, *Silene schafta*

11 Phlox subulata 'McDaniel's Cushion'
Moss phlox

The species, like *Phlox douglasii* (see above), is a low-growing evergreen perennial, but the late spring and early summer flowers are more starry and the petals are notched. The colour range in other named forms includes pink, mauve, scarlet and magenta. 'McDaniel's Cushion' has rich pink flowers. Hardy.
Height: 10cm (4in) **Spread:** 45cm (18in)
Site: Sun, partial shade. Fertile, well-drained soil
Use: Dry wall, paving, raised bed, rock garden
Good companions: *Armeria maritima* 'Dusseldorfer Stölz', *Hebe cupressoides* 'Boughton Dome', *Narcissus* 'Jenny'

red and russet

12 Saxifraga 'Peter Pan'
Mossy saxifrage

Tightly packed evergreen leaves form dense hummocks. These are topped in spring by wiry stems carrying saucer-shaped flowers that can be white, yellow, pink or red. The crimson-flowered 'Peter Pan' makes a tidy plant. 'Pixie', another compact hybrid, has deep red flowers. Hardy.
Height: 8cm (3in) **Spread:** 30cm (12in)
Site: Partial shade. Moist but well-drained soil
Compost: Soil-based (John Innes No. 2) with added grit and leaf-mould
Use: Edging, paving, raised bed, rock garden, trough
Good companions: *Alchemilla conjuncta*, *Phlox subulata*, *Viola biflora*

1 Aurinia saxatilis 'Dudley Nevill Variegated'
Gold dust

This evergreen shrubby perennial has variegated leaves and massed buff-yellow flowers. The species has bright yellow blooms while those of 'Citrina' are lemon-yellow. Hardy.

General care: To keep plants compact, trim when flowering has finished.

Height: 25cm (10in) **Spread:** 45cm (18in)

Site: Sun. Well-drained soil

Use: Dry wall, raised bed, rock garden, sunny bank

Good companions: *Achillea* x *lewisii* 'King Edward', *Aubrieta* 'Greencourt Purple', *Cytisus* x *beanii*

2 Cytisus x beanii
Broom

Like its relative the common broom (*Cytisus scoparius*), this dwarf deciduous shrub makes a sunny impression with sprays of golden pea flowers. It is short-lived, usually achieving its peak in its third year. Hardy.

General care: Prune lightly immediately after flowering.

Height: 60cm (2ft) **Spread:** 1m (3ft)

Site: Sun. Well-drained soil

Use: Front of border, raised bed, rock garden

Good companions: *Aubrieta* 'Doctor Mules', *Crocus tommasinianus*, *Helianthemum* 'Wisley Primrose', *Iris* 'George'

3 Raoulia australis Lutescens Group

A tight mat of very small blue-grey leaves, this evergreen perennial flows over irregularities. The minute yellow flowers are little more than a powdering in spring. Dislikes winter wet. Hardy.

Height: 1cm (½in) **Spread:** 45cm (18in)

Site: Sun, partial shade. Moist but well-drained and gritty soil

Compost: Soil-based (John Innes No. 1) with added leaf-mould and grit

Use: Paving, raised bed, rock garden, scree, trough

Good companions: *Armeria juniperifolia*, *Dianthus alpinus* 'Joan's Blood', *Salix boydii*

4 Viola biflora
Twin-flowered violet

The yellow flowers brighten up lightly shaded areas. This perennial has a creeping rootstock, so is likely to spread if it likes the conditions. Hardy.

Height: 8cm (3in) **Spread:** 30cm (12in)

Site: Partial shade. Humus-rich and moist but well-drained soil

Use: Raised bed, rock garden, woodland garden

Good companions: *Alchemilla conjuncta*, *Galanthus nivalis*, *Scilla siberica* 'Spring Beauty'

cream and white

5 Arabis alpina subsp. caucasica 'Schneehaube'
Rock cress

The species is a robust evergreen perennial that produces numerous spikes of four-petalled white flowers. It tends to bully less vigorous plants. 'Schneehaube' is more compact, as is 'Flore Pleno', which has double flowers. Hardy.

Height: 15cm (6in) **Spread:** 45cm (18in)

Site: Sun. Well-drained soil

Use: Dry wall, paving, raised bed, rock garden

Good companions: *Aubrieta* 'Doctor Mules', *Aurinia saxatilis* 'Citrina', *Cytisus* x *beanii*, *Juniperus communis* 'Green Carpet'

6 Iberis sempervirens 'Weisser Zwerg'
Candytuft

The pure white flowers clustered in rounded heads on this evergreen shrubby perennial are dazzling in spring and early summer. The species, does well on a sunny bank, but this compact cultivar is more suitable for growing with other small plants. Hardy.

General care: To keep plants compact, trim when flowering has finished.

Height: 15cm (6in) **Spread:** 25cm (10in)

Site: Sun. Moist but well-drained soil, even poor, and preferably limy

Use: Dry wall, paving, raised bed, rock garden

Good companions: *Gypsophila repens* 'Rosa Schönheit', *Juniperus squamata* 'Blue Star', *Sedum* 'Bertram Anderson'

water & waterside plants

Most of the plants that relish reliably moist conditions are
perennials. Some like the ground really wet and others will even grow
in shallow water. Plant in the dormant season.

yellow and orange

1 Caltha palustris 'Flore Pleno'
Kingcup, Marsh marigold
Instead of the single, rich yellow flowers shining
above deep green kidney-shaped leaves, this
double form of the beautiful wild perennial has
long-lasting yellow flowers that are tinted green
at the centre of tightly packed petals. Hardy.
Height: 40cm (16in) **Spread:** 30cm (12in)
Site: Sun, partial shade. Humus-rich and
permanently moist soil or water 10cm (4in) deep
Use: Bog garden, water margin
Good companions: *Acorus calamus*
'Variegatus', *Myosotis scorpioides*, *Zantedeschia
aethiopica* 'Crowborough'

2 Euphorbia palustris
Milkweed, Spurge
This herbaceous perennial makes an impressive
clump of bright green leaves topped by clusters of
greenish yellow flower-like bracts, which remain
attractive well beyond spring. The foliage turns
yellow and orange-brown in autumn. Hardy.
Height and spread: 1m (3ft)
Site: Sun. Humus-rich, permanently moist soil
Use: Bog garden, waterside
Good companions: *Iris laevigata* 'Variegata',
Rodgersia pinnata 'Superba', *Trollius europaeus*

3 Iris pseudacorus 'Variegata'
Yellow flag
The yellow flag is a vigorous plant to
fringe a large body of water. Its
yellow irises flutter among the tall
blades in summer and are followed
by attractive seedpods. In this less
vigorous variegated form, the fans of
young leaves are soft yellow striped
with green in spring before turning
full green in summer. Hardy.

Height: 1m (3ft) **Spread:** 60cm (2ft)
Site: Sun. Humus-rich and reliably moist soil or
water up to 15cm (6in) deep
Use: Bog garden, moist border, waterside
Good companions: *Ligularia* 'The Rocket',
Lysichiton americanus, *Matteuccia struthiopteris*

green

4 Matteuccia struthiopteris
Ostrich fern, Shuttlecock fern
In spring the greenish yellow new fronds form
a symmetrical 'shuttlecock' on a short trunk,
usually less than 30cm (12in) high. Later, a
plume of dark, fertile fronds, which carry the
spores, rises in the centre to remain as a
distinctive feature right through winter, after the
outer fronds have died. Spreads freely by
underground roots. Hardy.
Height: 1.5m (5ft) **Spread:** 1m (3ft)
Site: Partial shade, sun. Reliably moist, even
boggy soil
Use: Bog garden, damp border, waterside
Good companions: *Alnus glutinosa* 'Imperialis',
Osmunda regalis, *Rheum palmatum*
'Atrosanguineum'

herbs, vegetables & fruit

Culinary plants are often very ornamental, especially when in blossom or making fresh growth, but the first reason for growing early maturing vegetables and fresh herbs is their produce.

herbs

1 Chive
Allium schoenoprasum

A clump-forming perennial herb with slender, grass-like green leaves that have a mild onion flavour. Spherical bright purple flowers are borne throughout summer. Garlic or Chinese chives (*A. tuberosum*) has broader, garlic-flavoured leaves and white flowers. Snipped chives are a useful garnish for salads, soups and sandwiches. Hardy.
General care: Ensure plants do not dry out, particularly when grown in containers.
Height and spread: 30cm (12in)
Site: Sun, partial shade. Fertile and moist but well-drained soil
Compost: Soil-based (John Innes No. 3) or soil-less
Use: Border edging, container, underplanting roses

2 Fennel
Foeniculum vulgare

A tall-growing perennial, fennel has soft green feathery foliage. In summer it bears flat heads of small yellow flowers, attracting hoverflies that eat aphids. Bronze fennel (*F. vulgare* 'Purpureum') is even more handsome. Fennel leaves are used to season meat and the seeds to flavour sauces and fish dishes. Hardy.
General care: Fennel self-seeds freely so harvest before they have a chance to scatter, or remove the flowers if the seeds are not required.
Height: 1.5m (5ft) **Spread:** 45cm (18in)
Site: Sun. Well-drained soil, preferably fertile
Compost: Soil-based (John Innes No. 3) with added bark and grit
Use: Border, container

3 Lemon balm, variegated
Melissa officinalis 'Aurea'

Grown for its wrinkled green leaves, which give off a lemon scent if crushed, lemon balm looks most attractive in spring when it forms low clumps of neat foliage. This variegated form is one of the most decorative, with green-and-gold leaves. Stems of pale yellow to white flowers, which are attractive to bees, are borne in summer. The leaves are used to make tea. Hardy.
General care: In cold areas plants benefit from winter protection with fleece or straw.
Height: 60cm (2ft) **Spread:** 45cm (18in)
Site: Sun. Fertile and moist soil
Compost: Soil-less with added grit
Use: Border, container

4 Mint, Spearmint
Mentha spicata

This is the most popular of the large and varied mint family. The long, toothed green leaves are borne along upright stems and clusters of mauve flowers appear in summer. Mint is a very invasive perennial, spreading by means of underground runners, so grow it in a large bottomless container sunk in the ground. The leaves are commonly used in mint sauce and drinks. Hardy.
General care: Trim the edges of the clump regularly to limit its spread.
Height: 60cm (2ft) **Spread:** Indefinite
Site: Sun, partial shade. Any soil, except dry
Compost: Soil-based (John Innes No. 3)
Use: Border, container

5 Sorrel
Rumex acetosa

A tall-growing plant, sorrel produces stems clothed with large, lance-shaped, mid-green leaves. In early to midsummer these are topped with inconspicuous greenish flowers that age to reddish brown. The plant has little decorative value, but the strongly flavoured leaves can be used sparingly in soups and omelettes and with meat; the young, more mildly flavoured foliage can be mixed into salads. Hardy.
General care: Remove flowerheads when they appear, as sorrel has a tendency to run to seed early. In warm areas grow in partial shade.
Height: 1.2m (4ft) **Spread:** 30cm (12in)
Site: Sun, partial shade. Acid, humus-rich and moist soil
Use: Border

vegetables

6 Asparagus
Asparagus officinalis

A perennial vegetable with succulent young shoots that grow from asparagus roots or 'crowns'. Although expensive to buy, the plants will crop for many years. 'Fileas' is the earliest variety. Hardy.
Site: Sun. Well-drained soil with plenty of well-rotted manure or compost added
How to grow: In mid-spring plant year-old crowns 45cm (18in) apart in ridges 60cm (24in) apart. Harvest when spears are 15cm (6in) high from mid-spring to early summer; it will be several years before the plants begin to crop well. Feed with a general fertiliser after harvesting is complete, and in autumn cut back top growth and top-dress with manure.

7 Broccoli, late purple-sprouting
Brassica oleracea

Grown for its leafy flowerheads, late purple-sprouting broccoli is a useful vegetable that follows on from winter-cropping varieties. Hardy.
Site: Sun. Fertile, moist and slightly acid soil
How to grow: Sow thinly into a seedbed in mid to late spring. Transplant in early summer to midsummer, allowing 45cm (18in) between each plant and row, and keep well watered until established. Protect from cabbage root fly by fitting 'collars' around the base of individual plants. Harvest from mid to late spring when the flowerheads are well formed but before the flowers begin to open. Pick off flowerheads regularly as production will cease if the flowers are left to develop.

8 Carrot, early
Daucus carota

Carrots can be sown under protection in late winter to provide an early crop. Early varieties include 'Minicor' (syn. 'Amsterdam Forcing', 'Baby Nantes'), 'Early Nantes' and 'Paris Market'. Hardy.
Site: Sun. Well-drained and stone-free soil that has been manured but not in the past year
How to grow: Sow seed thinly under cloches or in frames, in rows 15cm (6in) apart. If necessary, thin seedlings to 5cm (2in) apart. Round-rooted varieties can be sown in a greenhouse, in modular trays with four seeds per cell, and planted out later. Plant out cell-grown clumps 15cm (6in) apart. Keep well watered during dry spells. In spring when the

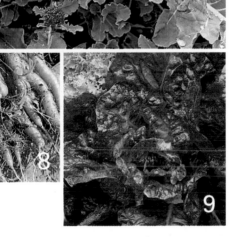

cloche or frame is removed, cover with fleece to protect from carrot root fly. Harvest from late spring onwards.

9 Lettuce, overwintered
Lactuca sativa
Autumn-sown lettuce can be grown under the protection of cloches or frames or in an unheated greenhouse over winter to give a good spring crop. Select a hardy variety that is suitable for winter cultivation.
Site: Sun. Fertile and well-drained soil
How to grow: Sow thinly in rows 23cm (9in) apart from very late summer to mid-autumn. Thin as soon as the seedlings are large enough to handle to 15–23cm (6–9in) apart. Ventilate when weather permits to avoid disease. Harvest as soon as plants are sufficiently large.

10 Radish
Raphanus sativus
A quick-growing salad vegetable that can be grown as a late spring crop by sowing in winter under protection. Hardy.

Site: Sun. Humus-rich and well-drained soil, not freshly manured
How to grow: Sow seed in mid to late winter under cloches or frames in rows 15cm (6in) apart, then thin seedlings to 2–3cm (1in) apart. Or, sow broadcast in a drill 10cm (4in) wide. For the best flavour, pull the radishes when the roots are no larger than 2–3cm (1in) in diameter.

11 Salad onion, Spring onion
Allium cepa
These are young onion plants that are grown close together. If successive sowings are made, spring onions can be harvested for much of the year. Sow seed at fortnightly intervals from late winter to mid-summer. Hardy.
Site: Sun. Well-drained and fertile soil, not freshly manured
How to grow: For a spring crop, sow thinly during midsummer, allowing 10cm (4in) between rows, or sow broadcast in a broad drill up to 10cm (4in)

wide in a sheltered site. Water the drill before sowing in dry weather. Thin if necessary to 1–2cm (½–1in) apart. For the best flavour, pull onions before their bases swell.

12 Salad rocket
Eruca vesicaria
An easy and useful leaf vegetable for salads, rocket has a delicious spicy flavour. It can be sown from late winter right through to autumn for harvesting almost all the year round. Hardy.
Site: Sun. Fertile and moist but well-drained soil
How to grow: Sow in late summer for a very early crop the following spring. Allow 30cm (12in) between rows, and thin seedlings to 10cm (4in) apart. Keep plants well watered to avoid them running to seed early. In cold areas, protect plants over winter with cloches. Harvest frequently.

fruit

13 Rhubarb
Rheum x hybridum
Rhubarb is classified as a vegetable but its stalks are eaten as a fruit. Its large green leaves are highly poisonous if eaten. It crops naturally during spring and early summer, but can be forced for a late winter crop. The variety 'Timperley Early' produces the earliest crops outdoors without being forced. Hardy.
Site: Sun. Any soil, preferably heavy and acid
How to grow: Plant a new crown in autumn or spring. Leave the plant untouched for the first year and harvest only a little in the second. From then on, always leave three to four stems on the plant to avoid weakening it. Mulch with well-rotted compost or manure in late winter.

the greenhouse

Tender plants can be grown in a protected environment to provide spring interest. In summer some can be moved outdoors to patios and terraces. Plant dimensions given here indicate average container–grown proportions.

pink and mauve

4 Aporocactus flagelliformis
Rat's tail cactus

In the wild, this perching (epiphytic) cactus grows on trees and rocks. In cultivation the cylindrical stems are best allowed to trail from a hanging basket. The trumpet-shaped purplish red blooms are borne in profusion along the stems. Tender.
Height: 15cm (6in) **Spread:** 1.5m (5ft)
Under glass: Full light. Soil-based compost (John Innes No. 2) with added grit and leaf-mould
Use: Conservatory or greenhouse minimum 7°C (45°F)

5 Echinocereus pectinatus
Cactus

Cylindrical, sometimes branching cactus with ribs marked out with dense rows of white spines. The funnel-shaped, bright pink flowers are about 8cm (3in) across and appear in late spring or early summer. Tender.
Height: 20cm (8in) **Spread:** 15cm (6in)
Under glass: Full light. Soil-based compost (John Innes No. 2) with added grit, or cactus compost
Use: Conservatory or greenhouse minimum 5°C (41°F), houseplant

6 Leptospermum scoparium 'Kiwi'
Manuka, New Zealand tea tree

This dwarf evergreen makes a good companion for spring bulbs under glass. The aromatic leaves are purplish when young and almost hidden by the five-petalled, deep crimson flowers, which bloom

purple, blue and violet

1 Arisaema sikokianum

Tuberous perennial producing dark, three and five-lobed leaves. The sinisterly beautiful flower-like structures, purple-brown on the outside consist of a funnel-shaped part (the spathe), and an open lid marked with pale purple striations. The spathe interior is white, as is the club-like part (spadix) at its centre. Not fully hardy but can be grown outdoors in mild woodland conditions on lime-free, humus-rich, moist but well-drained soil.
General care: Plant in winter with the top of the tuber 20cm (8in) deep. Shade from direct sun.
Height: 45cm (18in) **Spread:** 20cm (8in)
Under glass: Lime-free (ericaceous) compost with added leaf-mould and grit
Outdoor site: Partial shade.
Use: Unheated greenhouse, lightly shaded border, woodland garden

2 Prostanthera rotundifolia
Round-leaved mint bush

A bushy and aromatic evergreen shrub with small rounded leaves. Profuse bell-shaped purple flowers are borne in late spring and early summer. Half hardy.
Height and spread: 2m (6ft)
Under glass: Full light. Soil-based compost (John Innes No. 2)
Use: Conservatory or greenhouse minimum 2°C (36°F), sunny patio

3 Streptocarpus 'Kim'
Cape primrose

The Streptocarpus hybrids flower from spring to summer. They are perennials with a tuft of rather crinkled leaves and sprays of tubular flowers with five lobes at the mouth. The colour range includes purple, blue, white, pink or red, and flowers are usually striped with a contrasting colour. 'Kim' has small, white-centred deep blue flowers. Tender.
General care: Shade from direct sun.
Height and spread: 25cm (10in)
Under glass: Full light. Soil-less compost.
Use: Conservatory or greenhouse minimum 7°C (45°F), houseplant

into early summer. Needs a very favourable position if grown outdoors. Half hardy.
Height and spread: 1m (3ft)
Under glass: Full light. Soil-based compost (John Innes No. 3)
Outdoor site: Sun. Well-drained soil
Use: Conservatory or greenhouse minimum 2°C (36°F), sunny sheltered border

7 Schizanthus 'Hit Parade'
Poor man's orchid
Half-hardy annual with ferny leaves and showy, orchid-like flowers that can be purple, pink, red or white and usually have yellow throats with dark markings. The strong contrast of clear colours is

a feature of this selection. Time of flowering depends on time of sowing.
General care: Sow seed at 16°C (61°F) in late summer and early autumn for winter and spring flowers. Can be sown outdoors in mid-spring for summer and autumn flowers into fertile, moist but well-drained soil.
Height: 30cm (12in) **Spread:** 25cm (10in)
Under glass: Full light. Soil-based compost (John Innes No. 2)
Outdoor site: Sun. Fertile, moist but well-drained soil
Use: Conservatory or greenhouse minimum 2°C (36°F), formal bedding

8 Veltheimia bracteata
Tender evergreen bulb with glossy strap-like leaves.

The flowers, which are down-turned, tubular and purplish pink, are carried in a cluster at the top of a purplish stem. The effect is similar to the spike of a red-hot poker (*Kniphofia*). *V. capensis*, a similar species with more variable flower colour, needs a dry resting period in summer. Tender.
General care: Plant bulbs in autumn with the neck just above the compost surface.
Height: 45cm (18in) **Spread:** 30cm (12in)
Under glass: Full light. Soil-based compost (John Innes No. 2) with added sharp sand
Use: Conservatory or greenhouse minimum 7°C (45°F), houseplant

red and russet

9 Clianthus puniceus
Lobster claw, Parrot's bill
Where the climate is mild enough this evergreen shrub can be grown outdoors trained against a warm wall. The slender stems also need training under glass. The clusters of brilliant red flowers, which resemble lobster claws, continue into early summer. The equally attractive 'Albus' has greenish white flowers. Not fully hardy.
Height and spread: 2m (6ft)
Under glass: Full light. Soil-based compost (John Innes No. 3) with added grit
Outdoor site: Sun. Well-drained soil
Use: Conservatory or greenhouse minimum 2°C (36°F), warm wall outdoors

10 Cymbidium Showgirl
Orchid
Hundreds of winter and spring-flowering *Cymbidium* hybrids can be grown with very little heat. They grow with their roots in soil but have pseudobulbs – swollen stems that store food and water – above ground. The long-lasting flowers are available in many shades and colour combinations.

Showgirl has pink-tinted white flowers with a red-marked lip. Magnificent waxy blooms stand among or arch out from the leaves. Tender.
General care: Shade from hot sun in summer.
Height and spread: 45cm (18in)
Under glass: Indirect light. Various free-draining compost mixtures, for example equal parts loam, rough leaf-mould or peat substitute and sand
Use: Conservatory or greenhouse minimum 7°C (45°F), houseplant

11 Pelargonium 'Grand Slam'
Regal pelargonium
The showy Regals are evergreen bushy plants with large, often frilled, single or double flowers up to 5cm (2in) across and produced in clusters. The colour range includes red, orange, pink, white and purple, and plants flower from spring to autumn. The flowers of Grand Slam are crimson and violet-red. Tender.
Height: 45cm (18in) **Spread:** 30cm (12in)
Under glass: Full light. Soil-based compost (John Innes No. 2) or soil-less compost (coir-based) with added grit
Use: Conservatory or greenhouse minimum 2°C (36°F), houseplant

12 Sprekelia formosissima
Aztec lily, Jacobean lily
Bulb producing one unusually shaped scarlet or crimson flower per stem in late spring or early summer. The strap-shaped leaves die down in autumn. Tender.
General care: Plant bulbs in autumn with the neck above the compost surface. Keep almost dry when the bulb is dormant, and begin watering in spring.
Height: 30cm (12in) **Spread:** 20cm (8in)
Under glass: Full light. Soil-based compost (John Innes No. 3)
Use: Conservatory or greenhouse minimum 7°C (45°F), houseplant

PLANT SELECTOR

1 Calceolaria Anytime Series
Pouch flower, Slipper flower, Slipperwort

The calceolaria hybrids are mainly compact plants grown as biennials for their crowded heads of pouched flowers in shades of yellow, orange and red, often speckled or blotched with a darker colour. The Grandiflora Group have flowers as much as 8cm (3in) across. The Multiflora Group, which includes the Anytime Series, have heads packed with slightly smaller flowers. Grow outdoors in moist but well-drained and preferably acid soil.
Height: 20cm (8in) **Spread:** 30cm (12in)
Under glass: Full or indirect light. Soil-based compost (John Innes No. 2)
Outdoor site: Sun, partial shade. Moist but well-drained soil, preferably acid
Use: Conservatory or greenhouse minimum 7°C (45°F), houseplant, formal bedding

2 Lotus maculatus

Trailing evergreen perennial with mid-green foliage, the leaves consisting of several narrow leaflets. The yellow pea flowers, which are produced in spring and early summer, have strongly beaked keels that are tipped with red or orange. This is an attractive container plant for growing both under glass and outdoors in a sunny position. When grown outdoors this plant is often treated as an annual. Tender.
Height: 15cm (6in) **Spread:** 1m (3ft)
Under glass: Full light. Soil-based compost (John Innes No. 2) with added grit
Use: Conservatory or greenhouse minimum 2°C (36°F), sunny patio

3 Strelitzia reginae
Bird of paradise, Crane flower

Evergreen perennial with a fan of long-stalked leathery leaves, above which are poised orange-and-blue flowers that emerge like a crest from beak-like bracts. Tender.
General care: In summer move container-grown plants outdoors.
Height: 1.2m (4ft) **Spread:** 1m (3ft)
Under glass: Full light. Soil-based compost (John Innes No. 3)
Use: Conservatory or greenhouse minimum 10°C (50°F), sunny patio

4 Streptosolen jamesonii
Marmalade bush

The slender stems of this tender evergreen shrub can be trained against a wall or allowed to trail from a hanging basket. The flowers have a yellow tube and a flared orange mouth. They are borne in clusters from late spring through summer.

General care: Shade from hot sun.
Height: 2m (6ft) **Spread:** 1.2m (4ft)
Under glass: Full light. Soil-based compost (John Innes No. 3)
Use: Conservatory or greenhouse minimum 7°C (45°F)

cream and white

5 Gladiolus tristis
Gladioli

Winter-growing, half-hardy bulbous plant (strictly speaking the 'bulb' is a corm) that generally requires cool greenhouse protection, although in the mildest areas it can be grown outdoors in well-drained soil. Between late winter and late spring spikes carry ten or more creamy white to yellow flowers arching out on narrow tubes. The blooms, which are sweetly scented in the evening, have green tints and are variably flushed or marked mauve, red-brown or purple.
General care: Pot annually with the top of the corm about 10cm (4in) deep and start into growth in late summer or early autumn.
Height: 45cm (18in) **Spread:** 8cm (3in)
Under glass: Full light. Soil-based compost (John Innes No. 1) with added sharp sand

Use: Conservatory or greenhouse minimum 2°C (36°F), sunny border

6 Hymenocallis x festalis
Spider lily

Tender evergreen bulb with strap-shaped leaves. These are topped in late spring or summer by stems carrying up to five white scented flowers that look like spidery daffodils.
General care: Plant in autumn or early winter with

the neck of the bulb just above the surface of the compost.
Height: 75cm (2ft 6in) **Spread:** 30cm (12in)
Under glass: Full light. Soil-based compost (John Innes No. 2)
Use: Conservatory or greenhouse minimum 7°C (45°F)

7 Ornithogalum thyrsoides
Chincherinchee
This half-hardy bulb sends up an erect stem carrying as many as 30 cream or white cup-shaped flowers that are very long-lasting. The fleshy leaves wither before the flowers open.
General care: Plant with the top of the bulb about 10cm (4in) deep in autumn. Shade from hot sun.
Height: 45cm (18in) **Spread:** 15cm (6in)

Under glass: Full light. Soil-based compost (John Innes No. 2)
Use: Conservatory or greenhouse minimum 2°C (36°F)

8 Pittosporum tobira
Japanese mock orange
In mild areas, this half-hardy evergreen shrub often does well planted at the base of a warm wall. It has dark and shiny leathery leaves that set off the clusters of small creamy white flowers in late spring and early summer. Their scent is deliciously fruity.
General care: In summer move container-grown plants outdoors.
Height: 3m (10ft) **Spread:** 2.5m (8ft)
Under glass: Full light. Soil-based compost (John Innes No. 3)
Outdoor site: Sun. Moist but well-drained soil
Use: Conservatory or greenhouse minimum 2°C (36°F), sunny patio, sheltered sunny border

silver and grey

9 Primula auricula 'Lovebird'
Show auricula
Show auriculas are hardy evergreen perennials with leathery leaves that are often covered with a white powdery meal (farina). Erect stems carry heads of saucer-shaped flowers in a variety of colours. Each flower has a central circle of white meal ('paste') around the eye. 'Lovebird' has a yellow eye and a black zone feathering out from the circle of meal to a grey-green edge.
General care: Shade from hot sun. Keep water off foliage and flowers.
Height and spread: 15cm (6in)

Under glass: Full light. Soil-based compost (John Innes No. 2)
Use: Conservatory or greenhouse minimum 2°C (36°F)

green

10 Araucaria heterophylla
Norfolk Island pine
In the wild this half-hardy evergreen conifer can grow to 60m (200ft), but in a container its growth is inhibited. Young specimens have bright green needles, and the branches are arranged in tiered whorls to give a conical outline. Year-round interest and useful as a foliage plant in spring.
General care: Move pot-grown specimens outdoors in summer.
Height: 1.5m (5ft) **Spread:** 1m (3ft)
Under glass: Full light. Soil-based compost (John Innes No. 2)
Use: Conservatory or greenhouse minimum 5°C (41°F), houseplant, sunny patio

11 Sedum morganianum
Stonecrop
Under cultivation this tender plant is usually grown in a hanging basket or tall container so that the lax stems, 60cm (2ft), or more in length, hang down. They are covered with fleshy grey-green leaves that are neatly packed. Grown principally as a foliage plant, but clusters of pink or red starry flowers appear in spring.
Height: 60cm (2ft) **Spread:** 30cm (12in)
Under glass: Full light. Soil-based compost (John Innes No. 2) with added leaf-mould and a generous quantity of grit
Use: Conservatory or greenhouse minimum 5°C (41°F), houseplant

choosing the best plants

The following plant lists draw on all the plants described on the preceding pages of the Plant Selector, but they are grouped together here to help you choose plants for particular conditions, situations and uses to bring interest to your garden in late spring.

plants for clay soil

Although the following plants generally succeed on close-textured clay soils, they do better when the ground has been improved by the addition of grit and organic matter such as well-rotted garden compost.

- *Acer* (all)
- *Berberis* (all)
- *Caltha palustris* 'Flore Pleno'
- *Cardamine pratensis* 'Flore Pleno'
- *Choisya ternata*
- *Cornus florida* 'Cherokee Chief'
- *Crataegus* (all)
- *Doronicum orientale* 'Magnificum'
- *Epimedium* (all)
- *Filipendula ulmaria* 'Aurea'
- *Fritillaria meleagris*
- *Hosta* (all)
- *Philadelphus coronarius* 'Aureus'
- *Pleioblastus auricomus*
- *Polygonatum* x *hybridum*
- *Sorbus aria* 'Lutescens'
- *Viburnum* (all)

Viburnum opulus

plants for dry chalky soil

A large number of plants are automatically excluded from this list because they will not tolerate alkaline (limy) soil. The improvement of shallow chalky soil by the addition of moisture-retaining organic matter allows lime-tolerant but moisture-loving plants, notably clematis, to be grown successfully.

- *Aethionema* 'Warley Rose'
- *Aubrieta* 'Greencourt Purple'
- *Aurinia saxatilis* (all cultivars)
- *Berberis* (all)
- *Bergenia* 'Beethoven'
- *Cercis siliquastrum*
- *Cheiranthus* (all)
- *Choisya ternata*
- *Crataegus* (all)
- *Euphorbia polychroma*
- *Gypsophila cerastioides*
- *Iris* (all bearded)
- *Malus* (all)
- *Muscari* (all)
- *Philadelphus coronarius* 'Aureus'
- *Phlox douglasii* (all cultivars)
- *Phlox subulata* (all cultivars)
- *Prunus* (all ornamental cherries)
- *Pulsatilla vulgaris*
- *Sorbus aria* 'Lutescens'
- *Syringa vulgaris* (all cultivars)
- *Waldsteinia ternata*

Waldsteinia ternata

plants for sandy or gravelly soil

The following plants require free drainage and are mostly drought tolerant, although bulbs generally require a good supply of moisture in the growing season. The range of plants that can be grown in dry sunny gardens will be enlarged if the soil is improved by the addition of well-rotted organic matter.

- *Achillea* x *lewisii* 'King Edward'
- *Aethionema* 'Warley Rose'
- *Arabis alpina* subsp. *caucasica* (all cultivars)
- *Armeria juniperifolia*
- *Asphodelus albus*
- *Aubrieta* 'Greencourt Purple' (and other cultivars)
- *Aurinia saxatilis* (all cultivars)
- *Ceanothus* (all)
- *Cytisus* (all)
- *Erica arborea* var. *alpina*
- *Erysimum* (all)
- *Euphorbia polychroma*
- Fennel (*Foeniculum vulgare*)
- *Gladiolus tristis*
- *Iberis* (all)
- *Iris* (all bearded)
- *Lathyrus vernus*
- *Phlox douglasii* (all cultivars)
- *Raoulia australis* Lutescens Group

Iris 'Holden Clough'

plants for acid soil

Plants marked with an asterisk* will only grow satisfactorily on soils that are free of lime. Other plants in the list thrive on acid soils, but may also grow on neutral or slightly alkaline soils.

- *Acer palmatum* (all cultivars)
- *Bergenia* 'Beethoven'
- *Brunnera macrophylla* (all cultivars)
- *Camellia japonica* (all cultivars)*
- *Cornus florida* 'Cherokee Chief'
- *Disporum sessile* 'Variegatum'
- *Doronicum orientale* 'Magnificum'
- *Enkianthus campanulatus**
- *Erica arborea* var. *alpina**
- *Erythronium* (all)
- *Fothergilla major* Monticola Group*
- *Gentiana* (all)
- *Halesia carolina**
- x *Heucherella tiarelloides**
- *Ledum groenlandicum**
- *Magnolia* (all)
- *Meconopsis cambrica**
- *Meconopsis quintuplinervia**
- *Pieris* 'Forest Flame'*
- *Primula auricula* (all cultivars)
- *Primula japonica* 'Postford White'*
- *Primula sieboldii**
- *Smilacina racemosa**
- *Tellima grandiflora* (all cultivars)

plants for dry shade

The following plants grow most vigorously where there is a regular supply of water, but generally succeed in such difficult conditions as the shady base of walls or where roots of overhead trees and shrubs are near the surface.

- *Ajuga reptans* (all cultivars)
- *Bergenia* 'Beethoven'
- *Brunnera macrophylla*
- *Convallaria majalis*
- *Dicentra* 'Luxuriant'
- *Epimedium* (all)
- *Geranium phaeum*
- *Hyacinthoides non-scripta*
- *Lunaria annua*
- *Polygonatum* x *hybridum*
- *Prunus laurocerasus* (all cultivars)
- *Waldsteinia ternata*

plants for moist shade

The following plants thrive in moist soils and tolerate partial shade and, in a few cases, full shade. Many will also grow in full sun provided the soil is reliably moist.

- *Acer palmatum* (all cultivars)
- *Aquilegia* (all)
- *Brunnera macrophylla* (all cultivars)
- *Camellia japonica* (all cultivars)
- *Dicentra* (all)
- *Disporum sessile* 'Variegatum'
- *Dryopteris affinis*
- *Dryopteris erythrosora*
- *Epimedium* (all)
- *Erythronium* (all)
- *Filipendula ulmaria* 'Aurea'
- *Hosta* (all)
- *Leucojum aestivum* 'Gravetye Giant'
- *Matteuccia struthiopteris*
- *Milium effusum* 'Aureum'
- *Myosotis sylvatica* (all cultivars)
- *Omphalodes cappadocica*
- *Primula* (most)
- *Pulmonaria* 'Mawson's Blue'
- *Rhododendron* (all)
- *Smilacina racemosa*
- *Trillium* (all)
- *Uvularia grandiflora*
- *Viola* (all)

plants for ground cover

The following plants can be used to create an attractive weed-excluding cover if planted in weed-free soil.

- *Ajuga reptans* 'Purple Torch'
- *Bergenia* 'Beethoven'
- *Convallaria majalis*
- *Dicentra* 'Luxuriant'
- *Epimedium* x *rubrum*
- *Epimedium* x *versicolor* 'Sulphureum'
- *Epimedium* x *youngianum* 'Niveum'
- *Euphorbia amygdaloides* 'Purpurea'
- *Geranium macrorrhizum* 'Ingwersen's Variety'
- x *Heucherella tiarelloides*
- *Hosta fortunei* var. *albopicta*
- *Hosta undulata* var. *univittata*
- *Omphalodes cappadocica*
- *Pulmonaria* 'Mawson's Blue'
- *Tellima grandiflora* 'Purpurteppich'

plants for coastal sites

Where windbreaks and hedges give protection from salt-laden winds, a wide range of plants can be grown in coastal gardens. Many benefit from the sea's moderating influence on temperatures.

- *Acer pseudoplatanus* 'Brilliantissimum'
- *Arabis alpina* subsp. *caucasica* (all cultivars)
- *Armeria juniperifolia*
- *Aubrieta* 'Greencourt Purple' (and other cultivars)
- *Aurinia saxatilis* (all cultivars)
- *Berberis* (all)
- *Bergenia* 'Beethoven'
- *Ceanothus* (all)
- *Cheiranthus* (all)
- *Choisya ternata*
- *Crataegus* (all)
- *Cytisus* (all)
- *Erica arborea* var. *alpina*
- *Hyacinthoides non-scripta*
- *Iberis* (all)
- *Laburnum* x *watereri* 'Vossii'
- *Leptospermum scoparium* 'Kiwi'
- *Lunaria annua* (and cultivars)
- *Mysotis sylvatica* (all cultivars)
- *Prostanthera rotundifolia*
- *Pulsatilla vulgaris*
- *Sorbus aria* 'Lutescens'

Choisya ternata

choosing the best plants/2

trees for small gardens

The following are suitable for all but very small gardens, where climbers on structures such as arches are a better way of creating height and shade.

- *Cercis siliquastrum*
- *Cornus florida* 'Cherokee Chief'
- *Crataegus laevigata* 'Paul's Scarlet'
- *Halesia carolina*
- *Laburnum* x *watereri* 'Vossii'
- *Magnolia denudata*
- *Magnolia* 'Elizabeth'
- *Magnolia* x *kewensis* 'Wada's Memory'
- *Magnolia soulangeana*
- *Malus floribunda*
- *Malus* x *moerlandisii* 'Profusion'
- *Prunus* 'Kanzan'
- *Prunus* 'Shôgetsu'
- *Sorbus aria* 'Lutescens'

spring-flowering plants for containers

As well as the plants listed here as suitable for general container gardening, a number of rock garden, or alpine, plants are suitable for troughs, and all the greenhouse plants described on pages 64–68 can be grown in containers.

- *Bellis perennis*
- *Camellia japonica* (all cultivars)
- *Clematis alpina* (all cultivars)
- *Clematis alpina* subsp. *sibirica* 'White Moth'
- *Clematis macropetala*
- *Erysimum* x *allioni*
- *Erysimum cheiri* (all cultivars)
- *Fritillaria meleagris*
- *Hyacinthus orientalis* (all cultivars)
- *Muscari botryoides* 'Allbum'
- *Myosotis sylvatica*
- *Primula* Gold-laced Group
- *Primula* 'Guinevere
- *Tulipa* (all)
- *Viola* Sorbet Series

Tulipa 'Spring Green' and
Tulipa 'West Point'

flowers for cutting

In addition to the following, shrubs such as camellias, choisya, ornamental cherries and common lilac, if judiciously cut, provide material suitable for large flower arrangements.

- *Anthericum liliago*
- *Aquilegia* (all)
- *Bellis perennis*
- *Bergenia* 'Beethoven'
- *Brunnera macrophylla*
- *Convallaria majalis*
- *Dicentra spectabilis*
- *Doronicum orientale* 'Magnificum'
- *Erysimum* (most)
- x *Heucherella tiarelloides*
- *Hyacinthus orientalis* (all cultivars)
- *Iris* 'Florentina'
- *Iris* 'Holden Clough'
- *Leucojum aestivum*
- *Muscari armeniacum*
- *Myosotis sylvatica* 'Royal Blue'
- *Paeonia* (most)
- *Polemonium* 'Lambrook Mauve'
- *Polygonatum* x *hybridum*
- *Primula* (all)
- *Smilacina racemosa*
- *Tulipa* (all cultivars)
- *Viola* Sorbet Series

Paeonia
suffruticosa

plants with aromatic foliage

In the case of many aromatic plants, the scent of the leaves is only detectable when they are bruised.

- Chives (*Allium schoenoprasum*)
- *Choisya ternata*
- Fennel (*Foeniculum vulgare*)
- *Geranium macrorrhizum* 'Ingwersen's Variety'
- *Leptospermum scoparium* 'Kiwi'
- *Prostanthera rotundifolia*
- Spearmint (*Mentha spicata*)

plants with fragrant flowers

The age of a flower, time of day and temperature all affect the strength of floral scents. These plants are all worth siting carefully so that their perfumes can be enjoyed.

- *Choisya ternata*
- *Clematis montana* var. *rubens* 'Elizabeth'
- *Convallaria majalis*
- *Daphne cneorum* 'Eximia'
- *Erica arborea* var. *alpina*
- *Erysimum cheiri* (all cultivars)
- *Fothergilla major* Monticola Group
- *Gladiolus tristis*
- *Hyacinthus orientalis* (all cultivars)
- *Magnolia denudata*
- *Osmanthus delavayi*
- *Paeonia lactiflora* 'White Wings'
- *Philadelphus coronarius* 'Aureus'
- *Pittosporum tobira*
- *Rhododendron* 'Loderi King George'
- *Syringa vulgaris* (all cultivars)
- *Viburnum carlesii* 'Aurora'

Hyacinthus orientalis

trees and shrubs for autumn colour

In addition to their late spring flowers, in most years the foliage of the following plants colours well in autumn, particularly in a frost-free climate.

- *Acer palmatum* (all cultivars)
- *Cornus florida* 'Cherokee Chief'
- *Enkianthus campanulatus*
- *Fothergilla major* Monticola Group
- *Prunus* 'Shirofugen'
- *Prunus* 'Shôgetsu'
- *Prunus* 'Ukon'
- *Viburnum plicatum* 'Mariesii'

plants with variegated foliage

The leaves of the following plants are edged, spotted or otherwise marked in white, cream or yellow.

- *Acer pseudoplatanus* 'Brilliantissimum'
- *Ajuga reptans* 'Burgundy Glow'
- *Disporum sessile* 'Variegatum'
- *Hosta fortunei* var. *albopicta*
- *Hosta undulata* var. *univittata*
- *Iris pseudacorus* 'Variegata'
- *Lunaria annua* 'Alba Variegata'
- *Pieris* 'Forest Flame'
- *Pleioblastus auricomus*

Pieris 'Forest Flame'

evergreen shrubs

The following, all of which grow to a height of 1m (3ft) or more, are useful for creating year-round structure.

- *Berberis darwinii*
- *Berberis* x *stenophylla*
- *Camellia japonica* (all cultivars)
- *Ceanothus* 'Puget Blue'
- *Choisya ternata*
- *Erica arborea* var. *alpina*
- *Ledum groenlandicum*
- *Osmanthus delavayi*
- *Photinia* x *fraseri* 'Red Robin'
- *Pieris* 'Forest Flame'
- *Prunus laurocerasus* 'Otto Luyken'
- *Rhododendron* 'Bow Bells'
- *Rhododendron* 'Loderi King George'

plants with colourful foliage

The colour of leaves often changes significantly from one season to the next. The red, purple, copper, yellow, blue or cream foliage colour of plants in the following list is generally strongest in spring and early summer. For other colourful foliage see Trees and Shrubs for Autumn Colour, above left.

- *Acer pseudoplatanus* 'Brilliantissimum'
- *Acer palmatum* 'Corallinum'
- *Ajuga reptans* 'Burgundy Glow'
- *Clematis montana* var. *rubens* 'Elizabeth'
- *Dicentra* 'Langtrees'
- *Epimedium* (most)
- *Euphorbia amygdaloides* 'Purpurea'
- *Filipendula ulmaria* 'Aurea'
- *Leptospermum scoparium* 'Kiwi'
- *Milium effusum* 'Aureum'
- *Paeonia mlokosewitschii*
- *Photinia* x *fraseri* 'Red Robin'
- *Philadelphus coronarius* 'Aureus'
- *Pieris* 'Forest Flame'
- *Sorbus aria* 'Lutescens'
- *Tellima grandiflora* 'Purpurteppich'
- *Valeriana phu* 'Aurea'
- *Viola riviniana* Purpurea Group

plants with large or boldly shaped leaves

The leaves of the following plants are of architectural value in the garden and useful as cut foliage for indoors.

- *Bergenia* 'Beethoven'
- *Brunnera macrophylla*
- *Dryopteris affinis*
- *Filipendula ulmaria* 'Aurea'
- *Hosta* (all)
- *Iris* 'Florentina'
- *Iris pseudacorus* 'Variegata'
- *Matteuccia struthiopteris*
- *Paeonia delavayi* var. *ludlowii*
- *Podophyllum hexandrum*
- *Wisteria sinensis*

plants with ornamental fruit, berries and seed heads

The plants in the following list are worthwhile because they have more than one feature of ornamental value.

- *Asphodelus albus*
- *Berberis darwinii*
- *Berberis* x *stenophylla*
- *Clematis macropetala*
- *Cornus florida* 'Cherokee Chief'
- *Crataegus laevigata* 'Paul's Scarlet'
- *Halesia carolina*
- *Lunaria annua* (all cultivars)
- *Lunaria rediviva*
- *Malus floribunda*
- *Malus* x *moerlandsii* 'Profusion'
- *Paeonia mlokosewitschii*
- *Pulsatilla vulgaris*
- *Sorbus aria* 'Lutescens'

Matteuccia struthiopteris

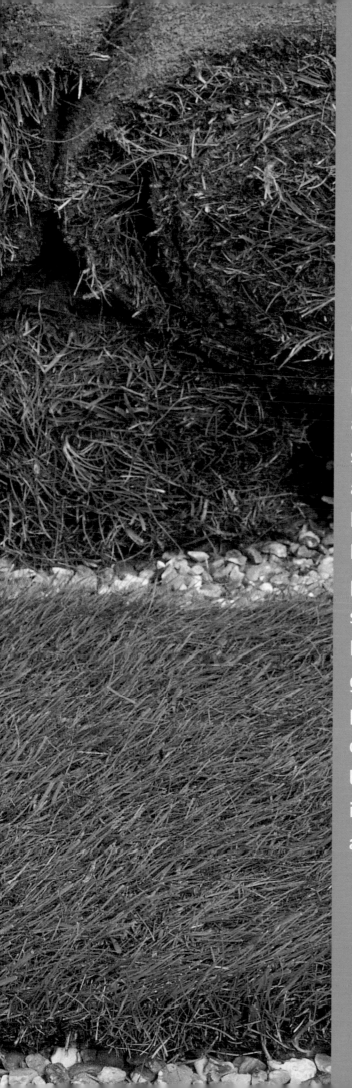

As the enthusiasm for gardening builds up in late spring, this is a good time to contemplate a major improvement to your garden. If you are feeling ambitious, you might decide to create a wildlife pond or a bog garden. Or perhaps you need to lay a new lawn from turf or seed. If your garden is already well developed and has a wealth of features, how about planting up the patio or terrace with something scented, or laying out a new gravel garden? Dreaming up new projects is not only a way of improving your garden, but also of ensuring that it stays fresh, dynamic and alive.

garden projects

creating focal points

To please the eye, every open space needs its focal point. Unless there is something relatively strong to catch the attention in the garden, the view, however well planted or laid out, can become directionless or dull. Focal points can take many forms and need not, in themselves, be particularly dominant, as long as they have enough presence to bind the rest of the design together.

something to look at

In a natural landscape, the focal point of a view may be something as simple as a tree on a skyline, a fold in the cliffs or a church nestling in a dip in the hills. Such features help to stop the eye from searching aimlessly and draw it to repose; well placed they can transform a scene from the humdrum to the beautiful. Photographers and landscape illustrators choose focal points when they compose their pictures, and for gardeners the same rules apply.

A focal point may be something as basic as a door, a path or a pillar festooned with a climbing plant, or it could be a tree with a distinctive outline or a large rock.

existing focal points

To understand focal points better, imagine a back garden dominated by a mature tree. Whatever design improvements are planned, the tree should always be at the centre of things, a main focal point. There are ways in which you could make the tree more pleasing. You could thin out the canopy to improve its shape and allow a clearer view through. You might grow a clematis or rambling rose up through the branches, or hang a nicely crafted swing from one of its boughs.

Another very simple focal point is the front door. By planting honeysuckle or other climbers to arch over the top, you are not only framing that focal point and softening the architecture, but you are also adding character, fragrance and colour.

Adding paired pots, filled with aromatic plants, on either side of the entrance, will heighten the impact, but don't make the scene too fussy; err on the side of simplicity.

placing is important

Choose where to introduce a focal point with care. If you have a long straight path leading to the bottom of your garden, what is in view at the end of it? If the backdrop is featureless, place a big vase, a little seat or a raised pot of pelargoniums against the boundary, and the path instantly becomes an enticing vista with a distinct end point.

using arches and arbours

Arches and arbours are, themselves, potential focal points, but if used to frame other objects, they help to draw attention to them. An arch over a statue immediately doubles the impact of the sculpture by creating a niche. An arbour always beckons and, if placed at the end of a pathway or vista, provides a perfect focal point in itself.

exits and entrances

Transition points in a garden can be transformed into a focal point. A simple wicket gate or just a narrow gap in a hedge or fence can be developed into a feature by constructing an arch over the top. Or you can arrange the planting to lead one's eye towards a tempting entrance that promises a new vista on the other side. Mirrors and trompe l'oeil often use this sense of promise to create an impression of

A modest water feature becomes the focal point of a sunken area.

additional space in a garden when, in fact, they terminate a vista.

design dynamics

A garden design that works well is not static but suggests plenty of movement. This does not mean having features that physically move, although waving grasses and flowing water certainly help to bring things to life. 'Movement' in design refers to the dynamics of the layout itself.

Arranging sight lines with care, and carefully placing eye-catching plants or

The **sundial** in a box-edged parterre (below) is strategically placed to draw the eye.

The **framed mirror** set into a wooden gate is the focus of a small garden. Its reflections dramatically 'increase' the garden's depth.

objects in particular positions will entice you to explore and discover a hidden seat or view. Focal points are all part of the intriguing game you can play.

A visitor to a well-designed small garden might think at first glance that it is all visible at once. But if the primary view is channelled down a narrow vista, you can create surprises along its length. Well-placed seats, for example, might tempt you to rest and, as you sit, you enjoy a new scene you might otherwise have missed.

make your focal points work

When you are planning a focal point consider the following:

A FOCAL POINT

• **need not be visible** from all over the garden.

• **can be a device** to lead the eye away from unsightly objects.

• **can trick the eye** to overlook a part of the garden that you want viewed from a different place or angle.

• **may be functional,** such as a seat or swing. Also, a functional but unsightly object could be transformed into a focal point: might the garage become a superb frame for climbing plants?

• **may need other clues** to point the way: a pathway could be flanked by pairs of containers, or 'portholes' cut in a hedge to frame a view.

• **may not be** in your garden at all: a more distant object such as a tower or spire or your neighbour's tree could make a fine backdrop for your garden, with vistas leading directly to the view.

providing scent

The sense of smell evokes the strongest memories and you can exploit this in the garden. In winter, before the main rush of early spring flowers, fragrance occurs here and there in the garden, mainly from individual plants. In summer, cocktails of different flower perfumes will waft on the warmer air, blending with the pleasing smells of mown grass, fresh foliage and soil after rain.

fragrant ideas

The scent of lilacs carried on the still warm air of a spring evening, or the spicy waft of early honeysuckle, promote a sense of restfulness and well-being. The smell of lime trees in full bloom, humming with feasting bees, is redolent of midsummer, while during the dark, cold months, a sprig or two of mahonia or wintersweet brought indoors will fill an entire room with the promise of spring. Here are some more ideas on how to make fragrance work a little harder in your garden.

- **add scent to your selection** criteria when purchasing your plants. If there is a choice, as in roses or lilies, go for species or varieties with the best fragrance rather than selecting merely for flower colour.
- **don't forget winter fragrance;** plant Christmas box (*Sarcococca*) or a daphne by a path or patio.
- **include plants** which, though not sweetly perfumed, contribute a smell that blends with the general cocktail of aromas. Even elderflowers, rue and hyssop have much to contribute, as they help to develop other perfumes (as do civet or musk in manufactured fragrances).
- **include something fragrant** for every season. Some smells evoke specific seasons: that of chrysanthemums belongs to misty, chilly autumn mornings, while violets and scented pansies (*Viola*) have the sweet odour of early spring.

- **add plenty of short-term,** strongly perfumed plants for summer, when you will be spending most time relaxing outdoors: stocks, pinks, lemon verbena, heliotrope and alyssum.
- **place sweetly fragrant plants** such as honeysuckle or jasmine near doorways and windows or over arches so that they can be enjoyed close-up.
- **combine plants** to produce a delicious olfactory harmony: honeysuckle with the sharper fragrance of mock orange (*Philadelphus*); sweet peas with roses.

Indoors try placing sweet peas near a vase containing lavender.
- **grow flowers for cutting,** such as the old-fashioned annual sweet mignonette (*Reseda*), sweet williams (*Dianthus barbatus*), lupins and phlox, as well as the king of fragrant summer cutting flowers, the sweet pea.
- **a rose without fragrance** is not worth growing. Extra sweet-scented varieties include pink 'Madame Isaac Pereire' and the old moss rose *R.* x *centifolia* 'Muscosa', dark red 'Papa Meilland' or

Lavender and
box hedging

Aromatic qualities of foliage are
quite as important as flower
fragrance. Mint, thyme, sage,
lavender, rosemary, basil, dill and
coriander are as welcome on a
patio or in a herb garden as they
are in the kitchen. Plant them
near hot paving, where their
aromatic oils will evaporate
better to release their fragrance.
Include non-culinary herbs such as
balm of Gilead (*Cedronella*), curry plant
(*Helichrysum angustifolium*), pineapple sage
(*Salvia elegans*) and scented-leaved pelargoniums.

Scented
pelargonium

Wisteria blossoms have a
delicate fragrance (above). As
they usually hang, as here over
an arch, the scent wafts down
enticingly.

Sitting areas are enhanced by
scented plants (left), here
Ceanothus arboreus 'Trewithen
Blue' with aromatic rosemary at
ground level.

Hyacinths have an intensely
sweet smell and *Narcissus* 'Tête
à Tête' a more subtle fragrance
(far left).

'Etoile de Hollande'. For apricot in
both colour and scent, look for 'Lady
Hillingdon'.
● **concealed fragrances** are fun. The
modest evergreen shrub *Daphne
laureola* has uninteresting green
flowers, but on a still day in late winter
its lovely scent is carried quite some
distance. Conversely, the South African
pineapple lily (*Eucomis bicolor*) looks as
though it should have the sweetest
fragrance but in fact its smell is
extremely rank.

scented plants **for all seasons**

LATE SPRING ● daphnes: *D. mezereum*, a small shrub with sweetly fragrant purple
flowers; also *D. bholua, D.* x *burkwoodii, D. laureola* subsp. *philippi* ● wild cowslip
(*Primula veris*), golden blooms with a freesia-like scent.

EARLY SUMMER ● heliotrope, a tender small shrubby bedding plant with purple
blooms and a strong vanilla fragrance ● lilac (*Syringa*), with variable
fragrance: *S. vulgaris* is best (right) ● mock orange (*Philadelphus*): all
species and varieties are fragrant.

LATE SUMMER ● butterfly bush (*Buddleja
davidii*) has a lovely, sweet fragrance
● madonna lily (*Lilium candidum*), with pure
white, richly perfumed flowers ● tobacco plant
(*Nicotiana*), select old-fashioned varieties such
as *N. sylvestris*, which are strongly fragrant
at night.

Nicotiana sylvestris

AUTUMN ● honeysuckle: *Lonicera japonica* is best for
late flowering into autumn; *L.* x *purpusii*, a shrub
honeysuckle with sweetly fragrant paired white blossoms from late autumn on
● katsura tree (*Cercidiphyllum japonicum*): as its beautiful leaves begin to fall, they
smell strongly of hot fudge.

WINTER ● christmas box (*Sarcococca humilis*), an evergreen shrub with tufty flowers
smelling of honey ● viburnums (*V. farreri* and *V.* x *bodnantense*), winter-blooming
shrubs with pale pink to white blooms ● winter aconite (*Eranthis hyemalis*), with a
subtle, musky fragrance, best enjoyed when the little stems are picked.

EARLY SPRING ● *Mahonia japonica*, a prickly leaved shrub with pale yellow fragrant
flowers ● wintersweet (*Chimonanthus praecox*), a tall shrub with pale flowers in
parchment and purple colours and a sweet, intense fragrance ● witch hazel
(*Hamamelis mollis*), with golden-yellow flowers.

pergolas

Pergolas may be large or small, simple or elaborate, sturdy or delicate. Used to cover a path or link two areas of the garden, they tend to become a focus and must be sited with care as well as being soundly built.

siting a pergola

Bear in mind that any eye-catching structure can look silly and intrusive if sited in the wrong place, so take care over its postion in the open garden.
- **a pergola is usually built to cover a path,** enticing you to explore or lead you to some important destination. This might be a focal point (see page 118) or a separate area of the garden.
- **straight pergolas extend vistas** and frame views, whereas a curving structure is intriguing, its end mysteriously hidden from sight.
- **if lavishly decked with plants,** perhaps swags of roses or fruit, a pergola can become an airy, colourful tunnel or mark a crossing of paths.
- **left bare,** it can have the ornamental quality of sculpture.
- **when sited as a lean-to structure** against a wall, a pergola can make an elegant transition from indoors to outdoors, especially if designed to harmonise with the style of house.
- **a pergola can simply cover a patio** to make an intimate outdoor sitting and eating area.

materials for pergolas

- **for large, substantial** free-standing pergolas use square pillars of brick or stone to support heavy overhead timber cross beams. For smaller structures you can use the same timber for both posts and beams.
- **for a more decorative finish,** pitch the roof beams upwards to produce a pointed central apex, or you can tilt, curve or shape the ends to give an oriental look.
- **rustic poles** are an attractive alternative to prepared timber, best

suited to cottage and rural gardens. Use natural poles complete with their bark for a truly rustic appearance, or choose stripped, treated poles for longer life.
- **tubular metal arches,** with a flat, rounded or pointed profile, are modern and unobtrusive; galvanised or plastic-sheathed arches last longer than wood.

- **a long-lasting composite** material made from recycled plastic is now available. It looks and behaves like timber but is entirely synthetic.

Clothed in wisteria, this sturdy pergola casts cool dappled shade beneath its overhead framework of timbers.

choosing the right structure

A pergola is possibly the easiest and cheapest kind of house extension you can build. Flat-topped designs are functional and easy to make. A simple wooden pergola is a project that might be undertaken by anybody with some experience of DIY. The task is made easier if two people are working together. The most popular pergola is built from finished timber, planed and treated with preservative. Either make your own (see page 124) or buy a kit, usually available in modular units to let you customise it.

SOME DEFINITIONS

ARBOUR A structure enclosing a seat but open at the front; may simply use climbing plants trained on trellis or posts to create a sheltered, intimate retreat.

ARCADE A simple pergola, built in the same way as a loggia, but open to the elements and usually intended as a support for climbing plants.

ARCH A structure made from a pair of upright posts or pillars joined at the top by an overhead cross-beam; used to frame or straddle a path or gateway.

COLONNADE An arcade that covers a path linking one building to another.

LOGGIA A formal pergola built against the side of the house, usually glazed or roofed overhead and sometimes with glazed sides to form a long garden room.

PERGOLA A general term for a series of arches spaced at regular intervals and joined to form a continuous tunnel over a path or patio, or a lean-to structure against a wall.

choosing climbers

Give some thought to the cultural needs as well as style of the climbing plants you select. Bear in mind the following:

- **always match the vigour** of the climber to the style and size of the support.
- **climbers will have to tolerate** full exposure to wind and frost.
- **they should not** be so vigorous that major annual pruning is needed.

- **choose roses** with pendulous flowers so their fragrance can be enjoyed.
- **select evergreens** that are not so leafy that they will shower you with drips in autumn and winter.
- **climbing annuals** like sweet peas, runner beans and morning glories, and clematis varieties that are pruned hard in spring, will allow you to clear away all topgrowth annually if you wish.

climbers for larger structures

CLIMBING AND RAMBLING ROSES • *Rosa* 'Compassion' • *R.* 'Lady Hillingdon'
• *R.* 'Madame Alfred Carrière' • *R.* 'Maigold' • *R.* 'Mermaid' • *R.* 'New Dawn'
• *R.* 'Paul's Lemon Pillar' • *R.* 'Wedding Day' • *R. filipes* 'Kiftsgate' • *R. mulliganii.*

CLEMATIS • *Clematis* x *durandii* • *C.* 'Ernest Markham' • *C.* 'Etoile Rose' • *C. flammula*
• *C.* 'Huldine' • *C.* 'Jackmanii' • *C. rehderiana* • *C. viticella*

IVIES • *Hedera helix* 'Buttercup' • *H. helix* 'Goldheart' • *H. helix* 'Ivalace'.

HONEYSUCKLES • *Lonicera* x *brownii* 'Dropmore Scarlet' • *L. japonica* 'Halliana'
• *L. splendida* • *L. tragophylla*

PERENNIALS FOR LIGHT STRUCTURES • *Abutilon megapotamicum* • *Akebia quinata*
• *Campsis radicans* • *Cobaea scandens* • *Jasminum officinale* • *Lathyrus latifolius*
• *Passiflora caerulea* • *Solanum laxum* • *Wisteria floribunda*

One half of this sculptural pergola (above) is left unplanted, revealing its strong architectural presence, while clematis softens the other half.

The urn on a plinth (top) makes a classic focal point at the end of a tunnel clad in roses and wisteria, sited over a gravel path.

pergolas/2
building a timber pergola

YOU WILL NEED for a timber
pergola 4m long x 2m wide x 2.2m
high (13 x 6 x 7ft):
• 10cm x 10cm (4 x 4in) timber,
treated with preservative, as follows:
6 upright posts 2.7m (9ft) long,
2 bearers (main beams) 4m (13ft)
long, 5 cross beams 2.2m (7ft) long
• 8cm (3in) screws • 20cm (8in)
screws or carriage bolts • 6 metal
post spikes • sledgehammer • spirit
level • chisel • mallet • spanner • drill

1 **Using short lengths of timber**, mark
positions for the posts, three on each
side and spaced 1.5m (5ft) apart each way.

2 **Drive metal post spikes** into the
ground to support the squared timber
uprights. Use a sledgehammer and protect
the top of the spike with a wooden 'dolly'
(which can be bought) or a suitably sized
offcut of timber.

3 **Wedge the posts** in the metal spikes and
tighten the two bolts on either side to
secure each one; check they are vertical.

4 **Position a**
bearer along the
tops of the posts on
one side of the
pergola, with an
equal amount
overhanging at each
end. Using a spirit
level check that it is horizontal. Mark the
position of three posts on the bearer and the
two midway points between the posts.

5 **Using a**
chisel and
mallet, cut out
five half-joints at
these marks,
10cm (4in) wide
and 5cm (2in)
deep, to house
the cross beams.
Do the same for the other bearer. Mark and
cut corresponding half joints in the cross
beams, again allowing for an equal
overhang, about 15cm (6in), at each end.

6 **Set the bearers in position**, together
with the three cross beams that join
them, over the tops of the posts. Drill
through the joints and use 20cm (8in)
screws or carriage bolts to fix them to the
posts. Join the intervening two cross
beams to the bearers with 8cm (3in) screws.

A simple wooden
pergola can be
assembled from the
instructions given here,
sturdy enough to carry
the weight of climbing
plants. You can
personalise or embellish
the basic design in a
variety of ways, such as
creating the 'ladder'
effect on the upright
posts (left).

design tips

- For a balanced appearance, plan the length so that the distance between each arch is the same as the span across the entrance to the pergola.
- A height of 2.2–2.5m (7–8ft) under the roof beams, and an entrance width of 1.5m (5ft) between posts, is the minimum for comfortable passage, especially if the pergola is covered with plants.
- Err on the side of strength when choosing materials and dimensions, so the structure can withstand the force of strong winds and the heavy weight of wet foliage.
- Keep your design simple to show off plants to best effect.
- Slope the top of a lean-to pergola downwards, in case you decide later on to glaze or roof it in as a loggia or garden room.

structural hints

- **for increased strength,** reinforce all the joints with T-shaped brackets or angle brackets.
- **diagonal reinforcing poles** or corner braces also add strength, especially on rustic pole structures.
- **with lean-to structures,** support one end of the cross beams on a 10cm x 5cm (4in x 2in) wall plate screwed or bolted to the wall. Either half-joint the ends or rest them in metal joist hangers.
- **use a spirit level and plumb line** for accurate positioning of posts and beams.
- **you can strengthen the joints** on planed timber with waterproof glue.
- **posts can be farther apart,** up to about 2.7–3m (9–10ft), but the greater the distance between them, the thicker both they and the bearers need to be.
- **for a heavy structure,** and in lighter soils, you will have to bed the posts in concrete foundations rather than metal spikes. Dig a hole for each post, 60cm (2ft) deep and 30cm (12in) square. Wedge the post in position and vertical, and fill the surrounding gap with concrete. Leave to set hard before continuing with the construction of the pergola.

alternative materials and methods

Pergolas may be heavy or light, as well as either formal or rustic in their appearance. Bear in mind, however, that if the pergola is to support climbers, it should not be too flimsy. Vary the materials used for the upright posts and the beams to achieve the pergola of your choice.

vertical supports
- **rustic poles** should be made of larch or chestnut, 10cm (4in) in diameter.
- **brick piers** need to be 30cm (12in) square, on solid footings, or 45cm (18in) square for very wide pergolas.

the beams
- **for more delicate, lightweight structures,** 10cm x 5cm (4in x 2in) bearers can be used, laid flat against the outside of the posts; cross beams can be the same dimension or 15cm x 5cm (6in x 2in), laid on edge and joined with halving joints.
- **double bearers** of thinner timber, bolted together with one outside and the other inside the post, give a light, modern feel to the structure.

the foundations
- **metal structures** can be concreted in at the base or simply driven into the ground provided they are long enough to bed securely.

planting on pergolas

Once you have finished all the building work, you can prepare the ground for planting your chosen climbers. Make sure any concrete and timber treatment has completely dried before you start and remove any excavated subsoil. Mark planting positions at least 23cm (9in) away from the posts if you have concrete foundations, and allow room for any later replacement or maintenance of the posts.

- **prepare** about 1m² (1sq yd) of ground for each plant. Dig down two spade depths and remove all weeds and root fragments. Fork in plenty of garden compost or well-rotted manure, with 60–90g per m² (2–3oz per sq yd) of balanced slow-release fertiliser.
- **dig out a hole** about twice the width of the plant's rootball and deep enough for the climber, once planted, to be fractionally deeper than it was before.
- **position the plant** so that it leans towards the post, then back-fill around the roots, and firm the soil into place. Water thoroughly, then spread an organic mulch 5–10cm (2–4in) deep around the plant.
- **most climbers** need tying in to their supports, and even clinging or twining varieties benefit from some early assistance before they are self-reliant. Fix vertical wires to the posts or wrap wire netting around them for plants like roses that need regular tying. Direct twining plants towards the post by tying their stems to a short cane, wedged into the ground at an angle.

trellis screens

A screen can be an important influence in a garden, changing its appearance by hiding an unwanted view, shielding plants from wind or salt spray, or creating a sense of privacy. Of all the suitable screening materials, trellis is perhaps the most popular, offering decoration and plant support as well as seclusion.

choosing the structure

Treillage, or the art of using trellis, has been used since Roman times to create free-standing barriers, fences and ornamental pillars in the garden, and to provide a background or support for plants on existing walls. You can make trellis yourself or buy it as prefabricated panels in a range of patterns, shapes and sizes, and in various materials such as coated steel, hard plastic, or soft or hard wood.

using standard square trellis

This has a neutral impact on the garden, and is the best kind for supporting plants. It is available in regular panels 30cm–2m (1–6ft) wide at a standard length of 2m (6ft), and with a variable mesh size of 10–20cm (4–8in).

● **attach panels** to vertical battens for training plants on walls, and to increase wall height.

● **use trellis as an open fence** or screen supported at each end with 10 x 10cm (4 x 4in) posts.

● **use to extend the height** of an existing fence by attaching it to vertical battens, or to horizontal strips along the top of the fence.

diamond mesh trellis

Its lattice pattern is more decorative and stronger visually, but it can look intrusive or self-conscious if simplicity is your aim. Buy expanding panels or adapt it from flexible square trellis by rotating it through 45°. For stability and durability, frame diamond panels on all sides with wooden battens.

special shapes

Eye-catching shapes or romantic screens can be made from different sized slats and battens in varying patterns; they are often intended as structural or painted features in their own right, unadorned with plants.

● **use elaborate,** high-profile designs (panels for these can be bought or custom-made) to create arches or windows that frame a view or a glimpse of the garden beyond. In trompe l'oeil, trellis is used as a frame for trick effects to give the illusion of more space.

● **use rigid trellis** to form wigwams or obelisk panels.

fixing trellis to walls

Do not attach trellis panels direct to walls, because painting and other maintenance is then more difficult, and plants suffer from lack of free ventilation behind the foliage.

The simplest way to fix trellis is to use spacer blocks or battens, cut from 4 x 5cm (1½ x 2in) or 4 x 4cm (1½ x 1½in) treated softwood. Fix these to the wall, about 1m (3ft) apart, with brass screws inserted in pre-drilled and fibre-plugged holes; attach the trellis with brass screws or galvanised nails.

Alternatively, attach the trellis to the battens with screw eyes and hooks for easy removal (especially where trellis is intended for seasonal use only). If you need to repaint the wall occasionally, hinge the trellis to a horizontal lower batten, and secure at the top with screws or hooks.

complementary climbers

Trelliswork is a light, relatively airy structure unsuited to vigorous, heavy climbers, and it is too ornamental to hide beneath a dense canopy of foliage. Choose instead climbers with an open growth or with elegant leaves:

● **climbing roses,** which enjoy the free circulation of air, but check their ultimate height before buying. Miniature climbers such as 'Laura Ford', 'Nice Day' and 'Warm Welcome' are attractive and grow to only about 2m (6ft) high. Some older shrub roses, like

putting up a trellis screen

YOU WILL NEED • 2 panels standard square trellis • brass screws • screwdriver • outdoor paint or stain

1 **Screw one panel** of trellis against the fence. Position the free-standing panel at a 90° angle to the first. Adjust it until the horizontal laths line up.

2 **Mark the position** for fixing, and screw the panels together.

3 **Finish off** by painting or staining the trellis the colour of your choice.

using trellis

• **avoid the cheapest types** of trellis made with thin, rickety laths that have little strength or durability.

• **use close-mesh panels** to create a high-density screen for privacy or shelter, and wide-mesh panels for plant supports and formal divisions.

• **you can make free-standing trellis** look more interesting by embellishing the tops of support posts with carved or moulded finials or small spheres.

• **always tie plants horizontally** or at an angle to the trellis; this gives more rapid and effective coverage and a more impressive display.

Trellis panels are used to enclose and screen a contemplative, orient-inspired gravelled area of the garden.

Painted trellis has been used decoratively (above) to make obelisks and an arbour as well as screening. Mounted on a railway sleeper, a trellis panel allows views through to a more formal area of the garden (top left). A home-made rustic screen (top right) divides the garden.

'Nevada', are suitable when trained and secured in the same way as climbers.

• **clematis,** especially small-leaved species like *C. alpina* and *C. tangutica*.

• **wall shrubs and other shrubs,** such as honeysuckles and espalier-trained cotoneaster and ornamental quince, as well as annual sweet peas, morning glories, canary creeper and rhodochiton.

permanent containers

Trees and shrubs will survive many years in containers as long as they are well tended. Choose plants carefully to stand alone or use them in groups to set off more transient displays of seasonal bedding.

year-round containers

Growing permanently in containers allows you to enjoy plants that require different soil and conditions from those found in your garden. Rhododendrons and pieris, for example, would not thrive in alkaline soil, but you can grow them to perfection in a pot of lime-free ericaceous compost. Spreading plants like many bamboos could overwhelm a small garden, but in a pot they look lovely and are less trouble.

This form of gardening is also very versatile, as you can create different effects with just one permanent plant by surrounding it with temporary plants in smaller pots, changing them from year to year and from season to season (see pages 50–53).

selecting plants

Choose trees and shrubs that are naturally slow growing, require little pruning and have appeal throughout the year. Flowering is not essential as evergreens give foliage interest in winter and provide a quiet background to brilliant summer bedding. Some, particularly conifers, have a distinct conical or rounded form; others, like box and small-leaved privets, can be trained as topiary.

Container-grown trained box, in pairs, bring formality to this spring garden (above).

Shapely perennials such as this agave (right) will give form to a summer patio planting.

Standard plants are another good choice. Fuchsias, ivies, *Hydrangea paniculata* and even wisteria can be grown this way, although they usually need permanent staking.

Do not overlook deciduous trees either. Japanese maples are shapely in and out of leaf and have wonderful foliage that changes with the seasons.

choosing containers

A container must be large enough for the plant to spread its roots and grow well for at least two years. It should be sturdy, broad-based for stability and flaring to the rim, so the rootball can be slid out easily for repotting. Drainage is essential, ideally one hole 2–3cm (1in) across for every 30cm (12in) diameter of rim. Ceramic or terracotta pots must be frost-proof if they are outdoors all winter.

planting a container

The best time to do this is in April. Before you start, water your plant thoroughly and allow to drain. Position the pot where it is to stand (unless you have a wheeled pot trolley) and raise it on bricks or 'pot feet'. Crocking the base creates crevices where adult vine weevils can hide, so instead cover the drainage hole with geotextile membrane to prevent pests from entering and compost from being washed through. Use loam-based rather than soil-less

---

grow trees **alone**

Trees and other permanent plants are best grown alone in a container. Any additional plants, particularly bedding and bulbs, not only compete for the limited amount of moisture and nutrients, but often require different watering and feeding regimes.

A mature pittosporum forms the centrepiece of a container grouping, together with a black-stemmed bamboo and an olive tree.

potting compost. As well as being heavier and giving stability, loam-based composts retain nutrients and moisture for longer, and are easier to re-wet.

trees and shrubs for containers

bamboos • bay (*Laurus nobilis*) • box (*Buxus sempervirens*) • camellias • *Cordyline australis* • *Hydrangea paniculata* 'Grandiflora' • japanese maples (*Acer palmatum* var. *dissectum* types) • *Ligustrum lucidum* • pieris • pittosporum • rhododendrons (azalea types)

after planting

• **insert supports** for climbers so that the plants can grow through them from the start. By summer, the supports should be almost invisible amid the flowers.

• **protect the plants** from frost, even if they are hardy. Keep some fleece handy to throw over them, but remove it in the morning as temperatures begin to rise.

• **mulch to conserve moisture,** suppress weeds and improve the pot's appearance. Use an organic material like cocoa shells, or something decorative such as pebbles or fir cones (see also page 134).

• **regular watering** is essential; erratic delivery causes stress to the plant.

• **feed** by lightly forking in a slow-release granular fertiliser that will last all season, or water on liquid feed at regular intervals.

in the following years

Routine pruning of trees and conifers should be unnecessary other than to remove any dead or damage shoots, or crossing branches. Climbers and topiary will need attention (see pages 36 and 50), and flowering shrubs require deadheading (see page 41).

Leave woody plants undisturbed for two to three years before repotting, then move young plants into a larger container; you can leave more mature plants up to five years. 'Refresh' compost annually in March or April by scraping off the top 5cm (2in) of old compost and replacing it with fresh, mixed with a slow-release fertiliser.

In repotting years you may need to do a little root pruning on established shrubs while they are dormant.

planting a tree in a container

1 Place a square of geotextile over the drainage hole and cover with 2–3cm (1in) coarse grit, for good drainage. Add some loam-based compost mixed with a little bone meal, to come about halfway up the sides of the container.

2 Position the plant centrally. Pack compost round the sides of the rootball, shaking the plant gently to eliminate air gaps. Push the compost down securely but without over-compacting it.

3 Fill the container with more compost and water thoroughly. This will cause the compost to sink to the correct level. Add the mulch of your choice.

planting a patio

All patios benefit from planting, but with a little extra thought and care you can transform
an outdoor seating area into a delightful oasis of colour and fragrance.

Patio space is usually limited, so it is important to select compact plants that will not sprawl too much. Since patios are usually sited in the sun, aromatic shrubs such as sage, rosemary or lavender should thrive. They make useful 'structure' plants, since they are evergreen, whether they are left free-growing, or perhaps clipped as a low perimeter hedge. Slow-growing small trees can also give structure, as can box (*Buxus*), holly (*Ilex*) or bay (*Laurus nobilis*) carefully clipped into shape once a year.

In a very hot spot, you may wish to consider constructing a trellis or pergola, on which to train climbers. As well as providing shade, these will furnish lovely displays with a mix of plants to ensure interest through the growing season.

making planting pockets

Improve the looks of your paving by introducing some larger plants that will fit in 'pockets'. The simplest way is to remove either part or all of a paving slab – but think carefully before you decide which ones to remove. Small,

close groups of plants are often prettier than singletons dotted at random. And some sites will be more favoured than others. Pick the warmest spot for tender plants or those of borderline hardiness, and the most sheltered for those, such as Japanese maples, which hate the wind.

● **it is usually a simple matter** to chip out a paver, or to crack one across and lift part of it.

● **the ground beneath** may be poor, so remove as much hardcore as you can and make sure the ground drains adequately. Back-fill the hole with good garden soil, or a mix of soil and potting compost.

Raised beds using wooden planks (left) are ideal for a rooftop terrace or a balcony, where there is no soil. Check the roof for structural safety before planting up a roof garden and always keep the weight round the edges.

Dwarf tulips (below left) are planted in pockets with grass to brighten this patio in late spring.

Dwarf plants such as this *Sisyrinchium depauperatum* (below right) grow in little soil in the gaps between granite setts.

good plants **for cracks**
● acaena ● aubrieta ● *Campanula cochleariifolia* ● *Erinus alpinus*
● pratia ● thyme

good shrubs **for pockets**
● azalea ● bay (*Laurus nobilis*)
● box (*Buxus sempervirens*)
● daphne ● hebe ● *Ilex crenata*
● patio roses ● *Phlomis fruticosa*

making a raised brick bed

YOU WILL NEED • bricks • mortar • trowel • spirit level

1 Mark out the area and calculate how many bricks you need; allow four and a half bricks per metre per course (four per yard). Lay the first course of bricks on a thin layer of stiffish mortar spread on the paving.

2 As you work, keep checking levels with a spirit level. Adjust the thickness of the mortar to compensate for a very slight fall. Leave gaps between bricks at intervals to allow excess water to drain out.

3 When you lay the second course, place the corner brick endways on, in order to make a strong bond.

4 Lay the top course of bricks upside down, so that the top is flush. Leave for two days until the mortar has set hard. Then fill with soil, using a good quality, free-draining loam or a mixture of loam and peat (or peat substitute).

planting in paving cracks

Fully paved patios will still allow for plenty of planting. Cracks between pavers are adequate for sustaining a wide range of drought-tolerant plants, including some alpine plants and most thymes. Spring is the ideal time for this sort of planting, but autumn is almost as good. Avoid planting in the extremes of summer heat or winter cold.

• **for planting in cracks** the ideal 'mortar', or material between paving slabs, is sand, or a sand/soil mixture. However, cement mortar, unless it is new and very hard, should be relatively easy to chip away in places to make cavities for the plants. If your patio is yet to be paved, be sure to leave space between pavers (2–3cm/1in is plenty) and to fill the cracks with a mix of sand and soil, or sand and potting compost.

• **if the slabs have been bedded** firmly onto a weak sand/cement mix laid over levelled hardcore, there is no need for anything stronger to grout them. When the plants are established, they will help to hold the pavers in position.

• **if you purchase alpine plants** for setting between the cracks, their rootballs may be too big to fit. Trim away some of the roots, using an old knife, until the rootball is small enough to slot in. Make sure that the plants are set deeply enough: the base of the stem should be flush with the paving. Firm them in gently before brushing away any surplus soil. Water well, not only at planting time, but regularly until the plants have had time to develop their root systems.

patio tips

• **to check drainage,** empty a bucket of water into the planting hole and take a coffee break; if the water is still there when you return, do not plant.

• **use old or recycled bricks** for a raised bed; they will give a more mellow look.

• **if you are unsure** whether you want a permanent raised bed, make a small one with unmortared bricks.

• **allow self-seeding plants** like wild violets, forget-me-nots and alchemilla to seed themselves around the patio.

Fill a raised bed with plants, such as alpines, that particularly enjoy the free-draining conditions it offers.

lightening dark areas

A dark passage or a gloomy corner may be challenging, especially if the site catches the wind or there is too little light for most plants to grow. But there are ways of bringing light into dark areas and there will always be a few plants that can cope with these tricky conditions.

identify your problem

As degrees of shade and growing needs vary enormously, it is difficult to know which plants will tolerate a particular situation. The first test is to see which plants, if any, are growing there now. Their appearance will give you an idea of the growing conditions. Every plant you are able to establish will be a step towards converting a dark, barren area into a small but lovely garden feature. Then consider possible solutions.

light levels Does the area receive direct sun at any time of day?

solutions: Improve light levels by painting surfaces white or a light colour. You might also install outdoor mirrors to reflect light. Trim, or at least thin out, any overhanging trees or bushes to let in more daylight.

wind How much is there? Narrow passages are often subject to wind funnelling between buildings, which is damaging to almost all plants, and can be miserable for people who are passing through the area.

solutions: Plant robust shrubs, or erect screens at points along the passage to slow down wind speed. Even in a narrow, confined spot, you would be surprised at how a slender, upright conifer in a big container can help to reduce the effect of wind. Openwork fencing or hedging will slow down wind speeds more effectively than a solid screen or wall, which will only cause eddying currents.

extra tough plants for dark corners

EVERGREEN SHRUBS AND CLIMBERS • holly: variegated forms such as 'Golden King' or 'Belgica Aurea' • ivy: pale variegated cultivars such as 'Glacier' or 'Adam' • lesser periwinkle: *Vinca minor* f. *alba* is a pretty white-flowered form • mahonias: *M. japonica* is the most fragrant, but try also 'Charity' and 'Winter Sun' • spotted laurel: *Aucuba japonica* 'Crotonifolia' is gold splashed.

EVERGREEN HERBACEOUS PLANTS These are surprisingly tolerant of gloom. • bergenias: *B.* 'Beethoven' has white flowers and 'Abendglut' purple-pink • epimedium (*E.* x *versicolor*) • lungwort (*Pulmonaria*) • spurge (*Euphorbia amygdaloides* var. *robbiae*)

FERNS Surprisingly resilient and disliking exposure to direct sun, they will grow in cracks in paving, on walls or squeezed in the gap between floor and wall. • hard fern (*Blechnum spicant*) • hart's tongue fern (*Asplenium scolopendrium*) • soft shield fern (*Polystichum setiferum* Divisilobum Group)

Vinca minor
f. *alba*

WHITE OR LIGHT-COLOURED FLOWERS White flowers are excellent in shady places as they stand out and reflect light. • cimicifuga (*C. simplex*) • daffodils (*Narcissus* 'Mount Hood', *N.* 'Thalia', *N. poeticus* var. *recurvus*) • goatsbeard (*Aruncus dioicus*) • hyacinths: *Hyacinthus orientalis* 'Carnegie', 'City of Haarlem' and 'L'Innocence' • Japanese anemone (*A.* x *hybrida* 'Honorine Jobert') • lily of the valley (*Convallaria majalis*) • snowdrops (*Galanthus nivalis*) • Solomon's seal (*Polygonatum* x *hybridum*) • tulips: *Tulipa* 'Purissima', with white flowers, and *T.* 'Spring Green', with flowers of white and green

All these have a good chance of surviving in even the most sunless spot.

White-painted walls and light coloured paving slabs (left) maximise the amount of light and enable plants to be grown here.

A chequerboard tiled floor and the minimal use of tough, shapely cordylines (right) in containers brings interest into this narrow passageway.

tendency to dryness Soil in passages can be dry, especially if shielded from rain by roof overhangs or the proximity of high buildings.

solutions: Since this is a small area and near the house, it will be easy to water by hand. It would also be relatively inexpensive to install a basic automatic watering system.

Agaves will grow in very dry conditions, so make a good choice for these stylish galvanised containers (above).

This side passage (left) has been designed in oriental style, using pale gravel and railway sleepers. Plants such as bamboo, planted through the gravel, screen the fence.

privacy Is the passageway public and, if so, might any garden development be subject to vandalism or accidental damage by passers-by? Take care not to block the passageway with annoying obstructions; instead, try to beautify the place so that people enjoy it and consequently respect it more.

solutions: Containers can be secured against theft by chains and locks, discreetly placed. Remember that damage is less likely to be perpetrated on thorny plants such as hollies, berberis or pyracantha.

walled areas Is the space both enclosed and severely restricted? The amount you can do here may be limited, but even a tiny site can be made to look slightly larger by creating some optical illusions.

solutions: How about fixing a trellis 'trompe l'oeil' on the wall? With the right shape, it is possible to make the flat surface resemble an arch. If you place a pot containing a handsome plant in the right spot, it will look like a special niche. And if nothing else will grow in this dark, hemmed-in space, you can always try ivy.

decorative aggregates

From crunchy gravel and iridescent slate to coloured glass nuggets and metal granules, your choice of surfacing materials has never been wider and is limited only by cost and your own imagination.

After centuries of use, crushed stone of various kinds remains popular as an inexpensive ground-cover material, more versatile than slabs and more durable than brick. The colour and texture varies according to the rock from which it is derived: from marble and granite to limestone, slate and spar. This variety allows you to create a well-integrated design with surfaces that reflect nearby building materials.

Alternative aggregates have more specific uses. Cobbles and pebbles, for example, harmonise immediately in water gardens, yet they may also be

bedded in concrete as a deterrent, since they are uncomfortable to walk over. Products of recycling include glass gravel, often brightly coloured, and metal granules, both stimulating ingredients for a contemporary design.

Using aggregates to mulch containers and small beds is a practical way to integrate them with their surroundings. Pebbles and small cobbles suit larger plants and beds, echoing the Oriental practice of stone mulching at the base of trees. Glass gravels, marble chippings and metal granules complement minimalist planting and patio schemes.

quantities to buy
- **gravel** is sold by the cubic metre or yard: 1m³ covers up to 40m² when laid 2–3cm (1in) deep (1cu yd covers 36sq yd).
- **cobbles and pebbles** are sold in the same quantities as gravel.
- **specialised aggregates** are usually bought in 25kg (56lb) bags. This covers about 1m² (1sq yd) laid loosely on a level surface at a depth of 2–3cm (1in).

Stars of blue glass are set into loose washed pebbles and gravel in an area that receives little wear.

laying aggregates for light use

YOU WILL NEED • tape measure • pegs and string • spade • spirit level • edging of your choice • geotextile membrane • wire hoops • sand • gravel • rake

1 Mark out the area with pegs and string; excavate to 5cm (2in) deep. Level the soil and install edging.

2 Lay a geotextile membrane and peg in place with wire hoops or staples.

3 Cover with a layer of sand 2–3cm (1in) deep, and roll or tamp firm.

4 Spread the gravel to a depth of 2–3cm (1in), then level and tread firm.

material choice

Gravel comprises irregular stone chippings, generally up to 12mm (½in) in size, that vary widely in colour and appearance. The loose surface can be painful for children and bare feet, and may attract cats, but makes a durable finish for drives and well-used paths. The crunching noise it makes under foot is a useful deterrent to intruders. Self-binding gravel is composed of different grades, including dust, and is rolled to a firm, permanent finish.

Shingle or 'pea gravel' (1) consists of smooth, rounded stones in a range of sizes from 0.5–2cm (¼–¾in), suitable for small paths and decorative areas around plants. However, it migrates down slopes and easily ruts if laid too deeply.

Glass gravel (2) is produced from recycled bottles, crushed to standardised fragments, sterilised and polished to form beads or a smooth, translucent shingle. It is very hard-wearing, but better suited to decorative

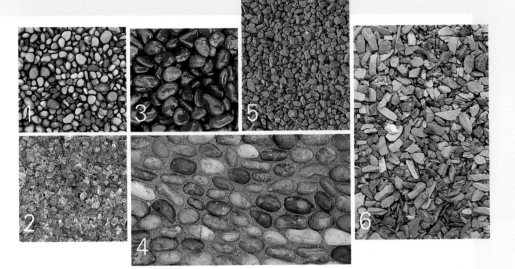

mulches, infills and surface designs, than paving, unless bonded in concrete.

Pebbles and cobbles are smooth, usually water-worn stones, sold in standard sizes and colours or in mixtures. Though the terms are interchangeable, cobbles are rounded and almost spherical, whereas pebbles are flatter. Lay them loose **(3)** or arrange in patterns and bed them in concrete **(4)** (see below).

Stone chippings are available in various natural stones, such as limestone, or as dyed chippings in vivid hues **(5)**.

Slate (6) is durable, smooth and iridescent when wet. It comes in greyish shades of red, green or blue, as small fragments of varying size. Lay it loose for a stable surface that suits a range of informal and contemporary settings.

Metal granules are available as copper, recycled from pylon cables, or light-weight aluminium. Use these angular aggregates loose as mulches and infills, or bond them with mortar or resin for harder wear and to provide a tough innovative surface around decking.

providing an edge

Unless bedded in concrete or resin, loose aggregates are mobile materials. They scatter under foot into adjacent beds or, more hazardously, onto lawns, causing damage to mowers and injury to you. An edging will restrain them.
bands of brick, edging tiles, cobbles and slates on edge provide complementary, formal edgings. Lay or, preferably, mortar them on a firm foundation of compacted hardcore or sand.
treated timber edging or gravel boards, sunk on edge into the ground, are practical and inexpensive, but have a relatively short life and may not match the aggregate.
wooden railway sleepers bedded firmly on

hardcore are durable and make a strong visual frame within a geometric design.

laying aggregates

The method adopted depends on the amount of surface-wear received.
for a well-used path
● **mark out the area** with pegs and string and excavate to 12cm (5in) deep; level the ground and install the edging.
● **spread hardcore** or mixed gravel almost to the surface of the excavation and level it. Roll or use a compacter until it is 5cm (2in) below the surroundings.
● **spread gravel** 5–8cm (2–3in) deep, starting from one side and levelling as you go; roll or tread the surface firm. Spray with water to settle the dust.

for light use

For a path that will receive only light wear, the foundations need not be so deep (see opposite).

bedding in concrete

● **excavate and prepare** a solid foundation, in the same way as for a well-used path (see above), leaving space to spread a 5cm (2in) layer of dry mortar (one part cement to four parts sand, or buy it ready-mixed).
● **press in the cobbles** or pebbles to half their depth, packing them tightly together.
● **finish by sifting** over a little more mortar. Spray with water to clean the stones and set the mortar.

planting in gravel

Gravel is an adaptable material that has many practical advantages in the garden. It can protect drought-loving plants from suffering in wet climates, re-create desert or alpine conditions, and even offer a solution for coping with desperately dry soils.

As ground-covering mulch, gravel can be used in a number of imaginative ways to create specialised habitats for plants that naturally grow in dry surroundings. Many of these, especially rock and alpine plants, and Mediterranean species, resent water lying where their stems meet the roots, and have difficulty surviving a wet winter unless provided with very efficient drainage. A gravel mulch allows water to drain fast and, when laid over a geotextile membrane, it also helps plants to survive hot dry summers by keeping their roots cool and moist.

creating a gravel bed

If your soil drains well, start by digging and removing the topsoil to a depth of about 8cm (3in), and take out any weeds. If the soil is very dry fork in some leaf-mould or garden compost. Replace the topsoil with 5cm (2in) unwashed gravel, and tread firm to consolidate the finer particles. Finish with a 2–3cm (1in) layer of shingle or 'pea gravel', which also needs rolling or treading.

Heavy clay or wet ground needs deeper preparation. Dig out the topsoil to a full spade's depth, and loosen the exposed subsoil with a fork. Then spread a 15cm (6in) layer of rubble, broken bricks or similar hardcore, and tread or ram firm. Cover this with a layer of inverted turves or plastic sheeting well perforated with a fork for drainage. Infill the bed with a free-draining planting mixture (see opposite), tread firm and top up if necessary, but leave space for the 2–5cm (1–2in) gravel mulch.

planting in gravel beds

To plant in a shallow gravel bed through a geotextile membrane, follow the steps shown opposite.

A gravelled area is planted with irises, verbascums and ornamental grasses, all of which enjoy hot, dry conditions.

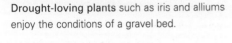

planting mixture for a gravel bed

Plants sensitive to excessive moisture need a well-mixed, free-draining planting compost, otherwise their roots could rot.

FOR HEAVY CLAY SOIL 1 part weed-free topsoil, 1 part sharp sand or coarse grit.

ON DRY GROUND 1 part weed-free topsoil, 1 part sharp sand, 1 part leaf-mould or garden compost.

FOR ALPINE PLANTS 1 part weed-free topsoil, 2–3 parts coarse grit.

Universal potting compost can be used instead of soil.

Drought-loving plants such as iris and alliums enjoy the conditions of a gravel bed.

To make planting pockets in a deep gravel bed you will need a crowbar, or strong metal rod, as well as a trowel.

● **scrape the gravel** to one side; drive the crowbar through the base layer and stir it round to enlarge the hole.

● **fill the hole** with planting mixture (see above) and firm with your fingers.

● **make a hole** in the mixture with a trowel, a little larger than the rootball, and position the plant so that the top of the rootball is level with the surface.

● **fill round the rootball** with planting mixture and firm gently. Replace the gravel round the plant stem, level and water well. You may need to water the plant again in dry weather until new growth is visible.

caring for gravel gardens

● **raking** will roughly level gravel and shingle, but a more uniform finish can be obtained by scraping across the gravel surface with the edge of a flat wooden board.

● **clear autumn leaves** and other plant debris from a gravel garden before it decomposes. Lightly brush it off with a stiff broom, or use a powered leaf blower.

● **top up bare patches** with fresh gravel in autumn and spring, especially around the base of plants, and re-level the surface with a rake or a board.

● **pull up weeds** as soon as you see them. Do not allow them to become established.

gravel-planting tips

● **do not use limestone** chippings around acid-loving plants, which will react to the presence of lime with poor growth and leaves turning yellow.

● **on steep slopes** use ground-cover plants such as bugle (*Ajuga reptans*) or creeping jenny (*Lysimachia nummularia*) to help stabilise the gravel and prevent it from creeping downhill.

● **lift and divide** mat-forming and other spreading perennials every few years to keep them young and vigorous. After replanting, water them in with a diluted liquid feed and mulch with fresh gravel.

planting through a membrane

1 **Scrape away** the gravel and use a sharp knife to cut a cross in the geotextile membrane.

2 **Turn back** the cut edges and plant so the top of the rootball is level with the soil surface. Tuck the cut material around the plant. Replace and level the gravel, and water well.

3 **For very small** or alpine plants, cut a circular hole in the membranes using a plastic pot as a template.

mulches

Mulching brings many benefits over and above its primary role in improving the soil. It gives your garden a neat, well-tended finish and reduces the amount of time and effort you need to spend on routine care.

Extreme weather is unkind to bare soil. Hot sunshine and winds dry and harden the surface, which causes heavy ground like clay to crack. Pounding rain turns the surface to a caked crust, and it washes away plant foods and even the topsoil itself. To protect your soil from these effects, cover the surface with a mulch. Depending on the material you use, mulching can also:

- **improve** soil texture
- **increase** the soil's ability to retain water and nutrients
- **suppress** weeds
- **provide** plant nutrients
- **deter** some pests
- **protect** plant roots from temperature extremes, including moderate frost
- **give** a decorative finish to beds or containers, especially for alpines.

using mulches

All bare cultivated soil benefits from mulching. Mulches tend initially to preserve the conditions they cover; for example, moist soil is prevented from drying out, while cold soil takes longer

loose inorganic mulches

gravel (1), **shingle** and other loose aggregates, such as crushed shells **(2)**, help to keep soil cool and moist, and improve the drainage around plants that need dry conditions, such as alpines and herbs. They also give a decorative finish to beds and containers (see page 134). Grit mulches protect plants from slugs.

small pebbles (3) and **cobbles (4)** form a decorative mulch around plants (see page 134).

loose organic mulches

shredded bark (5) must decompose for a year or be bought ready composted, as fresh bark removes nitrogen from the soil when it decays. It is a decorative mulch for shrubs, borders and herb gardens, often laid over geotextile membrane.

mushroom compost is a mixture of manure and straw or wood shavings left over from commercial mushroom cultivation. Use it around all plants except acid-lovers, because it contains lime, and make sure it is sterilised.

to warm up. So the best times to mulch are late spring, when soil temperatures are rising, and early autumn, before they begin to fall. Before covering the soil with a mulch, remove weeds, apply any fertilisers and ensure that the ground is thoroughly moist.

types of mulch

There are permanent inorganic mulches, such as gravel and shingle, and seasonal mulches, which include the various organic materials applied while plants are growing as well as being forked in later to improve the soil. There are also synthetic sheet mulches that are effective at suppressing weeds but which tend to look unattractive.

For maximum benefit spread loose organic mulches 5–10cm (2–4in) deep, depending on the plants. Young perennials, for example, need only a shallow mulch, which can be topped up as the plants develop, whereas shrubs, trees, fruit and potatoes can have a thicker layer. Leave a 5–8cm (2–3in) gap round the stems of trees and shrubs when spreading an organic mulch, to prevent rotting.

It is easier to mulch after sowing and planting but, where a mulch is in place, just scrape it aside to reveal the soil and replace it once you finish planting. Mulches are more effective insulators if they are kept loose, so check organic materials after heavy rain and gently loosen any compacted surfaces with a garden fork.

sheet mulches

black plastic is widely used for mulching strawberries, potatoes and other crops. Lay the plastic over prepared soil and secure the edges by burying them in slits made with a spade, then plant through smaller slits, cut with a sharp knife. Black plastic absorbs heat and excludes light, effectively suppressing weeds, but it is impermeable. It can successfully be used to clear a large area of weedy ground, such as a new vegetable plot, if it is left in position for a year or two.

clear plastic is sometimes spread over the soil to warm it up in early spring or to protect a prepared seedbed until needed.

black mulching paper is permeable and, like black plastic, used for short-term vegetable crops.

geotextile membranes are long-lasting materials that suppress weeds while allowing water to penetrate. They are widely used under shredded bark and gravel (see pages 134 and 137).

floating mulches include fleece and thin perforated plastic sheeting. They are spread over plants to help retain heat and moisture. They also protect crops from many flying insect pests as long as the edges are well secured (see black plastic). Since the materials are permeable and very light, they can be laid in position immediately after sowing and will rise with the plants as they grow. Use them in early autumn to protect crops against one or two degrees of frost.

manure allowed to rot down for at least a year makes a nutritious mulch for spreading generously around fruit, vegetables and roses. Dried and composted manure in bags is expensive and too concentrated for mulching, so is best used as a soil improver.

garden compost is nourishing and free of charge, but it must be well made or it can introduce persistent weeds to previously clean soil.

leaf-mould is an excellent soil conditioner. Sieve out the finer material for making potting compost, and use the coarse residue for mulching around any type of plant.

cocoa shells are a waste material that is light, pleasant to handle and both decorative and natural looking. This mulch may form an impervious surface after heavy rain.

grass cuttings are a useful mulch around well-established acid-loving plants such as rhododendrons and raspberries. Do not use for several mowings after weedkiller has been applied to the lawn.

straw (6) is spread around strawberries, cucumbers and squashes to ensure clean fruit. It is also useful for keeping greenhouse beds moist and for protecting frost-sensitive perennials in winter.

6

creating tropical effects

Many subtropical plants have superb architectural qualities and grow very large over quite a short period; some are also surprisingly hardy given a sheltered situation. They provide exotic-looking outlines, either with huge, distinctive leaves or with a striking growing habit. In a small garden, grow just one or two plants quite out of scale with the rest to create a sense of drama.

choosing grasses and grass-like plants

Grasses are universal, spanning the globe from the Equator to the arctic regions, but those from warm climates are bigger, lusher and more dramatic. Group them with unrelated, but grass-like plants, and the choice is extensive.

bamboos

Bamboos, the most exotic of all grasses, range from tiny, dwarf species to giants with stems like scaffold poles. The choice is vast, but only a limited number of species is hardy in cold climates and most of these are modest in height. *Fargesia murieliae*, easily the most vigorous and dependable, has stems up to 2–3m (6–10ft) and relatively small leaves. Less hardy, but able to tolerate light frost, is *Phyllostachys nigra* with glossy black stems to contrast with its foliage. (*P. nigra* var. *henonis* has stems of bright green, turning vivid gold as they mature.) In a subtropical border, a black-stemmed bamboo makes a strong but elegant feature, especially if it is contrasted with plants carrying bigger and broader foliage.

tall grasses

Tall lush-looking grasses that go well with bamboos and produce a softer, more shimmering effect include

The dramatic foliage of tree ferns, cannas and grasses (top) creates a lush 'tropical' setting. Red-leaved cannas mix well with the Japanese banana (*Musa*) and ferns (far left). The fiery-leaved grass *Imperata cylindrica* 'Red Baron' (left) suits an exotic-looking planting.

Miscanthus sinensis. A big, bold grass, it comes in a wide range of forms, but always displays the distinctive feature of a bold, silvery stripe down the centre of each leaf. Silky flowers are produced in late summer, often looking burnished or metallic as they emerge on stems that may exceed 2m (6ft).

Grasses with cane-like stems also have a tropical look. *Arundo donax* grows wild in the Mediterranean region, where it is used as a windbreak or hedge. Young plants dotted about a border make a striking display with their towering 3m (10ft) stems, furnished with leaves all the way up. Among grasses with flowers as well as good leaves, *Pennisetum alopecuroides* is low growing, with leaves sometimes blushed purple and flowers like furry squirrel tails. Combine any of these grasses with *Verbena bonariensis.* Although not a grass, its long-stemmed purple flowers provide a similar misty effect and it is an effective magnet for butterflies.

large-leaved exotics

Plants with huge, bold leaves always look tropical. These, whether grown as annuals or brought inside in winter, will make a valuable contribution to an exotic border:
- **castor oil plant** (*Ricinus communis*), has palmate leaves and is best when lush and young. Select a red-leaved form, such as 'Impala'.
- **the huge, tender perennial,** *Melianthus major* has large, compound leaves in a bewitching shade of blue-green, beautifully serrated along their margins. Contrast it with the red leaves of castor oil plant or canna (see below).
- **giant pelargonium** (*P. papilionaceum*) has huge rounded leaves and grows up to 2m (6ft) in a season. Its pretty purple-pink flowers are produced in clouds, like little butterflies.

brightly coloured flowers

Paddle-leaved cannas have the added advantage of summer flowers in strong colours, ranging through golds and oranges to red, pink or soft yellow; try contrasting the dark purple-leaved varieties such as 'Durban' with melianthus (see above).

Cannas also combine well with the brilliantly coloured salvias from South America. Among the most exotic-looking is *Salvia patens*, sporting bright peacock blue, hook-shaped flowers on 30–45cm (12–18in) stems; it is lovely at the front of a border, with cannas behind. At 2m (6ft) or so, huge *S. guaranitica* flowers later in summer with big, midnight blue to purple flowers. *S. involucrata* has nettle-shaped leaves of an unusual, almost fluorescent green and flowers of a rich plummy pink.

Temporary summer bedding blends well in a tropical border. Select the largest varieties available. Tobacco plants, especially the giant *Nicotiana sylvestris*, are impressive, as are African marigolds (*Tagetes*), multi-coloured coleus, salpiglossus and dahlias such as 'Bishop of Llandaff'.

tropical look-alikes

If you do not have a greenhouse or conservatory for winter protection, but still want that exotic mood, there are a number of plants that may look tender but are, in fact, surprisingly tough.
- **yuccas,** from the mountains of Central America, can withstand temperatures of -15°C (5°F) or less, yet give the impression of being desert plants. The most architectural species is *Yucca gloriosa*, but *Y. filamentosa* suits smaller spaces very well.
- **New Zealand flax** (*Phormium*) is resilient, too, though it will succumb to sustained frost and is vulnerable to winter wet unless the leaves are tied up for protection.
- **the tree** *Paulownia tomentosa,* if cut down almost to the ground each early spring, will produce fleshy stems with enormous heart-shaped leaves. It looks like a rainforest denizen, but is hardy.
- **the moisture-loving** *Rheum palmatum* has rhubarb-like leaves and tall flower spikes.
- **aralia** is grown for its large, much-divided foliage produced on curious thorny, stumpy trees.

tropical **focal points**

For extra height and exotic form, consider investing in a large tender shrub or tree. A banana is easy to grow, and the Japanese banana (*Musa basjoo*) is almost hardy. It can often be overwintered outdoors safely, especially in milder areas, by lagging the stem with fleece. Shrubs such as *Brugmansia* (with big hanging trumpet flowers), iochroma (with small, bright purple tubular flowers), tibouchina (purple-blue flowers) or mature citrus trees, can all be placed in strategic sunny positions outdoors in summer, but will need an indoor refuge in winter. Cannas have vibrant flowers in summer.

For exceptional leaf size, but totally unsuitable for small gardens, is *Gunnera manicata*, a giant hairy perennial (see page 153). Its 2m (6ft) wide leaves, carried on stems that may grow to almost 3m (10ft), die down in winter to protect the roots. Given poolside space, it could hardly be more dramatic.

Canna

new lawns

By late spring the soil is warm and moist, providing the ideal conditions for a new lawn to establish rapidly. Grass grows best from turf or seed in moist but well-drained soil, and good light is usually essential, although lawn mixtures that tolerate some shade are available.

planning your lawn

The size and shape of the lawn depends largely on the size and style of your garden: sweeping curves suit an informal setting while straight lines are more formal. If you are planning narrow strips of grass, make these multiples of the cutting width of your mower. This will make mowing easier and give a more even finish.

Whether grown from turf or seed, make a new lawn slightly larger than its ultimate planned size. This allows you to trim back the edges once the lawn is established to give a crisp outline.

seed or turf?

Before creating a new lawn, the big decision is whether to lay turf or sow seed. Turf provides an instant effect,

but it is much more expensive; on the other hand, seed is cheaper, but takes longer to establish. As the soil preparation for turfing a lawn and sowing seed is the same, the deciding factor tends to be how long you are prepared to wait.

preparing the ground

A lawn is a permanent garden feature, so it is worth preparing the ground thoroughly to avoid future problems. You do not want to be continually controlling established weeds or trying to rectify an uneven surface.

Deep and thorough digging is particularly important to ensure that the soil is well cultivated where most root activity occurs, and grass roots penetrate surprisingly deeply. It is

essential, first of all, to remove all traces of perennial weeds. Use a spade to dig the area to a depth of at least 25cm (10in). Carefully remove all weed roots and creeping stems. You can do this by hand as you dig, but where the ground contains a high proportion of pernicious perennial weeds, such as horsetail, you may need to use a chemical weedkiller based on glyphosate to eradicate weeds from the soil completely.

SOWING TIP Birds will not eat grass seeds that have been treated with an unpalatable chemical repellent. They may, however, 'dust bathe' in a seedbed before the lawn has started to grow. This is a nuisance, but it is easy to re-seed any resulting small bare patches.

Grass seed will start to germinate in 6–14 days after sowing (above), depending on the seed mixture and the weather.

Turf must be unrolled and laid as soon as possible, ideally within 24 hours of its delivery (left). To avoid unnecessary delay, agree on a delivery date that allows plenty of time to prepare the soil beforehand.

sowing seed

A seeded lawn may be slow to establish but, when sown at the optimum times in spring or autumn, the result is usually of a good quality. You can also select a seed mixture that suits your garden situation. Most reputable seed mixtures are a blend of two or more species of grass that will grow well together and provide an even, dense coverage. The species of grasses usually differ in their mode of growth and at least one will have a creeping habit. The sowing rate will vary depending on the seed mixture and the intended use for the lawn, so check the instructions on the packet.

SOWING TIP Sow at a slightly higher rate than recommended to achieve a thicker-looking lawn in a shorter period of time.

lawn seed mixtures

• **for fine ornamental lawns** These lawns look lush and beautiful, but will not stand up to hard wear. Mow with a cylinder mower for a fine close finish, and one with a roller for stripes. Sowing rate: 35–50g per m² (1–2oz per sq yd)
Mowing height: 1–1.5cm (½–⅝in)

• **for lightly shaded lawns** This is the best mix for lightly or partially shaded areas where the soil is moist, but unsuitable for deep shade, dry soils or under evergreen trees. Sowing rate: 35–50g per m² (1–2oz per sq yd)
Mowing height: 1.5–2cm (⅝–¾in)

• **for hard-wearing lawns** This mix produces a tough, good-looking lawn, tolerant of heavy use and children's games throughout the summer. Sowing rate: 25–35g per m² (¾–1oz per sq yd)
Mowing height: 1.5–2cm (⅝–¾in)

sowing a lawn

1 **After digging thoroughly,** use a garden fork to break up any compacted soil to improve drainage. Level the soil, then allow it to settle for about two weeks. Any emerging weeds can be hoed off or treated with a systemic weedkiller based on the chemical glyphosate.

2 **Rake the soil roughly level.** Incorporate a base dressing of fertiliser applied at the rate of 150–200g per m² (4–6oz per sq yd).

3 **Firm the soil thoroughly.** To do this, shuffle over the ground taking short steps and applying pressure with your heels. Rake the soil again and remove any stones.

4 **To sow the seed evenly,** mark out the area into 1-metre squares (1-yard squares) with canes and a string line. Weigh out enough seed for 1 square metre. Pour the seed into a plastic beaker and mark the level on the side. Use this measure to save weighing the seed every time.

5 **For each square,** sow half the seed in one direction and the remainder at right angles. Pour a manageable quantity into your hand at a time and scatter evenly.

6 **When you have sown** all the seed, lightly rake the entire area to incorporate the seed into the soil surface. Water well.

new lawns/2

lawns from turf

Laying turf is the gardener's equivalent of carpet laying and the job must be done just as carefully and as systematically for a good result. So first prepare the soil as described on page 142 and mark out the area slightly larger than required.

Turf may be expensive, but about six weeks from being laid, the lawn should be well established and ready for use. However, this method is not without its drawbacks during the early stages. Newly laid turf needs to be kept well watered, and in warm dry weather this could mean as much as 25 litres per m² (5 gallons per sq yd) each week. If turf is allowed to dry out it will shrink and lift, exposing a much greater surface and accelerating the drying process; whereas if there is a spell of dry weather immediately after grass seed has been sown to make a new lawn, the seeds will simply remain dormant until the conditions for germination improve, rather than beginning to grow immediately.

buying turf

Turves are usually sold in sections 1m x 30cm (3 x 1ft) and rolled along their length, which makes them easy to stack, transport and store. Many of the more expensive turves are reinforced with a biodegradable plastic mesh, so less soil is needed to hold the root structure together and the turves can be thinner and up to 2m (6ft) in length. For extensive lawns it is possible to buy turf as a large roll, which is laid out by a contractor and cut to the exact dimensions, like a fitted carpet.

turfing a lawn

1 **Starting from one corner**, lay the first row of turf alongside a plank or garden line to get a straight edge. For lawns with curved edges, lay a hosepipe or length of rope to define the boundaries.

2 **Go back to the starting point** to lay the second row of turves at right angles to the first. This ensures that the joints are staggered, like bricks in a wall; it is called 'keying' the turves together. As you work, butt the turves up close to each other.

3 **Work from a wooden plank**; this protects the turves from damage caused by walking on them as subsequent rows are laid. The uniform pressure will also gently firm the turves into position after they are laid, helping the grass to establish.

4 **When all the turves are down**, spread a lawn top-dressing (available from garden centres) over the entire area and brush it into any gaps or cracks with a besom broom or the back of a rake. This will help to stop the turf edges from drying out and shrinking.

care of new lawns

Whether your lawn has been laid from seed or turf, once established it will need regular mowing, watering and feeding to encourage the production of healthy green growth.

mowing new lawns

New lawns sown from seed early the previous autumn or in April will be ready for their first cut at the end of May, but only a very light topping is required for the first two or three cuts. If you use a rotary mower, sharpen the blades well beforehand so that they will cut the grass rather than drag it out by the roots. Rotary mowers rely on the speed of the blades to get a cutting action, but a combination of blunt blades and shallow-rooted grass seedlings can wreak total havoc on a newly establishing lawn.

Whichever type of mower you have, use one with a roller if possible, as the pressure of the roller will bend over the young blades of grass, thus checking their rate of growth. The plants respond by branching from the base to produce many more leaves, which thickens the coverage of the lawn considerably. Some gardeners even roll a new lawn two or three times before the first cut to encourage this branching growth (called 'tillering'). Checking the top growth and stimulating extra root development produces an established lawn more quickly.

The first three or four cuts of a new lawn should be made on a high blade setting, just to 'top' the grass leaves. As the grass starts to thicken, you can gradually lower the height of the cut,

but no more than a third of the total height should ever be removed in a single cut (see page 55).

watering new lawns

Young grass plants are very vulnerable in the early stages, before they become established. Freshly laid turf will dry out very quickly if not kept moist, and lawns raised from seed will also dry out rapidly because the grass leaves do not yet cover the soil surface sufficiently to stop it from drying out. One advantage of turf is that immediately after laying the turves and firming them into place, you can brush a 'top-dressing' of loam and sand into the joints to help reduce drying out and therefore shrinkage.

You should water all newly made lawns for at least two to three hours every three or five days if there is no significant rainfall. The gentlest, and most efficient, way to do this is to leave a soaker hose running at a gentle trickle on the lawn, moving it every half hour.

feeding lawns

Regular mowing gradually saps the strength of the grass. If the nutrients taken up by the grass then removed as clippings are not replaced, the lawn will lose its vigour and become vulnerable to attack from disease. Overcome this potential problem by feeding the grass as soon as growth starts in the spring.

All spring lawn feeds contain high levels of nitrogen to promote rapid, green leaf growth. Most consist of a mixture of fertilisers designed to release a constant supply of nutrients during spring and summer. If you are using fertiliser in powder or granular form, water it in if no rain falls within 48 hours of its application.

Apply solutions of lawn feed through a hose dilutor. For small lawns, use a watering can and dilute the solution according to the manufacturer's instructions on the label (see also page 55).

Consider making a hard mowing edge at the same time as laying a new lawn. This will enable the mower to glide smoothly over the lawn edges.

wildlife ponds

A wildlife pond looks more natural than any other type of water feature, but needs careful planning and construction if it is to blend into the landscape and last a long time.

Dense planting around the margins, including irises and flowering marsh marigolds, creates cover under which wildlife can approach the pond. Placing logs around the perimeter offers safe hiding places.

siting a wildlife pond

Water in any form will lure a certain amount of wildlife, but a pond designed specifically for wildlife will encourage more creatures and enable them to use it in safety. Think about these practical points before you decide on the position.

● **avoid shady sites.** Place the pond where it will get sun for most of the day.
● **site the pond in the open**, away from overhanging trees or large shrubs. Fallen leaves pollute the water, and those of evergreens such as yew and laurel are toxic; large roots may damage the liner.
● **choose a sheltered spot** away from cold winds so the water temperature is less likely to fluctuate, making it a healthier habitat for wildlife and aquatic plants.
● **avoid sites with a high water table** or any that become waterlogged, as the water in the soil could cause the liner to balloon upwards.

designing a wildlife pond

There are several key points for a successful wildlife pond.

● **the pond should not be too small**; about 2 x 2.5m (6 x 8ft) is a minimum size, but larger ponds are more interesting and it is easier to develop and maintain the ecological balance. An irregular, curved outline looks most natural.
● **there should be a point of easy access** in the form of a 'beach' that slopes gently down to an area of shallow water. Large stones in the water with their tops exposed allow birds to perch.
● **to accommodate a wide selection** of water plants, vary the pool depth. Part needs to be at least 60cm (2ft) deep for water lilies and other deep-water plants, while an underwater shelf running round part of the edge allows marginal, or shallow-water, plants to

pond safety
Ponds are a hazard for young children, but you can make a pond safe by building in a special metal grid that sits just below the surface of the water.

grow. These plants will also help wildlife to climb out of the pond.
● **some dense planting** adjacent to the pond allows creatures to approach in safety. The perfect companion to a wildlife pond is a bog garden, and one can be added as a natural extension of the watery habitat (see page 150).

choosing a liner

A flexible liner is the best material for constructing a wildlife pond as the design can then be made to suit the needs of different creatures, something less easily achieved with a preformed unit. A liner is also easier to install, and the pond can be made almost any size or shape to suit your garden.

Flexible liners are available in a range of materials, from pvc to butyl rubber, and it is worth buying the best that you can afford. Cheaper materials have a shorter life, mainly because of their poor resistance to the ultra-violet rays in sunlight. Always check the length of guarantee as a guide to a good liner; the best quality materials will be guaranteed for at least 20 years. Liners come in rolls of varying width, so take this into account when planning the dimensions of your pond.

Before you lay the pool liner, you will need to line the cavity with a cushioning underlay to protect it from sharp objects that could work through the soil. Other options include old carpet, though it is bulky and awkward to work with, or a 5cm (2in) layer of damp sand.

edging materials

Vary the edging of your pond to give the maximum benefit to wildlife and the most enjoyment for yourself. Make one part a shallow shelving 'beach' of small pebbles and gravel, with large cobbles in the water to stop the smaller stones slipping down into the depths. In other places lay turf up to the water's edge, and into this set a couple of paving slabs to provide a viewing platform for people to stand on. If the pond is large, build two or three such vantage points. Rocks or logs positioned at the edge and interspersed with bushy or trailing plants make excellent hiding places for frogs and other creatures.

Flowering marginal plants, including iris, candelabra primulas and arum lilies, bring colour to the edges of a pond in late spring.

wildlife ponds/2
building a wildlife pond

calculating the liner
To find the area of liner required multiply the length by the width as follows:
Length = maximum overall length + (2 x maximum depth) + 30cm (12in)
Width = maximum overall width + (2 x maximum depth) + 30cm (12in)
This formula works for all ponds, regardless of size or shape.
The extra 30cm (12in) is to allow for adequate overlap around the edges.

4 **Once digging is complete,** check over the entire cavity and remove any debris and protruding stones that could damage the liner. Firm the sides with your hands to avoid any soft spots that could subside later. Line the cavity with protective underlay.

2 **Dig out the pond cavity** just inside the sand mark. Make the sides slope outwards by at least 20° to stop the soil crumbling into the hole. Shape underwater shelves round the edge 30cm (12in) deep and 23–30cm (9–12in) wide. Outside the sand mark, remove a 45cm (18in) strip of soil or turf to a depth of 5cm (2in) to accommodate the overlap of liner.

3 **Use the spirit level** placed on the plank to check that the rim of the pond is level all round, as any discrepancies will show up dramatically when the pond is full of water. If you plan to have a bog garden next to the pond, make the adjoining edge 5cm (2in) lower than the rest of the rim. Check that the underwater shelves are level, too.

1 **Mark out the shape of the pond** using a hosepipe. View it from every angle, including from an upstairs window if possible. When you are completely happy with the shape and the overall position of the pond, trickle sand onto the ground (inset picture) to mark the outline, then remove the hosepipe.

5 **Cut the pond liner** to size, if necessary. Lay it loosely over the cavity and weigh down the edges temporarily with bricks. When handling the liner, take care that it does not catch on any sharp objects. This part of the job is best done by two people with plenty of time to get things right.

6 **Start running in water** from a hose once the liner is centred over the hole. The increasing weight of the water will mould the liner to the shape of the cavity. As the liner sinks, move the weights and fold the liner neatly around shelves and corners. Continue filling the pond until the water is just below the rim. Trim the liner to leave an overlap of 15cm (6in) all round. Bury the outside edge of liner in the soil, leaving a rim about 5–8cm (2–3in) wide, except where you plan to have a shallow sloping 'beach', as the liner here needs to extend at least 15cm (6in) out of the water.

7 **Edge the pond** with different materials to conceal the liner rim. Paving stones should project over the water by 5cm (2in) to conceal the liner; turf should butt up to the edge. Cover the beach area with pebbles or gravel.

introducing plants

A pond needs the right balance of planting to keep the water clear naturally or it will turn bright green with algae. The most important plants in this regard are water lilies (*Nymphaea*), whose leaves should shade a third to half of the water's surface, and oxygenating plants which take up nutrients that otherwise encourage algal growth. Water lilies range in size from dwarves to vigorous ones suitable for a small lake, so choose a variety to suit your pond. These and other water plants also provide vital shelter, breeding sites and feeding grounds for all sorts of creatures. A range of marginal plants can be grown on the underwater shelves around the pond (see box below). Plant them in plastic mesh baskets: they are easier to manage if grown individually (see page 49).

encouraging wildlife

The best way to stock a wildlife pond is to do nothing, as all sorts of creatures will find a new pond surprisingly quickly. Birds will come to drink and bathe, and hedgehogs will also stop to drink. Amphibians like frogs, toads and newts live in water most of the time, and many insects need water in which to live or breed. Never keep fish in a wildlife pond as they will feed on the tadpoles and insects.

water plants for wildlife

All these plants benefit wildlife in some way: nectar and pollen-producing flowers feed butterflies and bees, while plants with vertical stems play an important role in the breeding cycle of dragonflies and damselflies. • bogbean (*Menyanthes trifoliata*) • dwarf reedmace (*Typha minima*) • flowering rush (*Butomus umbellatus*) • lesser spearwort (*Ranunculus flammula*) • marsh marigold (*Caltha palustris*) • purple loosestrife (*Lythrum salicaria*) • skunk cabbage (*Lysichiton americanus*) • water forget-me-not (*Myosotis scorpioides*) • water iris (*Iris laevigata*) • water mint (*Mentha aquatica*) • water violet (*Hottonia palustris*) • yellow flag (*Iris pseudacorus* and *I. pseudacorus* 'Variegata')

Lysichiton americanus

bog gardens

A bog garden makes the perfect partner to an informal or wildlife pond and enables you to create a lush artificial wetland for plants that would not ordinarily thrive in your plot.

Moisture-loving plants, such as hostas, *Iris pseudacorus* and *Persicaria bistorta* 'Superba', brighten a bog garden in late spring.

creating a bog garden

Although very few gardens contain marshy ground, it is not difficult to replicate these conditions artificially. In this damp environment a rich selection of moisture-loving plants with bright flowers and luxuriant foliage will flourish, even in the height of summer. Ponds and bogs are complementary garden features. But an area of water is by no means essential and a bog garden can work extremely well in its own right. Constructing a bog garden is similar to, but simpler than, making a pond. It basically consists of excavating a hole, lining it with a waterproof membrane and filling with enriched soil.

siting a bog garden

The ideal site for a bog garden is in partial shade, as this enables you to grow the widest variety of plants. This may not be possible if you are making one in an open area next to a pond.

Fortunately, many plants, such as astilbes and hostas, recommended for shady situations, will tolerate a greater degree of sun, particularly in cooler areas of the country, if they grow in soil that is never allowed to dry out. Bear in mind that a bog garden in sun means more watering, and feeder ponds will need frequent topping up in summer.

At the edge of a bog garden, marginal plants include globe flower (*Trollius* x *cultorum* 'Orange Queen'), ferns and arums.

adjacent to a pond

From a practical point of view, siting a bog garden next to a wildlife pond means the overspill from the pond should keep the bog garden soil moist. There are wildlife benefits too, as many creatures like to approach the water under cover and also love a damp, leafy environment. Aesthetically, the lush foliage of many bog plants creates a natural visual transition from water to dry land and successfully integrates a pond into a surrounding garden.

Ideally, you should build a bog garden at the same time as the pond (see page 152), though it can be added to an existing pond later. A layout with bold, flowing curves looks in keeping with an informal pond. Make the bog garden's size no greater than the pond, to keep the features in balance.

a stand-alone bog garden

Without the constraints of a pond, a stand-alone bog garden can transform a dank shady area for much of the year with plants like candelabra primroses, irises and luxuriant ferns. Its success depends on careful placing. Although a position in light or dappled shade is desirable, if your garden is even slightly sloping, you should site the bog in the lower part of the plot where water would gather naturally, even if it is in the sun. This situation will look more convincing than on higher ground, and will collect more rainwater.

A stand-alone bog garden is made as described on page 152, except that no dividing wall is required. Check that the top and the floor are both level before laying an inexpensive flexible liner.

watering a bog garden

A feeder pond helps to keep the soil in the bog garden saturated. Without an adjacent pond, frequent watering is essential. One of the best ways to make the task less arduous is to tap into the guttering that collects rain from a nearby building. If the catchment area is small, such as the roof of a shed or greenhouse, you could extend the downpipe to empty directly into the bog garden, via an excavated channel in which the extra length of pipe is sunk. A large roof could provide too much water, in which case it would be preferable to install a water butt or two to collect the run-off. Connect the butts to the bog garden with a hosepipe, which can be turned on as required.

Water a bog garden gradually rather than in a huge flood. An easy way to ensure the whole area is thoroughly but gently watered is to lay a soaker hose (also known as leaky pipe) around the bog garden when it is being planted. Hide the hose with a layer of mulch.

bog gardens/2

making a bog garden

YOU WILL NEED

- flexible liner (see page 148 for calculating the size)
- garden hose and sand, for marking out the area • spade • scissors
- gravel, to line the base • large stones and fine plastic mesh
- garden fork, or knife, for making drainage holes • well-rotted organic matter, such as manure or garden compost

LINER TIP Use a cheap flexible liner for a bog garden as, unlike a pond liner, it does not need to be completely watertight.

1 Mark out the site (see page 148), then excavate the bog garden to around 45cm (18in) deep. Keep good-quality topsoil separate from subsoil. If the bog garden is adjoining a pond, leave a wall of soil (above) between the two holes, 10–15cm (4–6in) across the top and getting wider towards the bottom. The dividing wall should be 5cm (2in) lower than the pond rim. Firm all over and remove stones and other debris.

2 Cut the liner if needed, and lay it in the cavity, fitting it as for a pond liner (see page 148). Overlap the liners by a minimum of 15cm (6in). Make 1cm (½in) drainage holes in the liner with a sharp knife at 1m (3ft) intervals and 5cm (2in) up from the base. Puncture the liner around all sides, except for the wall between bog and pond.

3 Spread washed gravel in a 5cm (2in) layer over the floor of the bog garden. Mix excavated topsoil with a third by volume of organic matter such as well-rotted manure or compost. Fill the bog garden with this soil mixture, or to just below the dividing wall, firming it into the corners as you go.

4 Lay stones or pebbles on top of the dividing wall. Then place a piece of fine plastic mesh on the bog-garden side of this 'barrier' to prevent soil from washing into the pond. Add more soil until it is level with the surrounding garden. Omit this step for a stand-alone bog garden (see page 151).

5 Trim the liner to leave 10cm (4in) all round and fold the edge under, burying it in the ground so only a narrow rim remains visible. Water from the pond will trickle through the stone 'barrier' and saturate the soil.

6 You can plant your bog garden as soon as it is completed. After raking the soil surface, set out the plants in their pots until you are satisfied with their positions. Plant them at the same depth as they were growing previously. While planting, take care not to tread on the soil as this will cause compaction; if necessary, work from a plank to spread your weight. After planting, water the bog garden thoroughly to settle the soil around the plant roots.

choosing plants

Bog gardens are ideal for a wide variety of perennials: select them to give a succession of colour from early spring to the end of autumn. Select some plants for their long-lasting foliage interest, to contrast with and provide a background for the flowers. Include some ornamental grasses and sedges (*Carex*) to bring light, airy touches. Choose plants that are in scale with your bog garden, as they range from dainty dwarfs to huge, spreading giants.

Shrubs and trees are unsuitable for artificial bog gardens as their root systems are large. In the long term they could penetrate and damage the liner. Where a nearby framework of larger plants or those for winter interest is required, the answer is to choose those that thrive in ordinary garden soil, but are in keeping with water. Look for arching stems and bold or feathery foliage, such as shrubby willows (*Salix*), dogwoods (*Cornus alba* varieties), bamboos and tall ornamental grasses, such as *Miscanthus sinensis* and *Stipa gigantica*. Plant willows and bamboos about 2.5m (8ft) from the edge of the bog garden so their roots do not damage the buried liner in their search for moisture. Dogwoods and grasses can be planted a little closer.

routine care

The maintenance of a bog garden is similar to that of an ordinary border. You need to keep on top of weeds and to deadhead flowers regularly to encourage more blooms. Cut back dead foliage at any time between autumn and late winter, but in cold areas delay this until early spring, as the dead foliage will give the rootstocks extra protection from frost.

Every year in early spring mulch the bare ground between plants with an 8cm (3in) layer of rotted garden compost or composted bark. At the same time feed the plants in bog gardens next to a pond with slow-release fertiliser pellets. While you can use other garden fertilisers in stand-alone bog gardens, their use near ponds presents a risk of surplus nutrients washing into the water, encouraging the growth of algae and blanket weed.

some plants for seasonal interest in your bog garden

SPRING/EARLY SUMMER FLOWERS
- astilbe • bugle (*Ajuga reptans*)
- candelabra primulas (*Primula beesiana, P. bulleyana, P. pulverulenta*)
- cuckoo flower (*Cardamine pratensis* and *C. pratensis* 'Flore-Pleno')
- drumstick primula (*Primula denticulata*) • giant cowslip (*Primula florindae*) • globe flower (*Trollius*)
- himalayan cowslip (*Primula sikkimensis*) • marsh marigold or kingcup (*Caltha palustris*) • ragged robin (*Lychnis flos-cuculi*) • umbrella plant (*Darmera peltata*) • water avens (*Geum rivale*)

SUMMER/AUTUMN FLOWERS
- creeping jenny (*Lysimachia nummularia* and 'Aurea') • daylily (*Hemerocallis*) • *Iris ensata* hybrids
- joe pye weed (*Eupatorium purpureum*)
- *Lobelia* x *gerardii* 'Vedrariensis', *L. siphilitica, L.* 'Queen Victoria'
- *Mimulus guttatus, M. luteus*
- purple loosestrife (*Lythrum salicaria*) • rodgersia • siberian irises (*Iris sibirica*)

ATTRACTIVE FOLIAGE
- *Acorus gramineus* 'Ogon'
- *Filipendula ulmaria* 'Aurea'
- gunnera • hosta • *Imperata cylindrica* 'Rubra' • ligularias
- *Lobelia* 'Queen Victoria'
- ostrich fern (*Matteuccia struthiopteris*) • *Rheum palmatum* 'Atrosanguineum' • rodgersia • sedge (*Carex* spp.) • sensitive fern (*Onoclea sensibilis*) • umbrella plant (*Darmera peltata*)

PLANTS FOR WILDLIFE
While the environment of a pond provides a haven for many creatures, certain plants have added value to wildlife as their flowers attract bees, butterflies and insects. These include:
- bugle (*Ajuga reptans*) • creeping jenny (*Lysimachia nummularia*)
- cuckoo flower (*Cardamine pratensis*)
- purple loosestrife (*Lythrum salicaria*)
- ragged robin (*Lychnis flos-cuculi*).

A variety of hostas and large-leaved *Gunnera manicata* grow in a bog garden at the side of a stream.

late spring index

acknowledgments

Photographs were supplied by the following people and organisations. Where relevant, the number of the picture as it appears on a page is given. Abbreviations are used as follows: t top, c centre, b bottom, l left, r right. JB Jonathan Buckley, MB Mark Bolton, MBr Martin Brigdale, NB Nicola Browne, HSC Harry Smith Collection, SC Sarah Cuttle, GPL Garden Picture Library, JG John Glover, JH Jerry Harpur, MH Marcus Harpur, SH Sunniva Harte, NH N Holmes, AL Andrew Lawson, MM Marianne Majerus, S&OM S & O Mathews, MN Mike Newton, CN Clive Nichols, RD Reader's Digest, HR Howard Rice, GR Gary Rogers, MLS Mayer Le Scanff, MT Maddie Thornhill, MW Mark Winwood, SSP Sea Spring Photos, JS J Sira, JW Justyn Willsmore.

Front cover SC Back cover tl & tr MW, c & cr SC, bl MN, br RD 1 GPL/HR 2-3 GPL/M Mouchy 4-5 GPL/JG 8-9 GPL/HR (Design: B Chatto) 10 tl JB, tr & br MB, bl GPL/C Burrows 11 tl GPL/MB, tr RD, bl MM (Design: Peter Chan) br MM 12 tl MB, tr JH (Shute House, Design: G Jellicoe) 12-13 GPL/M Mouchy 13 tl JB (Design: S Raven, Pearch Hill Farm) tr & br JH (Design: B Chatto), bc MB, c RD 14 tl JB, b GPL/M Watson, 15 tl MM, tr AL (Eastgrove Cottage, Hereford), cl & cr GPL/HR, b GPL/MLS, c MB 16 tl AL, tr JH (Design: P Larson, Ladew, Maryland, USA), bl GPL/S Wooster, br JB (Design: C Rutherford) 17 l JH (Chateau de Corbeil, France), tr S&OM, br GPL/SH 18 tl SC, bl GPL/J Sorrell, bl GPL/L Burgess 19 tl MT, tr GPL/JG, cr GPL/J Sorrell, bl AL (RHS Chelsea 1996, Design: D Pearson), br GPL/F Strauss 20 t JH, bl JB (Design: H Yemm), br GPL/HR 21 tl GPL/S Wooster, tr GPL/MLS, bl GPL/JS, br SC 22 t GR, c GPL/HR, b GPL/J Ferro Sims 23 tl & br GPL/M Heuff, tr GPL/B Thomas, cr JB, bl AL, c GPL/HR (Design: B Chatto) 24-25 MBr 26 MW 27 l MW, t MB, b MN 28 SC 29 MW except br SC 30 SC 31 t SC, b RD 32 SC except c insert MW 33 t SC, b RD 34 CN 35 t MW, b SC 36 MB 37 MW 38 SC 39 l SC, r GPL/HR 40 MN 41 t SC, b MW 42 t JB, b MW 43 t SC, b MB 44 GPL/J Pavia 45 t & cr MN, bl & br SC, bc MW 46 GR 47 MW 48 t MB, bl NB, br SC 49 MW 50 GPL/L Brotchie 51 SC 52 SC 53 tl & tc SC, tr MN, b GPL/J Wade 54 l GPL/JG, r MW 55 MW 56 t GPL/HR, b GPL/M Howes 57 l MT, r SC 58 t SSP, b MW 59 t MBr, b MW 60 t MT, b MN 61 t MT, b SSP 62 GPL/A Lord 63 MW except t GPL/SH 64 MW 65 l MW, b GPL/P Windsor 66 MW 67 t GPL/M Howes, bc & bl SC, br MW, 68 l JH, r MT 69 l MW, r SC 70 l GPL/R Evans, r MW 71 t MB, b MW 72-73 RD 74-75 (1, 5, 6) HSC, (2, 4, 10) RD, (3) MB, (7) GPL/NH (8) GPL/JG, (9) GPL/JS, (11) GPL/M Heuff, (12) SC 76-77 (1) MT, (2) GPL/SH, (3, 4, 6, 10) RD, (5) HSC, (7) SC, (8) GPL/JS, (9, 12) MB, (11) S&OM 78-79 (1) JW, (2) GPL/JG, (3) GPL/JS, (4, 6, 10, 11) RD, (5) GPL/NH, (7) GPL/HR, (8) MB, (9) SC, (12) GPL/J Wade, (13) GPL/C Fairweather, (14) GPL/MLS 80-81 (1, 5, 6, 7, 12) RD, (2) GPL/HR, (3, 4) AL, (8, 9) GPL/JG, (10) GPL/J Pavia, (11) GPL/ D Willery 82-83 (1, 3, 10, 12) RD, (2) GPL/R Evans, (4) GPL/NH, (5, 7) GPL/ J Hurst, (6, 13) HSC, (8) GPL/JS, (9) GPL/J Pavia, (11) MB 84-85 (1, 4) GPL/JG, (2, 6, 8) GPL/SH, (3, 5) RD, (7, 9, 10, 11) HSC, (12) MB 86-87 (1, 2, 7) MB, (3, 11) GPL/HR, (4, 5, 8, 9, 10, 12) RD, (6) GPL/JG 88-89 (1, 9) SC, (2, 3, 4, 5) RD, (6, 7) GPL/C Burrows, (8) RD 90-91 (1) GPL/JS, (2) MB, (3, 5, 7, 9) GPL/HR, (4) GPL/JG,

(6, 8) RD, (10) GPL/B Carter, (11) HSC, (12) GPL/JS 92-93 (1, 4, 9) MB, (2, 5, 7, 8, 10) RD, (3, 6, 11) GPL/JG, (12, 13) GPL/B Carter 94-95 (1, 2, 3, 9, 10) RD, (4) HSC, (5) SC, (6) GPI/HR, (7) GPL/NH, (8, 11) MB, (12) S&OM 96-97 (1, 4) GPL/JG, (2, 10) MB, (3, 6, 7, 11, 12) RD, (5) Ray Cox/Glendoick Gardens Ltd, (8) GPL/D Clyne, (9) HSC 98-99 (1, 8, 9) MB, (2, 3) GPL/HR, (4) JW, (5, 6, 7, 10, 11) RD, (12) GPL/E Crichton 100 (1) GPL/R Sutherland, (2) GPL/JG, (3, 4) RD, (5) GPL/B Carter, (6) MB 101 (1) GPL/D Askham, (2, 7) RD, (3) GPL/B Carter, (4) Ray Cox/Glendoick Gardens Ltd, (5, 9) GPL/J Glover, (6) GPL/B Challinor, (8) GPL/D England 102-103 (1) GPL/J Hurst, (2, 3, 4, 6, 7, 11) RD, (5) GPL/S Harte, (8) GPL/JS, (9, 12) HSC, (10) SC 104 (1, 4) GPL/HR, (2, 6) RD, (3, 5) HSC 105 (1, 3, 4) RD, (2) MB 106-107 (1) HSC, (2) GPI/NH, (3) GPL/J Wade, (4) GPL/C Boursnell, (5) GPL/B Thomas, (6, 8, 13) GPL/M Howes, (7) GPL/HR, (9) C Carter, (10) GPL/M Watson, (11) SSP, (12) GPL/SH 108-109 (1) MH, (2) GPL/NH, (3, 4, 6, 7, 8, 9) RD, (5) GPL/J Pavia, (10) GPL/MB, (11) GPL/B Challinor, (12) GPL/D Cavagnaro 110-111 (1) MT, (2) GPL/JS, (3, 4) RD, (5) GPL/JG, (6) GPL/C Burrows, (7, 8, 9) HSC, (10) GPL/B Thomas, (11) J Dracup 112 l SC, c AL, r S&OM 113 MB 114 l RD, c GPL/B Carter, r GPL/HR 115 RD 116-117 GPL/J Legate 118 MB 119 l JB (Design: N Ryan), r MB 120 l GPL/JG, r JB (Design: H Yemm) 120-121 JH (Hermannshof, Weinheim, Germany) 121 ct M Harpur, tr NB, br SC, c MN 122 JH (Hakone, USA) 123 t GPL/JG (RHS Chelsea 1994), b NB (Design: J & M Kling) 124 MB 125 GPL/J Wade 126 AL (Lord Leycester Hospital, Warwick) 126-127 GPL/M Watson 127 MB except tl JB & br JB (Design: P Kelly) 128 t AL, b JB (RHS Chelsea 2001, Design: A Sturgeon) 129 SC except t MN) 130 t MB, br MN, bl JH (Design: B Clark, California) 131 MB except b GPL/R Evans 132 RD 132-133 JB (Design: P Kelly) 133 tl GPL/HR, tr C Boursnell/Country Life, b M Harpur (RHS Chelsea 2000) 134 MW except tr GPL/A Scaresbrook (RHS Chelsea 2000, Godstone Gardeners Club) 135 MW 136 GPL/JG (Design: F Lawrenson) 137 MW except t GPL/JG (RHS Chelsea 1997, Design: C Bradley Hole) 138 tl GPL/G Glynn-Smith, c MN, br SC, bl JB (Design: D Buckley) cl GPL/JS 139 MW 140 tl JH (Design: L Cochran), bl GPL/HR (RHS Chelsea 1999, Design: M Challis), br MW 141 JH (Design: R Hartiage) 142 l GPL/J Legate, r MW 143 MW 144 MW 145 GPL/JG 146 MM 147 S&OM 148 MW 149 MW except c GPL/R Sutherland, br S&OM 150 GPL/R Evans 151 GPL/R Sutherland (Design: A Paul) 152 MW 153 GPL/JS

Front cover: Tulipa 'Spring Green'. Back cover, clockwise from top left: pinching out sideshoot on a tomato plant; apple blossom; Viola sororia 'Freckles'; scattering lawn sand to control moss; Berberis darwinii; Sempervivum tectorum

Amazon Publishing would like to thank Adrian Hall Garden Centres, and the following individuals for allowing us to use their gardens for photography: Katia Demetriardi, Bridget Heal, Gaye Prescott, Jenny Raworth

Late Spring is part of a series of gardening books called the All-Season Guide to Gardening. It was created for Reader's Digest by Amazon Publishing Limited.

Series Editor Carole McGlynn
Art Director Ruth Prentice

Editors Barbara Haynes, Jackie Matthews; also Norma MacMillan, Alison Freegard
Design Jo Grey, Mary Staples; also Alison Shackleton
Photographic art direction Ruth Prentice
Special photography Sarah Cuttle, Mark Winwood
Writers Steve Bradley, Andi Clevely, Nigel Colborn, Sue Fisher, David Joyce
Picture research Clare Limpus, Mel Watson, Sarah Wilson
Consultant Jonathan Edwards
DTP Claire Graham
Editorial Assistant Elizabeth Woodland

FOR READER'S DIGEST
Project Editor Christine Noble
Pre-press Accounts Manager Penny Grose

READER'S DIGEST GENERAL BOOKS
Editorial Director Cortina Butler
Art Director Nick Clark

First Edition Copyright © 2002
The Reader's Digest Association Limited
11 Westferry Circus, Canary Wharf,
London E14 4HE
www.readersdigest.co.uk
Reprinted with amendments 2003

Copyright © 2002 Reader's Digest Association Far East Limited
Philippines copyright © 2002 Reader's Digest Association Far East Limited

We are committed to both the quality of our products and the service we provide to our customers. We value your comments, so please feel free to contact us on 08705 113366, or via our website at www.readersdigest.co.uk If you have any comments about the content of our books, you can contact us at gbeditorial@readersdigest.co.uk

Origination Colour Systems Limited, London
Printed and bound in the EEC by Arvato Iberia

ISBN 0 276 42708 4
BOOK CODE 621-001-2
CONCEPT CODE UK0087